A G E N D A   S E T T I N G
Readings on Media, Public Opinion, and Policymaking

COMMUNICATION
TEXTBOOK SERIES
Jennings Bryant — Editor

Journalism
Maxwell McCombs — Advisor

AGENDA SETTING
Readings on Media, Public Opinion, and Policymaking

Edited by

David L. Protess
Northwestern University

Maxwell McCombs
University of Texas at Austin

LEA LAWRENCE ERLBAUM ASSOCIATES, PUBLISHERS
1991   Hillsdale, New Jersey   Hove and London

Lawrence Erlbaum Associates, Inc., Publishers
365 Broadway
Hillsdale, New Jersey 07642

Library of Congress Cataloging-in-Publication Data

Agenda setting : readings on media, public opinion, and policymaking /
edited by David Protess, Maxwell McCombs.
    p. cm.
    Includes bibliographical references and indexes.
    ISBN 0-8058-0841-8 (pbk.)
    1. Journalism — Social aspects — United States. 2. Journalism —
Political aspects — United States. 3. Public opinion — United
States. I. Protess, David. II. McCombs, Maxwell E.
PN4888.S6A35 1991
302.23'0973 — dc20   90-26714
                                          CIP

Printed in the United States of America
10 9 8 7 6 5 4 3 2

Contents

Preface

The agenda-setting influence of the news media has attracted considerable attention in recent years. Although the idea now has considerable popular currency, the scholarly literature spelling out the precise details of how and to what extent the news media shape our pictures of the world is scattered in a great variety of journals and books. One purpose of this anthology is to make a broad sample of this rich literature accessible to advanced undergraduates and to beginning graduate students. More than two dozen selections advance this goal. Our second goal is to present an orderly introduction and overview to a research literature that now includes several hundred items. To advance this second goal — and to avoid the morass of repetitious citations and summaries that are inevitable in any collection of articles on the same subject — many of the selections in this anthology have been edited. Portions of the text and many, if not all, the footnotes and references have been omitted in order to guide the reader quickly through the selection to its principal points.

Finally, in order to secure both goals, an extensive bibliography is included at the end of this anthology. This set of citations is a major contribution in its own right. Although not everything ever published on the agenda-setting role of the news media is listed here, the vast majority of the journal articles and books reporting empirical results are included. Coupled with the selections included in this anthology, readers are presented with the opportunity for an extensive exploration of the agenda-setting influence of the news media.

Maxwell McCombs
David Protess

THE PUBLIC AGENDA

Each generation writes its own history of the world. This is not because of any pernicious desire to cast aside the worldview of their fathers and mothers or even to rewrite history more to their liking! Although these motives may not be totally absent, each generation creates a history differing in significant details from previous versions principally because they came of age under a new set of circumstances. Think of the differences between the college graduates of 1950 and those of 1975. One came of age during the economic prosperity of the quiescent Eisenhower years. The other came of age during the turbulent Vietnam era. Your generation will experience and create yet a different history. The experiences that bind the members of a generation, but separate them from others, do more than define immediate perspectives about public issues and politics. They also color historical perspectives about who Americans are and what kind of country we were and should be. The richness and variation of these experiences among individuals as well as between generations is captured in psychologist Kurt Lewin's concept of the lifespace, one of the key ideas in his book, *A Dynamic Theory of Personality*.

An individual's lifespace is the map or picture of the

significant elements in his or her life. It is those persons, places, and events that are significant to the individual's behavior. The famous *New Yorker* magazine cover illustrating the New Yorker's view of the United States or the souvenir maps depicting the Texan's view of the nation are caricatured versions of the lifespaces of New Yorkers and Texans. In terms of everyday reality, 45th Street does loom larger to a New York resident than does Nebraska or Kansas. To a Texan all the other states do seem like small clusters around a gigantic Lone Star state. Journalist Walter Lippmann expressed this same idea through his contrast of the environment and the pseudo-environment. Our behavior, he noted, is a response to the pseudo-environment, the world that is pictured in our mind.

There is a different set of pictures in the heads of each generation as a result of their direct personal experiences and their accumulated repertoire of historical and contemporary information. In more general terms, this has been called the construction of social reality. Individuals construct their own set of pictures from their direct personal experience, what they read in books, magazines and newspapers, and what they see on television and in movies. Through the transmission of traditional culture, the creation of contemporary culture, and the interpretation of public affairs, mass communication plays a major role in the construction of the pictures in our heads.

In recent decades scholars of mass communication have discovered that journalists' day-by-day judgments on the selection and display of news stories influence the public's perceptions of what the important issues of the day are. This influence of the news media on the perceived salience of key political issues is called the *agenda-setting* role of mass communication. The creation of these perceived saliences in the minds of the mass communication audience is a by-product of journalistic practice, shaped by the need to select and highlight a small number of topics each day. What journalists consider to be "newsworthy" provides efficient cues about the relative importance of the welter of issues in our time. Newspapers clearly communicate salience through page placement, headline size, and the amount of space alloted to a topic. Television news formats contain similar cues about the salience of issues.

The concept of agenda-setting is an assertion that the audience learns what issues are important from the priorities of the news media and incorporates a similar set of weights in their own personal agendas. Agenda-setting is a relational concept specifying a positive connection between the emphases of the news media and the perceived importance of these topics to the news audience. Establishing these saliences among the public, placing an issue or topic on the public agenda so that it becomes the focus of public attention, thought, and discussion is the first stage in the formation of public opinion. Consideration of public opinion usually focuses on the distribution of opinions pro and con after an issue is before the public. Agenda-setting directs our attention to an earlier stage in the public opinion process, the stage at which an issue emerges.

It is important to note that these cues created by the news media influence people's pictures of the world, not their feelings about these issues. Heavy news coverage on the topic of abortion is likely to increase the salience of this issue on the public agenda. This news coverage will not necessarily determine whether individuals advocate freedom of choice or pro-life.

Early concern with the effects of mass communication concentrated on people's attitudes and opinions. The benchmark Eire County and Elmira studies, which examined the impact of the mass media on voters in the 1940 and 1948 presidential elections, found little empirical evidence of any mass media influence. In fact, the contrary evidence was so pervasive that Joseph Klapper's classic, *The Effects of Mass Communication,* proclaimed the law of minimal consequences. But agenda-setting shifts the focus of attention away from immediate effects on attitudes and opinions to longer term effects on cognitions. Agenda-setting is about the transfer of saliences, the movement of issues from the media agenda to the public agenda.

Contrasting earlier concerns about the effects of mass communication on attitudes and opinion with the effects pertinent to agenda-setting, Bernard Cohen remarked in *The Press and Foreign Policy* that

> the press is significantly more than a purveyor of information and opinion. It may not be successful much of the time in telling people what to think, but it is stunningly successful in telling its readers what to think *about.* (p. 13)

This idea of agenda-setting has been articulated for well over a half century. Note that the opening chapter of Walter Lippmann's classic, *Public Opinion,* is titled "The World Outside and the Pictures in Our Heads." But it was only in 1968 that Maxwell McCombs and Donald Shaw first put this idea to empirical test. Most of the readings in this anthology represent the outpouring of research that has followed that first empirical foray 20 years ago.

In one of these readings, Ray Funkhouser analyses the key issues around which American public opinion coalesced during the turbulent 1960s. He examines the basic agenda-setting hypothesis across an entire decade, in contrast with the original McCombs and Shaw study that examined a brief moment among undecided voters during the 1968 presidential election. Together the pair of studies provide a microview and a macroview of the agenda-setting role of the news media.

Other selections in this introductory section on the public agenda provide context and perspective. Anthony Downs describes the stages in the natural history of each issue appearing on the public agenda. Together these four readings provide a broad introduction to the public agenda and its relationship to the daily coverage of public issues in the news media.

But a comprehensive portrait of public opinion and the agenda-setting role of the news media requires attention to a number of other questions. How does this process work? What factors inhibit or enhance this influence of the press on the public? Looking more broadly at the press and public opinion, what are the consequences of agenda-setting? Does extensive media coverage and a concerned public lead to action by government officials? Going the other way, so to speak, how is the media agenda created? Or, as it is sometimes put, who sets the media agenda? With only the capacity to cover a few issues at any moment, what influences determine the focus of news coverage? Answers to these questions — and many others that will occur to you — begin to construct a comprehensive portrait of the role played by the news media, public opinion and policymakers in the natural history of contemporary American public issues.

1 Public Opinion*

Walter Lippmann

THE WORLD OUTSIDE AND THE PICTURES
IN OUR HEADS

There is an island in the ocean where in 1914 a few Englishmen, Frenchmen, and Germans lived. No cable reaches that island, and the British mail steamer comes but once in sixty days. In September it had not yet come, and the islanders were still talking about the latest newspaper which told about the approaching trial of Madame Caillaux for the shooting of Gaston Calmette. It was, therefore, with more than usual eagerness that the whole colony assembled at the quay on a day in mid-September to hear from the captain what the verdict had been. They learned that for over six weeks now those of them who were English and those of them who were French had been fighting in behalf of the sanctity of treaties against those of them who were Germans. For six strange weeks they had acted as if they were friends, when in fact they were enemies.

But their plight was not so different from that of most of the population of Europe. They had mistaken for six weeks, on the continent the interval may have been only six days or six hours. There was an interval. There was a moment when the picture of Europe on which men were conducting their business as usual, did not in any way correspond to the Europe which was about to make a jumble of their lives. There was a time for each man when he was still adjusted to an environment that no longer existed. All over the world as late as July 25th men were making goods that they would not be able to ship, buying goods they would not be able to import, careers were being planned, enterprises contemplated, hopes and expectations entertained, all in the belief that the world as known was the world as it was. Men were writing books describing that world. They trusted the picture in their heads. And then over four years later, on a Thursday morning, came the news of an armistice, and people gave vent to their unutterable relief that the slaughter was over. Yet in the five days before the real armistice came, though the end of the war had been celebrated, several thousand young men died on the battlefields.

Looking back we can see how indirectly we know the environment in which nevertheless we live. We can see that the news of it comes to us now fast, now slowly; but that whatever we believe to be a true picture, we treat as if it were the environment itself. It is harder to remember that about the beliefs upon which we are now acting, but in respect to other peoples and other ages we flatter ourselves that it is easy to see when they were in deadly earnest about ludicrous pictures of the world. We insist, because of our superior hindsight, that the world as they needed to know it, and the world as they did know it, were often two quite contradictory things. We can see, too, that while they governed and fought, traded and reformed in the world as they imagined it to be, they produced results, or failed to produce any, in the world as it was. They started for the Indies and found America. They diagnosed evil and hanged old women. They thought they could grow rich by always selling and never buying. A caliph, obeying what he conceived to be the Will of Allah, burned the library at Alexandria.

Writing about the year 389, St. Ambrose stated the case for the prisoner in Plato's cave who resolutely declines to turn his head. "To discuss the nature and position of the earth does not help us in our hope of the life to come. It is enough to know what Scripture states. 'That He hung up the earth upon nothing' (Job xxvi. 7). Why then argue whether He hung it up in air or upon the water, and raise a controversy as to how the thin air could sustain the earth; or why, if upon the waters, the earth does not go crashing down to the bottom? . . . Not because the earth is in the middle, as if suspended on even balance, but because the majesty of God constrains it by the law of His will, does it endure stable upon the unstable and the void."

It does not help us in our hope of the life to come. It is enough to know what Scripture states. Why then argue? But a century and a half after St. Ambrose, opinion was still troubled, on this occasion by the problem of the antipodes. A monk named Cosmas, famous for his scientific attainments, was therefore deputed to write a Christian Topography, or "Christian Opinion concerning the World." It is clear that he knew exactly what was expected of him, for he based all his conclusions on the Scriptures as he read them. It appears, then, that the world is a flat parallelogram, twice as broad from east to west as it is long from north to south. In the center is the earth surrounded by ocean, which is in turn surrounded by another earth, where men lived before the deluge. This other earth was Noah's port of embarkation. In the north is a high conical mountain around which revolve the sun and moon. When the sun is behind the mountain it is night. The sky is glued to the edges of the outer earth. It consists of four high walls which meet in a concave roof, so that the earth is the floor of the universe. There is an ocean on the other side of the sky, constituting the "waters that are above the firmament." The space between the celestial ocean and the ultimate roof of the universe belongs to the blest. The space between the earth and sky is inhabited by the angels. Finally, since St. Paul said that all men are made to live upon the "face of the earth" how could they live on the back where the Antipodes are supposed to be? "With such a passage before his eyes, a Christian, we are told, should not 'even speak of the Antipodes.' "

Far less should he go to the Antipodes; nor should any Christian prince give him a ship to try; nor would any pious mariner wish to try. For Cosmas there was nothing in the least absurd about his map. Only by remembering his absolute conviction that this was the map of the universe can we begin to understand how he would have dreaded Magellan or Peary or the aviator who risked a collision with the angels and the vault of heaven by flying seven miles up in the air. In the same way we can best understand the furies of war and politics by remembering that almost the whole of each party believes absolutely in its picture of the opposition, that it takes as fact, not what is, but what it supposes to be the fact. And that therefore, like Hamlet, it will stab Polonius behind the rustling curtain, thinking him the king, and perhaps like Hamlet add:

> Thou wretched, rash, intruding fool, farewell!
> I took thee for thy better; take thy fortune.

Great men, even during their lifetime, are usually known to the public only through a fictitious personality. Hence the modicum of truth in the old saying that no man is a hero to his valet. There is only a modicum of truth, for the valet, and the private secretary, are often immersed in the fiction themselves. Royal personages are, of course, constructed personalities. Whether they themselves believe in their public character, or whether they merely permit the chamberlain to stage-manage it, there are at least two distinct selves, the public and regal self, the private and human. The biographies of great people fall more or less readily into the histories of these two selves. The official biographer reproduces the public life, the revealing memoir the other. The Charnwood Lincoln, for example, is a noble portrait, not of an actual human being, but of an epic figure, replete with significance, who moves on much the same level of reality as Aeneas or St. George. Oliver's Hamilton is a majestic abstraction, the sculpture of an idea, "an essay" as Mr. Oliver himself calls it, "on American union." It is a formal monument to the statecraft of federalism, hardly the biography of a person. Sometimes people create their own façade when they think they are revealing the interior scene. The Repington diaries and Margot Asquith's are a species of self-portraiture in which the intimate detail is most revealing as an index of how the authors like to think about themselves.

But the most interesting kind of portraiture is that which arises spontaneously in people's minds. When Victoria came to the throne, says Mr. Strachey, "among the outside public there was a great wave of enthusiasm. Sentiment and romance were coming into fashion; and the spectacle of the little girl-queen, innocent, modest, with fair hair and pink cheeks, driving through her capital, filled the hearts of the beholders with raptures of affectionate loyalty. What, above all, struck everybody with overwhelming force was the contrast between Queen Victoria and her uncles. The nasty old men, debauched and selfish, pigheaded and ridiculous, with their perpetual burden of debts, confusions, and disreputabilities—they had vanished like the snows of winter and here at last, crowned and radiant, was the spring."

M. Jean de Pierrefeu saw hero-worship at first hand, for he was an officer on Joffre's staff at the moment of that soldier's greatest fame:

For two years, the entire world paid an almost divine homage to the victor of the Marne. The baggage-master literally bent under the weight of the boxes, of the packages and letters which unknown people sent him with a frantic testimonial of their admiration. I think that outside of General Joffre, no commander in the war has been able to realize a comparable idea of what glory is. They sent him boxes of candy from all the great confectioners of the world, boxes of champagne, fine wines of every vintage, fruits, game, ornaments and utensils, clothes, smoking materials, inkstands, paperweights. Every territory sent its speciality. The painter sent his picture, the sculptor his statuette, the dear old lady a comforter or socks, the shepherd in his hut carved a pipe for his sake. All the manufacturers of the world who were hostile to Germany shipped their products, Havana its cigars, Portugal its port wine. I have known a hairdresser who had nothing better to do than to make a portrait of the General out of hair belonging to persons who were dear to him; a professional penman had the same idea, but the features were composed of thousands of little phrases in tiny characters which sang the praise of the General. As to letters, he had them in all scripts, from all countries, written in every dialect, affectionate letters, grateful, overflowing with love, filled with adoration. They called him Savior of the World, Father of his Country, Agent of God, Benefactor of Humanity, etc. . . . And not only Frenchmen, but Americans, Argentinians, Australians, etc. etc. . . . Thousands of little children, without their parents' knowledge, took pen in hand and wrote to tell him their love: most of them called him Our Father. And there was poignancy about their effusions, their adoration, these sighs of deliverance that escaped from thousands of hearts at the defeat of barbarism. To all these naif little souls, Joffre seemed like St. George crushing the dragon. Certainly he incarnated for the conscience of mankind the victory of good over evil, of light over darkness.

Lunatics, simpletons, the half-crazy and the crazy turned their darkened brains toward him as toward reason itself. I have read the letter of a person living in Sydney, who begged the General to save him from his enemies; another, a New Zealander, requested him to send some soldiers to the house of a gentleman who owed him ten pounds and would not pay.

Finally, some hundreds of young girls, overcoming the timidity of their sex, asked for engagements, their families not to know about it; others wished only to serve him.

This ideal Joffre was compounded out of the victory won by him, his staff and his troops, the despair of the war, the personal sorrows, and the hope of future victory. But beside hero-worship there is the exorcism of devils. By the same mechanism through which heroes are incarnated, devils are made. If everything good was to come from Joffre, Foch, Wilson, or Roosevelt, everything evil originated in the Kaiser Wilhelm, Lenin and Trotsky. They were as omnipotent for evil as the heroes were omnipotent for good. To many simple and frightened minds there was no political reverse, no strike, no obstruction, no mysterious death or mysterious conflagration anywhere in the world of which the causes did not wind back to these personal sources of evil.

Worldwide concentration of this kind on a symbolic personality is rare enough to be clearly remarkable, and every author has a weakness for the striking and irrefutable example. The vivisection of war reveals such examples, but it does not make them out of nothing. In a more normal public life, symbolic pictures are no less governant of behavior, but each symbol is far less inclusive because there are so many competing ones. Not only is each symbol charged with less feeling because at most it represents only a part of the population, but even within that part there is infinitely less suppression of individual difference. The *symbols of public opinion,* in times of moderate security, are subject to check and comparison and argument. They come and go, coalesce and are forgotten, never organizing perfectly the emotion of the whole group. There is, after all, just one human activity left in which whole populations accomplish the union sacrée. It occurs in those middle phases of a war when fear, pugnacity, and hatred have secured complete dominion of the spirit, either to crush every other instinct or to enlist it, and before weariness is felt.

At almost all other times, and even in war when it is deadlocked, a sufficiently greater range of feelings is aroused to establish conflict, choice, hesitation, and compromise. The symbolism of public opinion usually bears, as we shall see, the marks of this balancing of interest. Think, for example, of how rapidly, after the armistice, the precarious and by no means successfully established symbol of Allied Unity disappeared, how it was followed almost immediately by the breakdown of each nation's symbolic picture of the other: Britain the Defender of Public Law, France watching at the Frontier of Freedom, America the Crusader. And think then of how within each nation the symbolic picture of itself frayed out, as party and class conflict and personal ambition began to stir postponed issues. And then of how the symbolic pictures of the leaders gave way, as one by one, Wilson, Clemenceau, Lloyd George, ceased to be the incarnation of human hope, and became merely the negotiators and administrators for a disillusioned world.

Whether we regret this as one of the soft evils of peace or applaud it as a return to sanity is obviously no matter here. Our first concern with fictions and symbols is to forget their value to the existing social order, and to think of them simply as an important part of the machinery of human communication. Now in any society that is not completely self-contained in its interests and so small that everyone can know all about everything that happens, ideas deal with events that are out of sight and hard to grasp. Miss Sherwin of Gopher Prairie, is aware that a war is raging in France and tries to conceive it. She has never been to France, and certainly she has never been along what is now the battlefront. Pictures of French and German soldiers she has seen, but it is impossible for her to imagine three million men. No one, in fact, can imagine them, and the professionals do not try. They think of them as, say, two hundred divisions. But Miss Sherwin has no access to the order of battle maps, and so if she is to think about the war, she fastens upon Joffre and the Kaiser as if they were engaged in a personal duel. Perhaps if you could see what she sees with her mind's eye, the image in its composition might be not unlike an Eighteenth Century engravng of a great soldier. He stands there boldly unruffled and more than life size, with a shadowy army of tiny little figures winding off into the landscape behind. Nor it seems are great men oblivious to these expectations. M. de Pierrefeu tells of a photographer's visit to Joffre. The General was in his "middle class office, before the worktable without papers, where he sat down to write his signature. Suddenly it was noticed that there were no maps on the walls. But since according to popular ideas it is not possible to think of a general without maps, a few were placed in position for the picture, and removed soon afterwards."

The only feeling that anyone can have about an event he does not experience is the feeling aroused by his mental image of that event. That is why until we know what others think they know, we cannot truly understand their acts. I have seen a young girl, brought up in a Pennsylvania mining town, plunged suddenly from entire cheerfulness into a paroxysm of grief when a gust of wind cracked the kitchen window-pane. For hours she was inconsolable, and to me incomprehensible. But when she was able to talk, it transpired that if a window-pane broke it meant that a close relative had died. She was, therefore, mourning for her father, who had frightened her into running away from home. The father was, of course, quite thoroughly alive as a telegraphic inquiry soon proved. But until the telegram came, the cracked glass was an authentic message to that girl. Why it was authentic only a prolonged investigation by a skilled psychiatrist could show. But even the most casual observer could see that the girl, enormously upset by her family troubles, had hallucinated a complete fiction out of one external fact, a remembered superstition, and a turmoil of remorse, and fear and love for her father.

Abnormality in these instances is only a matter of degree. When an Attorney-General, who has been frightened by a bomb exploded on his doorstep, convinces himself by the reading of revolutionary literature that a revolution is to happen on the first of May 1920, we recognize that much the same mechanism is at work. The war, of course, furnished many examples of this pattern: the casual fact, the creative imagination, the will to believe, and out of these three elements, a counterfeit of reality to which there was a violent instinctive response. For it is clear enough that under certain conditions men respond as powerfully to fictions as they do to realities, and that in many cases they help to create the very fictions to which they respond. Let him cast the first stone who did not believe in the Russian army that passed through England in August, 1914, did not accept any tale of atrocities without direct proof, and never saw a plot, a traitor, or a spy where there was none. Let him cast a stone who never passed on as the real inside truth what he had heard someone say who knew no more than he did.

In all these instances we must note particularly one common factor. It is the insertion between man and his environment of a pseudo-environment. To that pseudo-environment his behavior is a response. But because it *is* behavior, the consequences, if they are acts, operate not in the pseudo-environment where the behavior is stimulated, but in the real environment where action eventuates. If the behavior is not a practical act, but what we call roughly thought and emotion, it may be a long time before there is any noticeable break in the texture of the fictitious world. But when the stimulus of the pseudo-fact results in action on things or other people, contradiction soon develops. Then comes the sensation of butting one's head against a stone wall, of learning by experience, and witnessing Herbert Spencer's tragedy of the murder of a Beautiful Theory by a Gang of Brutal Facts, the discomfort in short of a maladjustment. For certainly, at the level of social life, what is called the adjustment of man to his environment takes place through the medium of fictions.

By fictions I do not mean lies. I mean a representation of the environment which is in lesser or greater degree made by man himself. The range of fiction extends all the way from complete hallucination to the scientists' perfectly self-conscious use of a schematic model, or his decision that for his particular problem accuracy beyond a certain number of decimal places is not important.

A work of fiction may have almost any degree of fidelity, and so long as the degree of fidelity can be taken into account, fiction is not misleading. In fact, human culture is very largely the selection, the rearrangement, the tracing of patterns upon, and the stylizing of, what William James called "the random irradiations and resettlements of our ideas." The alternative to the use of fictions is direct exposure to the ebb and flow of sensation. That is not a real alternative, for however refreshing it is to see at times with a perfectly innocent eye, innocence itself is not wisdom, though a source and corrective of wisdom.

For the real environment is altogether too big, too complex, and too fleeting for direct acquaintance. We are not equipped to deal with so much subtlety, so much variety, so many permutations and combinations. And although we have to act in that environment, we have to reconstruct it on a simpler model before we can manage with it. To traverse the world men must have maps of the world. Their persistent difficulty is to secure maps on which their own need, or someone else's need, has not sketched in the coast of Bohemia.

THE NATURE OF NEWS

All the reporters in the world working all the hours of the day could not witness all the happenings in the world. There are not a great many reporters. And none of them has the power to be in more than one place at a time. Reporters are not clairvoyant, they do not gaze into a crystal ball and see the world at will, they are not assisted by thought-transference. Yet the range of subjects these comparatively few men manage to cover would be a miracle indeed, if it were not a standardized routine.

Newspapers do not try to keep an eye on all mankind. They have watchers stationed at certain places, like Police Headquarters, the Coroner's Office, the County Clerk's Office, City Hall, the White House, the Senate, House of Representatives, and so forth. They watch, or rather in the majority of cases they belong to associations which employ men who watch "a comparatively small number of places where it is made known when the life of anyone . . . departs from ordinary paths, or when events worth telling about occur. For example, John Smith, let it be supposed, becomes a broker. For ten years he pursues the even tenor of his way and except for his customers and his friends no one gives him a thought. To the newspapers he is as if he were not. But in the eleventh year he suffers heavy losses and, at last, his resources all gone, summons his lawyer and arranges for the making of an assignment. The lawyer posts off to the County Clerk's office, and a clerk there makes the necessary entries in the official docket. Here in step the newspapers. While the clerk is writing Smith's business obituary a reporter glances over his shoulder and a few minutes later the reporters know Smith's troubles and are as well informed concerning his business status as they would be had they kept a reporter at his door every day for over ten years."

When Mr. Given says that the newspapers know "Smith's troubles" and "his business status," he does not mean that they know them as Smith knows them, or as Mr. Arnold Bennett would know them if he had made Smith the hero of a three volume novel. The newspapers know only "in a few minutes" the bald facts which are recorded in the County Clerk's Office. That overt act "uncovers" the news about Smith. Whether the news will be followed up or not is another matter. The point is that before a series of events become news they have usually to make themselves noticeable in some more or less overt act. Generally too, in a crudely overt act. Smith's friends may have known for years that he was taking risks, rumors may even have reached the financial editor if Smith's friends were talkative. But apart from the fact that none of this could be published because it would be libel, there is in these rumors nothing definite on which to peg a story. Something definite must occur that has unmistakable form. It may be the act of going into bankruptcy, it may be a fire, a collision, an assault, a riot, an arrest, a denunciation, the introduction of a bill, a speech, a vote, a meeting, the expressed opinion of a well known citizen, an editorial in a newspaper, a sale, a wage-schedule, a price change, the proposal to build a bridge. . . . There must be a manifestation. The course of events must assume a certain definable shape, and until it is in a phase where some aspect is an accomplished fact, news does not separate itself from the ocean of possible truth.

Naturally there is room for wide difference of opinion as to when events have a shape that can be reported. A good journalist will find news oftener than a hack. If he sees a building with a dangerous list, he does not have to wait until it falls into the street in order to recognize news. It was a great reporter who guessed the name of the next Indian Viceroy when he heard that Lord So-and-So was inquiring about climates. There are lucky shots but the number of men who can make them is small. Usually it is the stereotyped shape assumed by an event at an obvious place that uncovers the run of the news. The most obvious place is where people's affairs touch public authority. De minimis non curat lex. It is at these places that marriages, births, deaths, contracts, failures, arrivals, departures, lawsuits, disorders, epidemics and calamities are made known.

In the first instance, therefore, the news is not a mirror of social conditions, but the report of an aspect that has obtruded itself. The news does not tell you how the seed is germinating in the ground, but it may tell you when the first sprout breaks through the surface. It may even tell you what somebody says is happening to the seed under ground. It may tell you that the sprout did not come up at the time it was expected. The more points, then, at which any happening can be fixed, objectified, measured, named, the more points there are at which news can occur.

So, if some day a legislature, having exhausted all other ways of improving mankind, should forbid the scoring of baseball games, it might still be possible to play some sort of game in which the umpire decided according to his own sense of fair play how long the game should last, when each team should go to bat, and who should be regarded as the winner. If that game were reported in the newspapers it would consist of a record of the umpire's decisions, plus the reporter's impression of the hoots and cheers of the crowd, plus at best a vague account of how certain men, who had no specified position on the field moved around for a few hours on an unmarked piece of sod. The more you try to imagine the logic of so absurd a predicament, the more clear it becomes that for the purposes of newsgathering, (let alone the purposes of playing the game) it is impossible to do much without an apparatus and rules for naming, scoring, recording. Because that machinery is far from perfect, the umpire's life is often a distracted one. Many crucial plays he has to judge by eye. The last vestige of dispute could be taken out of the game, as it has been taken out of chess when people obey the rules, if somebody thought it worth his while to photograph every play. It was the moving pictures which finally settled a real doubt in many reporters' minds, owing to the slowness of the human eye, as to just what blow of Dempsey's knocked out Carpentier.

Wherever there is a good machinery of record, the modern news service works with great precision. There is one on the stock exchange, and the news of price movements is flashed over tickers with dependable accuracy. There is a machinery for election returns, and when the counting and tabulating are well done, the result of a national election is usually known on the night of the election. In civilized communities deaths, births, marriages and divorces are recorded, and are known accurately except where there is concealment or neglect. The machinery exists for some, and only some, aspects of industry and government, in varying degrees of precision for securities, money and staples, bank clearances, realty transactions, wage scales. It exists for imports and exports because they pass through a custom house and can be directly recorded. It exists in nothing like the same degree for internal trade, and especially for trade over the counter.

It will be found, I think, that there is a very direct relation between the certainty of news and the system of record. If you call to mind the topics which form the principal indictment by reformers against the press, you find they are subjects in which the newspaper occupies the position of the umpire in the unscored baseball game. All news about states of mind is of this character: so are all descriptions of personalities, of sincerity, aspiration, motive, intention, of mass feeling, of national feeling, of public opinion, the policies of foreign governments. So is much news about what is going to happen. So are questions turning on private profit, private income, wages, working conditions, the efficiency of labor, educational opportunity, unemployment, monotony, health, discrimination, unfairness, restraint of trade, waste, "backward peoples," conservatism, imperialism, radicalism, liberty, honor, righteousness. All involve data that are at best spasmodically recorded. The data may be hidden because of a censorship or a tradition of privacy, they may not exist because nobody thinks record important, because he thinks it red tape, or because nobody has yet invented an objective system of measurement. Then the news on these subjects is bound to be debatable, when it is not wholly neglected. The events which are not scored are reported either as personal and conventional opinions, or they are not news. They do not take shape until somebody protests, or somebody investigates, or somebody publicly, in the etymological meaning of the word, makes an *issue* of them.

This is the underlying reason for the existence of the press agent. The enormous discretion as to what facts and what impressions shall be reported is steadily convincing every organized group of people that whether it wishes to secure publicity or to avoid it, the exercise of discretion cannot be left to the reporter. It is safer to hire a press agent who stands between the group and the newspapers. Having hired him, the temptation to exploit his strategic position is very great. "Shortly before the war," says Mr. Frank Cobb, "the newspapers of New York took a census of the press agents who were regularly employed and regularly accredited and found that there were about twelve hundred of them. How many there are now (1919) I do not pretend to know, but what I do know is that many of the direct channels to news have been closed and the information for the public is first filtered through publicity agents. The great corporations have them, the banks have them, the railroads have them, all the organizations of business and of social and political activity have them, and they are the media through which news comes. Even statesmen have them."

Were reporting the simple recovery of obvious facts, the press agent would be little more than a clerk. But since, in respect to most of the big topics of news, the facts are not simple, and not at all obvious, but subject to choice and opinion, it is natural that everyone should wish to make his own choice of facts for the newspapers to print. The publicity man does that. And in doing it, he certainly saves the reporter much trouble, by presenting him a clear picture of a situation out of which he might otherwise make neither head nor tail. But it follows that the picture which the publicity man makes for the reporter is the one he wishes the public to see. He is censor and propagandist, responsible only to his employers, and to the whole truth responsible only as it accords with the employers' conception of his own interests.

The development of the publicity man is a clear sign that the facts of modern life do not spontaneously take a shape in which they can be known. They must be given a shape by somebody, and since in the daily routine reporters cannot give a shape to facts, and since there is little disinterested organization of intelligence, the need for some formulation is being met by the interested parties.

2 The Agenda-Setting Function of Mass Media*

Maxwell McCombs
Donald Shaw

In our day, more than ever before, candidates go before the people through the mass media rather than in person.[1] The information in the mass media becomes the only contact many have with politics. The pledges, promises, and rhetoric encapsulated in news stories, columns, and editorials constitute much of the information upon which a voting decision has to be made. Most of what people know comes to them "second" or "third" hand from the mass media or from other people.[2]

Although the evidence that mass media deeply change attitudes in a campaign is far from conclusive,[3] the evidence is much stronger that voters learn from the immense quantity of information available during each campaign.[4] People, of course, vary greatly in their attention to mass media

---

*Reprinted from Public Opinion Quarterly (1972, Vol. 36, pp. 176–185) by permission of The University of Chicago Press.

[1]See Bernard R. Berelson, Paul F. Lazarsfeld, and William N. McPhee, *Voting,* Chicago, University of Chicago Press, 1954, p. 234. Of course to some degree candidates have always depended upon the mass media, but radio and television brought a new intimacy into politics.

[2]Kurt Lang and Gladys Engel Lang, "The Mass Media and Voting," in Bernard Berelson and Morris Janowitz, eds., *Reader in Public Opinion and Communication,* 2d ed., New York, Free Press, 1966, p. 466.

[3]See Berelson *et al., op. cit.,* p. 223; Paul F. Lazarsfeld, Bernard Berelson, and Hazel Gaudet, *The People's Choice,* New York, Columbia University Press, 1948, p. xx; and Joseph Trenaman and Denis McQuail, *Television and the Political Image,* London, Methuen and Co., 1961, pp. 147, 191.

[4]See Bernard C. Cohen, *The Press and Foreign Policy,* Princeton, Princeton University Press, 1963, p. 120.

political information. Some, normally the better educated and most politically interested (and those least likely to change political beliefs), actively seek information; but most seem to acquire it, if at all, without much effort. It just comes in. As Berelson succinctly puts it: "On any single subject many 'hear' but few 'listen'." But Berelson also found that those with the greatest mass media exposure are most likely to know where the candidates stand on different issues.[5] Trenaman and McQuail found the same thing in a study of the 1959 General Election in England.[6] Voters do learn.

They apparently learn, furthermore, in direct proportion to the emphasis placed on the campaign issues by the mass media. Specifically focusing on the agenda-setting function of the media, Lang and Lang observe:

> The mass media force attention to certain issues. They build up public images of political figures. They are constantly presenting objects suggesting what individuals in the mass should think about, know about, have feelings about.[7]

Perhaps this hypothesized agenda-setting function of the mass media is most succinctly stated by Cohen, who noted that the press "may not be successful much of the time in telling people what to think, but it is stunningly successful in telling its readers what to think *about*."[8] While the mass media may have little influence on the direction or intensity of attitudes, it is hypothesized that *the mass media set the agenda for each political campaign, influencing the salience of attitudes toward the political issues.*

METHOD

To investigate the agenda-setting capacity of the mass media in the 1968 presidential campaign, this study attempted to match what Chapel Hill voters *said* were key issues of the campaign with the *actual content* of the mass media used by them during the campaign. Respondents were selected randomly from

---

[5]Berelson *et al., op. cit.,* pp. 244, 228.

[6]Trenaman and McQuail, *op. cit.,* p. 165.

[7]Lang and Lang, *op. cit.,* p. 468. Trenaman and McQuail warn that there was little evidence in their study that television (or any other mass medium) did anything other than provide information; there was little or no attitude change on significant issues. "People are aware of what is being said, and who is saying it, but they do not necessarily take it at face value." See *op. cit.,* p. 168. In a more recent study, however, Blumler and McQuail found that high exposure to Liberal party television broadcasts in the British General Election of 1964 was positively related to a more favorable attitude toward the Liberal party for those with medium or weak motivation to follow the campaign. The more strongly motivated were much more stable in political attitude. See Jay G. Blumler and Denis McQuail, *Television in Politics: Its Uses and Influence,* Chicago, University of Chicago Press, 1969, p. 200.

[8]Cohen, *op. cit.,* p. 13.

lists of registered voters in five Chapel Hill precincts economically, socially, and racially representative of the community. By restricting this study to one community, numerous other sources of variation—for example, regional differences or variations in media performance—were controlled.

Between September 18 and October 6, 100 interviews were completed. To select these 100 respondents a filter question was used to identify those who had not yet definitely decided how to vote—presumably those most open or susceptible to campaign information. Only those not yet fully committed to a particular candidate were interviewed. Borrowing from the Trenaman and McQuail strategy, this study asked each respondent to outline the key issues as he saw them, regardless of what the candidates might be saying at the moment.[9] Interviewers recorded the answers as exactly as possible.

Concurrently with the voter interviews, the mass media serving these voters were collected and content analyzed. A pretest in spring 1968 found that for the Chapel Hill community almost all the mass media political information was provided by the following sources: Durham *Morning Herald,* Durham *Sun,* Raleigh *News and Observer,* Raleigh *Times,* New York *Times, Time, Newsweek,* and NBC and CBS evening news broadcasts.

The answers of respondents regarding major problems as they saw them and the news and editorial comment appearing between September 12 and October 6 in the sampled newspapers, magazines, and news broadcasts were coded into 15 categories representing the key issues and other kinds of campaign news. Media news content also was divided into "major" and "minor" levels to see whether there was any substantial difference in mass media emphasis across topics.[10] For the print media, this major/minor division was in terms of space and position; for television, it was made in terms of position and time allowed. More specifically, *major* items were defined as follows:

1. Television: Any story 45 seconds or more in length and/or one of the three lead stories.

2. Newspapers: Any story which appeared as the lead on the front page or on any page under a three-column headline in which at least one-third of the story (a minimum of five paragraphs) was devoted to political news coverage.

3. News Magazines: Any story more than one column or any item which appeared in the lead at the beginning of the news section of the magazine.

4. Editorial Page Coverage of Newspapers and Magazines: Any item in the lead editorial position (the top left corner of the editorial page) plus all items

---

[9]See Trenaman and McQuail, *op. cit.,* p. 172. The survey question was: "What are you *most* concerned about these days? That is, regardless of what politicians say, what are the two or three *main* things which you think the government *should* concentrate on doing something about?"

[10]Intercoder reliability was above .90 for content analysis of both "major" and "minor" items. Details of categorization are described in the full report of this project. A small number of copies of the full report is available for distribution and may be obtained by writing the authors.

in which one-third (at least five paragraphs) of an editorial or columnist comment was devoted to political campaign coverage.

Minor items are those stories which are political in nature and included in the study but which are smaller in terms of space, time, or display than major items.

FINDINGS

The over-all *major* item emphasis of the selected mass media on different topics and candidates during the campaign is displayed in Table 1. It indicates that a considerable amount of campaign news was *not* devoted to discussion of the major political issues but rather to *analysis of the campaign itself*. This

TABLE 1
Major Mass Media Reports on Candidates and Issues, by
Candidates

| | Quoted Source | | | | | | |
	Nixon	Agnew	Humphrey	Muskie	Wallace	Lemay[a]	Total
The issues							
Foreign policy	7%	9%	13%	15%	2%	—	10%
Law and order	5	13	4	—	12	—	6
Fiscal policy	3	4	2	—	—	—	2
Public welfare	3	4	(*)[b]	5	2	—	2
Civil rights	3	9	(*)[b]	0	4	—	2
Other	19	13	14	25	11	—	15
The campaign							
Polls	1	—	—	—	1	—	(*)[b]
Campaign events	18	9	21	10	25	—	19
Campaign analysis	25	17	30	30	35	—	28
Other candidates							
Humphrey	11	22	—	5	1	—	5
Muskie	—	—	—	—	—	—	—
Nixon	—	—	11	5	3	—	5
Agnew	—	—	(*)[b]	—	—	—	(*)[b]
Wallace	5	—	3	5	—	—	3
Lemay	1	—	1	—	4	—	1
Total percent	101%[c]	100%	99[c]	100%	100%	—	98%[c]
Total number	188	23	221	20	95	11	558

[a]Coverage of Lemay amounted to only 11 major items during the September 12-October 6 period and are not individually included in the percentages; they are included in the total column.
[b]Less than .05 per cent.
[c]Does not sum to 100% because of rounding.

may give pause to those who think of campaign news as being primarily about the *issues*. Thirty-five percent of the major news coverage of Wallace was composed of this analysis ("Has he a chance to win or not?"). For Humphrey and Nixon the figures were, respectively, 30 percent and 25 percent. At the same time, the table also shows the relative emphasis of candidates speaking about each other. For example, Agnew apparently spent more time attacking Humphrey (22 percent of the major news items about Agnew) than did Nixon (11 percent of the major news about Nixon). The over-all *minor* item emphasis of the mass media on these political issues and topics closely paralleled that of major item emphasis.

Table 2 focuses on the relative emphasis of each party on the issues, as reflected in the mass media. The table shows that Humphrey/Muskie emphasized foreign policy far more than did Nixon/Agnew or Wallace/Lemay. In the case of the "law and order" issue, however, over half the Wallace/Lemay news was about this, while less than one-fourth of the Humphrey/Muskie news concentrated upon this topic. With Nixon/Agnew it was almost a third — just behind the Republican emphasis on foreign policy. Humphrey of course spent considerable time justifying (or commenting upon) the Vietnam War; Nixon did not choose (or have) to do this.

The media appear to have exerted a considerable impact on voters' judgments of what they considered the major issues of the campaign (even though the questionnaire specifically asked them to make judgments without regard to what politicians might be saying at the moment). The correlation between the major item emphasis on the main campaign issues carried by the media and voters' independent judgments of what were the important issues was +.967. Between minor item emphasis on the main campaign issues and voters' judgments, the correlation was +.979. In short, the data suggest a very strong relationship between the emphasis placed on different campaign issues by the media (reflecting to a considerable degree the emphasis by candidates)

TABLE 2
Mass Media Report on Issues, by Parties

Issues	Republican Nixon/Agnew			Democratic Humphrey/Muskie			American Wallace/Lemay		
	Major	Minor	Total	Major	Minor	Total	Major	Minor	Total
Foreign policy	34%	40%	38%	65%	63%	64%	30%	21%	26%
Law and order	26	36	32	19	26	23	48	55	52
Fiscal policy	13	1	6	10	6	8	—	—	—
Public welfare	13	14	13	4	3	4	7	12	10
Civil Rights	15	8	11	2	2	2	14	12	13
Total percent[a]	101%	99%	100%	100%	100%	101%	99%	100%	101%
Total number	47	72	119	48	62	110	28	33	61

[a]Some columns do not sum to 100% because of rounding.

and the judgments of voters as to the salience and importance of various campaign topics.

But while the three presidential candidates placed widely different emphasis upon different issues, the judgments of the voters seem to reflect the *composite* of the mass media coverage. This suggests that voters pay some attention to all the political news *regardless* of whether it is from, or about, any particular favored candidate. Because the tables we have seen reflect the composite of *all* the respondents, it is possible that individual differences, reflected in party preferences and in a predisposition to look mainly at material favorable to one's own party, are lost by lumping all the voters together in the analysis. Therefore, answers of respondents who indicated a preference (but not commitment) for one of the candidates during the September–October period studied (45 of the respondents; the others were undecided) were analyzed separately. Table 3 shows the results of this analysis for four selected media.

The table shows the frequency of important issues cited by respondents who favored Humphrey, Nixon, or Wallace correlated (*a*) with the frequency of *all* the major and minor issues carried by the media and (*b*) with the frequency of the major and minor issues oriented to *each party* (stories with a particular party or candidate as a primary referent) carried by each of the four media. For example, the correlation is .89 between what Democrats see as the important issues and the New York *Times*'s emphasis on the issues in *all* its major news items. The correlation is .79 between the Democrats' emphasis on the issues and the emphasis of the New York *Times* as reflected *only* in items about the Democratic candidates.

If one expected voters to pay more attention to the major and minor issues oriented to their own party—that is, to read or view *selectively*—the correlations between the voters and news/opinion about their own party should be strongest. This would be evidence of selective perception.[11] If, on the other hand, the voters attend reasonably well to *all* the news, *regardless* of which candidate or party issue is stressed, the correlations between the voter and total media content would be strongest. This would be evidence of the agenda-setting function. The crucial question is which set of correlations is stronger.

In general, Table 3 shows that voters who were not firmly committed early in the campaign attended well to *all* the news. For major news items, correlations were more often higher between voter judgments of important issues and the issues reflected in all the news (including of course news about their favored candidate/party) than were voter judgments of issues reflected in news *only* about their candidate/party. For minor news items, again voters

---

[11]While recent reviews of the literature and new experiments have questioned the validity of the selective perception hypothesis, this has nevertheless been the focus of much communication research. For example, see Richard F. Carter, Ronald H. Pyszka, and Jose L. Guerrero, "Dissonance and Exposure to Arousive Information," *Journalism Quarterly*, Vol. 46, 1969, pp. 37–42; and David O. Sears and Jonathan L. Freedman, "Selective Exposure to Information: A Critical Review," *Public Opinion Quarterly*, Vol. 31, 1967, pp. 194–213.

TABLE 3
Intercorrelations of Major and Minor Issue Emphasis by
Selected Media with Voter Issue Emphasis

	Major Items		Minor Items	
Selected Media	All News	News Own Party	All News	News Own Party
New York Times				
Voters (D)	.89	.79	.97	.85
Voters (R)	.80	.40	.88	.98
Voters (W)	.89	.25	.78	− .53
Durham Morning Herald				
Voters (D)	.84	.74	.95	.83
Voters (R)	.59	.88	.84	.69
Voters (W)	.82	.76	.79	.00
CBS				
Voters (D)	.83	.83	.81	.71
Voters (R)	.50	.00	.57	.40
Voters (W)	.78	.80	.86	.76
NBC				
Voters (D)	.57	.76	.64	.73
Voters (R)	.27	.13	.66	.63
Voters (W)	.84	.21	.48	− .33

more often correlated highest with the emphasis reflected in all the news than
with the emphasis reflected in news about a favored candidate. Considering
both major and minor item coverage, 18 of 24 possible comparisons show
voters more in agreement with all the news rather than with news only about
their own party/candidate preference. This finding is better explained by the
agenda-setting function of the mass media than by selective perception.

Although the data reported in Table 3 generally show high agreement
between voter and media evaluations of what the important issues were in
1968, the correlations are not uniform across the various media and all groups
of voters. The variations across media are more clearly reflected in Table 4,

TABLE 4
Correlations of Voter Emphasis on Issues with Media Coverage

	Newsweek	Time	New York Times	Raleigh Times	Raleigh News and Observer
Major Items	.30	.30	.96	.80	.91
Minor Items	.53	.78	.97	.73	.93
	Durham Sun	Durham Morning Herald	NBC News	CBS News	
Major Items	.82	.94	.89	.63	
Minor Items	.96	.93	.91	.81	

which includes all survey respondents, not just those predisposed toward a candidate at the time of the survey. There also is a high degree of consensus among the news media about the significant issues of the campaign, but again there is not perfect agreement. Considering the news media as mediators between voters and the actual political arena, we might interpret the correlations in Table 5 as reliability coefficients, indicating the extent of agreement among the news media about what the important political events are. To the extent that the coefficients are less than perfect, the pseudo-environment reflected in the mass media is less than a perfect representation of the actual 1968 campaign.

Two sets of factors, at least, reduce consensus among the news media. First, the basic characteristics of newspapers, television, and newsmagazines differ. Newspapers appear daily and have lots of space. Television is daily but has a severe time constraint. Newsmagazines appear weekly; news therefore cannot be as "timely". Table 5 shows that the highest correlations tend to be among like media; the lowest correlations, between different media.

Second, news media do have a point of view, sometimes extreme biases. However, the high correlations in Table 5 (especially among like media) suggest consensus on news values, especially on major news items. Although there is no explicit, commonly agreed-upon definition of news, there is a professional norm regarding major news stories from day to day. These major-story norms doubtless are greatly influenced today by widespread use of the major wire services—especially by newspapers and television—for much

TABLE 5

Intercorrelation of Mass Media Presidential News Coverage for Major and Minor Items

	Newsweek	Time	New York Times	Raleigh Times	Raleigh News & Observer	Durham Sun	Durham Morning Herald	NBC	CBS
					Major Items				
Newsweek		.99	.54	.92	.79	.81	.79	.68	.42
Time	.65		.51	.90	.77	.81	.76	.68	.43
New York Times	.46	.59		.70	.71	.66	.81	.66	.66
Raleigh Times	.73	.66	.64		.85	.89	.90	.72	.62
Raleigh News and Observer	.84	.49	.60	.74		.84	.93	.82	.60
Durham Sun	.77	.47	.47	.70	.80		.94	.91	.77
Durham Morning Herald	.89	.68	.68	.80	.93	.73		.89	.76
NBC News	.81	.65	.38	.87	.73	.84	.75		.82
CBS News	.66	.60	.83	.88	.79	.76	.78	.72	
					Minor Items				

political information.[12] But as we move from major events of the campaign, upon which nearly everyone agrees, there is more room for individual interpretation, reflected in the lower correlations for minor item agreement among media shown in Table 5. Since a newspaper, for example, uses only about 15 percent of the material available on any given day, there is considerable latitude for selection among minor items.

In short, the political world is reproduced imperfectly by individual news media. Yet the evidence in this study that voters tend to share the media's *composite* definition of what is important strongly suggests an agenda-setting function of the mass media.

DISCUSSION

The existence of an agenda-setting function of the mass media is not *proved* by the correlations reported here, of course, but the evidence is in line with the conditions that must exist if agenda-setting by the mass media does occur. This study has compared aggregate units — Chapel Hill voters as a group compared to the aggregate performance of several mass media. This is satisfactory as a first test of the agenda-setting hypothesis, but subsequent research must move from a broad societal level to the social psychological level, matching individual attitudes with individual use of the mass media. Yet even the present study refines the evidence in several respects. Efforts were made to match respondent attitudes only with media actually used by Chapel Hill voters. Further, the analysis includes a juxtaposition of the agenda-setting and selective perception hypotheses. Comparison of these correlations too supports the agenda-setting hypothesis.

Interpreting the evidence from this study as indicating mass media influence seems more plausible than alternative explanations. Any argument that the correlations between media and voter emphasis are spurious — that they are simply responding to the same events and not influencing each other one way or the other — assumes that voters have alternative means of observing the day-to-day changes in the political arena. This assumption is not plausible;

---

[12]A number of studies have focused on the influence of the wire services. For example, see David Gold and Jerry L. Simmons, "News Selection Patterns among Iowa Dailies," *Public Opinion Quarterly*, Vol. 29, 1965, pp. 425–430; Guido H. Stempel III, "How Newspapers Use the Associated Press Afternoon A-Wire," *Journalism Quarterly*, Vol. 41, 1964, pp. 380–384; Ralph D. Casey and Thomas H. Copeland Jr., "Use of Foreign News by 19 Minnesota Dailies," *Journalism Quarterly*, Vol. 35, 1958, pp. 87–89; Howard L. Lewis, "The Cuban Revolt Story: AP, UPI, and Three Papers," *Journalism Quarterly*, Vol. 37, 1960, pp. 573–578; George A. Van Horn, "Analysis of AP News on Trunk and Wisconsin State Wires," *Journalism Quarterly*, Vol. 29, 1952, pp. 426–432; and Scott M. Cutlip, "Content and Flow of AP News — From Trunk to TTS to Reader," *Journalism Quarterly*, Vol. 31, 1954, pp. 434–446.

since few directly participate in presidential election campaigns, and fewer still see presidential candidates in person, the information flowing in interpersonal communication channels is primarily relayed from, and based upon, mass media news coverage. The media are the major primary sources of national political information; for most, mass media provide the best — and only — easily available approximation of ever-changing political realities.

It might also be argued that the high correlations indicate that the media simply were successful in matching their messages to audience interests. Yet since numerous studies indicate a sharp divergence between the news values of professional journalists and their audiences, it would be remarkable to find a near perfect fit in this one case.[13] It seems more likely that the media have prevailed in this area of major coverage. . . .

ACKNOWLEDGMENTS

This study was partially supported by a grant from the National Association of Broadcasters. Additional support was provided by the UNC Institute for Research in Social Science and the School of Journalism Foundation of North Carolina.

---

[13]Furthermore, five of the nine media studied here are national media and none of the remaining four originate in Chapel Hill. It is easier to argue that Chapel Hill voters fit their judgments of issue salience to the mass media than the reverse. An interesting study which discusses the problems of trying to fit day-to-day news judgments to reader interest is Guido H. Stempel III, "A Factor Analytic Study of Reader Interest in News," *Journalism Quarterly*, Vol. 44, 1967, pp. 326–330. An older study is Philip F. Griffin, "Reader Comprehension of News Stories: A Preliminary Study," *Journalism Quarterly*, Vol. 26, 1949, pp. 389–396.

3 Up and Down With Ecology: The "Issue-Attention Cycle"*

Anthony Downs

American public attention rarely remains sharply focused upon any one domestic issue for very long—even if it involves a continuing problem of crucial importance to society. Instead, a systematic "issue-attention cycle" seems strongly to influence public attitudes and behavior concerning most key domestic problems. Each of these problems suddenly leaps into prominence, remains there for a short time, and then—though still largely unresolved—gradually fades from the center of public attention. A study of the way this cycle operates provides insights into how long public attention is likely to remain sufficiently focused upon any given issue to generate enough political pressure to cause effective change.

The shaping of American attitudes toward improving the quality of our environment provides both an example and a potential test of this "issue-attention cycle." In the past few years, there has been a remarkably widespread upsurge of interest in the quality of our environment. This change in public attitudes has been much faster than any changes in the environment itself. What has caused this shift in public attention? Why did this issue suddenly assume so high a priority among our domestic concerns? And how long will the American public sustain high-intensity interest in ecological matters? I believe that answers to these questions can be derived from analyzing the "issue-attention cycle."

*Reprinted with permission of the author from: *The Public Interest,* No. 28 (Spring, 1972), pp. 38–50. Copyright 1972 by National Affairs Inc.

THE DYNAMICS OF THE "ISSUE-ATTENTION CYCLE"

Public perception of most "crises" in American domestic life does not reflect changes in real conditions as much as it reflects the operation of a systematic cycle of heightening public interest and then increasing boredom with major issues. This "issue-attention cycle" is rooted both in the nature of certain domestic problems and in the way major communications media interact with the public. The cycle itself has five stages, which may vary in duration depending upon the particular issue involved, but which almost always occur in the following sequence:

1. **The pre-problem stage.** This prevails when some highly undesirable social condition exists but has not yet captured much public attention, even though some experts or interest groups may already be alarmed by it. *Usually, objective conditions regarding the problem are far worse during the pre-problem stage than they are by the time the public becomes interested in it.* For example, this was true of racism, poverty, and malnutrition in the United States.

2. **Alarmed discovery and euphoric enthusiasm.** As a result of some dramatic series of events (like the ghetto riots in 1965 to 1967), or for other reasons, the public suddenly becomes both aware of and alarmed about the evils of a particular problem. This alarmed discovery is invariably accompanied by euphoric enthusiasm about society's ability to "solve this problem" or "do something effective" within a relatively short time. The combination of alarm and confidence results in part from the strong public pressure in America for political leaders to claim that every problem can be "solved." This outlook is rooted in the great American tradition of optimistically viewing most obstacles to social progress as *external* to the structure of society itself. The implication is that every obstacle can be eliminated and every problem solved *without any fundamental reordering of society itself,* if only we devote sufficient effort to it. In older and perhaps wiser cultures, there is an underlying sense of irony or even pessimism which springs from a widespread and often confirmed belief that many problems cannot be "solved" *at all* in any complete sense. Only recently has this more pessimistic view begun to develop in our culture.

3. **Realizing the cost of significant progress.** The third stage consists of a gradually spreading realization that the cost of "solving" the problem is very high indeed. Really doing so would not only take a great deal of money but would also require major sacrifices by large groups in the population. The public thus begins to realize that part of the problem results from arrangements that are providing significant benefits to someone—often to millions. For example, traffic congestion and a great deal of smog are caused by increasing automobile usage. Yet this also enhances the mobility of millions of

Americans who continue to purchase more vehicles to obtain these advantages. In certain cases, technological progress can eliminate some of the undesirable results of a problem without causing any major restructuring of society or any loss of present benefits by others (except for higher money costs). In the optimistic American tradition, such a technological solution is initially assumed to be possible in the case of nearly every problem. Our most pressing social problems, however, usually involve either deliberate or unconscious exploitation of one group in society by another, or the prevention of one group from enjoying something that others want to keep for themselves. For example, most upper-middle-class whites value geographic separation from poor people and blacks. Hence any equality of access to the advantages of suburban living for the poor and for blacks cannot be achieved without some sacrifice by middle-class whites of the "benefits" of separation. The increasing recognition that there is this type of relationship between the problem and its "solution" constitutes a key part of the third stage.

4. **Gradual decline of intense public interest.** The previous stage becomes almost imperceptibly transformed into the fourth stage: a gradual decline in the intensity of public interest in the problem. As more and more people realize how difficult, and how costly to themselves, a solution to the problem would be, three reactions set in. Some people just get discouraged. Others feel positively threatened by thinking about the problem; so they suppress such thoughts. Still others become bored by the issue. Most people experience some combination of these feelings. Consequently, public desire to keep attention focused on the issue wanes. And by this time, some other issue is usually entering Stage Two; so it exerts a more novel and thus more powerful claim upon public attention.

5. **The post-problem stage.** In the final stage, an issue that has been replaced at the center of public concern moves into a prolonged limbo — a twilight realm of lesser attention or spasmodic recurrences of interest. However, the issue now has a different relation to public attention than that which prevailed in the "pre-problem" stage. For one thing, during the time that interest was sharply focused on this problem, new institutions, programs, and policies may have been created to help solve it. These entities almost always persist and often have some impact even after public attention has shifted elsewhere. For example, during the early stages of the "War on Poverty," the Office of Economic Opportunity (OEO) was established, and it initiated many new programs. Although poverty has now faded as a central public issue, OEO still exists. Moreover, many of its programs have experienced significant success, even though funded at a far lower level than would be necessary to reduce poverty decisively.

Any major problem that once was elevated to national prominence may sporadically recapture public interest; or important aspects of it may become attached to some other problem that subsequently dominates center stage. Therefore, problems that have gone through the cycle almost always receive a higher average level of attention, public effort, and general concern than those still in the pre-discovery stage.

WHICH PROBLEMS ARE LIKELY TO GO THROUGH THE CYCLE?

Not all major social problems go through this "issue-attention cycle." Those which do generally possess to some degree three specific characteristics. First, the majority of persons in society are not suffering from the problem nearly as much as some minority (a *numerical* minority, not necessarily an *ethnic* one). This is true of many pressing social problems in America today—poverty, racism, poor public transportation, low-quality education, crime, drug addiction, and unemployment, among others. The number of persons suffering from each of these ills is very large *absolutely*—in the millions. But the numbers are small *relatively*—usually less than 15 per cent of the entire population. Therefore, most people do not suffer directly enough from such problems to keep their attention riveted on them.

Second, the sufferings caused by the problem are generated by social arrangements that provide significant benefits to a majority or a powerful minority of the population. For example, Americans who own cars—plus the powerful automobile and highway lobbies—receive short-run benefits from the prohibition of using motor-fuel tax revenues for financing public transportation systems, even though such systems are desperately needed by the urban poor.

Third, the problem has no intrinsically exciting qualities—or no longer has them. When big-city racial riots were being shown nightly on the nation's television screens, public attention naturally focused upon their causes and consequences. But when they ceased (or at least the media stopped reporting them so intensively), public interest in the problems related to them declined sharply. Similarly, as long as the National Aeronautics and Space Administration (NASA) was able to stage a series of ever more thrilling space shots, culminating in the worldwide television spectacular of Americans walking on the moon, it generated sufficient public support to sustain high-level Congressional appropriations. But NASA had nothing half so dramatic for an encore, and repetition of the same feat proved less and less exciting (though a near disaster on the third try did revive audience interest). So NASA's Congressional appropriations plummeted.

A problem must be dramatic and exciting to maintain public interest because news is "consumed" by much of the American public (and by publics everywhere) largely as a form of entertainment. As such, it competes with other types of entertainment for a share of each person's time. Every day, there is a fierce struggle for space in the highly limited universe of newsprint and television viewing time. Each issue vies not only with all other social problems and public events, but also with a multitude of "non-news" items that are often far more pleasant to contemplate. These include sporting news, weather reports, crossword puzzles, fashion accounts, comics, and daily horoscopes. In fact, the amount of television time and newspaper space devoted to sports coverage, as compared to international events, is a striking commentary on the relative value that the public places on knowing about these two subjects.

When all three of the above conditions exist concerning a given problem that has somehow captured public attention, the odds are great that it will soon move through the entire "issue-attention cycle" — and therefore will gradually fade from the center of the stage. The first condition means that most people will not be continually reminded of the problem by their own suffering from it. The second condition means that solving the problem requires sustained attention and effort, plus fundamental changes in social institutions or behavior. This in turn means that significant attempts to solve it are threatening to important groups in society. The third condition means that the media's sustained focus on this problem soon bores a majority of the public. As soon as the media realize that their emphasis on this problem is threatening many people and boring even more, they will shift their focus to some "new" problem. This is particularly likely in America because nearly all the media are run for profit, and they make the most money by appealing to the largest possible audiences. Thus, as Marshall McLuhan has pointed out, it is largely the audience itself — the American public — that "manages the news" by maintaining or losing interest in a given subject. As long as this pattern persists, we will continue to be confronted by a stream of "crises" involving particular social problems. Each will rise into public view, capture center stage for a while, and then gradually fade away as it is replaced by more fashionable issues moving into their "crisis" phases . . .

THE FUTURE OF THE ENVIRONMENTAL ISSUE

Concern about the environment has passed through the first two stages of the "issue-attention cycle" and is by now well into the third. In fact, we have already begun to move toward the fourth stage, in which the intensity of public interest in environmental improvement must inexorably decline. And this raises an interesting question: Will the issue of environmental quality then move on into the "post-problem" stage of the cycle?

My answer to this question is: Yes, but not soon, because certain characteristics of this issue will protect it from the rapid decline in public interest typical of many other recent issues. First of all, many kinds of environmental pollution are much more visible and more clearly threatening than most other social problems. This is particularly true of air pollution. The greater the apparent threat from visible forms of pollution and the more vividly this can be dramatized, the more public support environmental improvement will receive and the longer it will sustain public interest. Ironically, the cause of ecologists would therefore benefit from an environmental disaster like a "killer smog" that would choke thousands to death in a few days. Actually, this is nothing new; every cause from early Christianity to the Black Panthers has benefited from martyrs. Yet even the most powerful symbols lose their impact if they are constantly repeated. The piteous sight of an oil-soaked seagull or a dead soldier pales after it has been viewed even a dozen times. Moreover, some of the worst environmental threats come from forms of pollution that are invisible. Thus, our propensity to focus attention on what is most visible may cause us to clean up the pollution we can easily perceive while ignoring even more dangerous but hidden threats.

Pollution is also likely to be kept in the public eye because it is an issue that threatens almost everyone, not just a small percentage of the population. Since it is not politically divisive, politicians can safely pursue it without fearing adverse repercussions. Attacking environmental pollution is therefore much safer than attacking racism or poverty. For an attack upon the latter antagonizes important blocs of voters who benefit from the sufferings of others or at least are not threatened enough by such suffering to favor spending substantial amounts of their money to reduce it.

A third strength of the environmental issue is that much of the "blame" for pollution can be attributed to a small group of "villains" whose wealth and power make them excellent scapegoats. Environmental defenders can therefore "courageously" attack these scapegoats without antagonizing most citizens. Moreover, at least in regard to air pollution, that small group actually has enough power greatly to reduce pollution if it really tries. If leaders of the nation's top auto-producing, power-generating, and fuel-supplying firms would change their behavior significantly, a drastic decline in air pollution could be achieved very quickly. This has been demonstrated at many locations already.

Gathering support for attacking any problem is always easier if its ills can be blamed on a small number of "public enemies"—as is shown by the success of Ralph Nader. This tactic is especially effective if the "enemies" exhibit extreme wealth and power, eccentric dress and manners, obscene language, or some other uncommon traits. Then society can aim its outrage at a small, alien group without having to face up to the need to alter its own behavior. It is easier to find such scapegoats for almost all forms of pollution than for other major problems like poverty, poor housing, or racism. Solutions to those problems would require millions of Americans to change their own behavior patterns, to accept higher taxes, or both.

The possibility that technological solutions can be devised for most pollution problems may also lengthen the public prominence of this issue. To the extent that pollution can be reduced through technological change, most people's basic attitudes, expectations, and behavior patterns will not have to be altered. The traumatic difficulties of achieving major institutional change could thus be escaped through the "magic" of purely technical improvements in automobile engines, water purification devices, fuel composition, and sewage treatment facilities . . .

All the factors set forth above indicate that circumstances are unusually favorable for launching and sustaining major efforts to improve the quality of our environment. Yet we should not underestimate the American public's capacity to become bored — especially with something that does not immediately threaten them, or promise huge benefits for a majority, or strongly appeal to their sense of injustice. In the present mood of the nation, I believe most citizens do not want to confront the need for major social changes on any issues except those that seem directly to threaten them — such as crime and other urban violence. And even in regard to crime, the public does not yet wish to support really effective changes in our basic system of justice. The present Administration has apparently concluded that a relatively "low-profile" government — one that does not try to lead the public into accepting truly significant institutional changes — will most please the majority of Americans at this point. Regardless of the accuracy of this view, if it remains dominant within the federal government, then no major environmental programs are likely to receive long-sustained public attention or support.

Some proponents of improving the environment are relying on the support of students and other young people to keep this issue at the center of public attention. Such support, however, is not adequate as a long-term foundation. Young people form a highly unstable base for the support of any policy because they have such short-lived "staying power." For one thing, they do not long enjoy the large amount of free time they possess while in college. Also, as new individuals enter the category of "young people" and older ones leave it, different issues are stressed and accumulated skills in marshaling opinion are dissipated. Moreover, the radicalism of the young has been immensely exaggerated by the media's tendency to focus attention upon those with extremist views. In their attitudes toward political issues, most young people are not very different from their parents.

There is good reason, then, to believe that the bundle of issues called "improving the environment" will also suffer the gradual loss of public attention characteristic of the later stages of the "issue-attention cycle." However, it will be eclipsed at a much slower rate than other recent domestic issues. So it may be possible to accomplish some significant improvements in environmental quality — if those seeking them work fast.

4 The Issues of the Sixties: An Exploratory Study in the Dynamics of Public Opinion*

G. Ray Funkhouser

Of all the things that may be said about the years from 1960 to 1970, one that will provoke little argument is that they had their share of issues. Indeed, reviewing the various issues of those eleven years — Vietnam, civil rights, black militancy, crime, riots, campus unrest, the sex revolution, smoking and lung cancer, inflation, ecology, slums and poverty, women's liberation — it is astounding that they all took so few years to happen.

This study seeks to relate news media coverage to public opinion and to the realities underlying the various issues of the sixties, examining trends in each of these as a means of exploring the dynamics of public opinion. Fortunately, the sixties were the best-surveyed years in history, with public opinion data regularly gathered and reported. For the first time it is possible to construct trends of nationwide opinion on a broad selection of issues over a series of consecutive years.

METHODOLOGY

Each of the three factors examined here is complex. The precise nature of "public opinion" is still a mystery, a large part of the mystery being whether or not it even has a precise nature. While it is easy to talk glibly about the "mass media," a comprehensive analysis of the total range of communications which

*Reprinted from *Public Opinion Quarterly* (1973, Vol. 37, pp. 62-75) by permission of The University of Chicago Press.

play a role in forming and influencing nationwide public opinion is probably impossible and certainly beyond the capabilities of any single research effort. "Reality," as it relates to public issues, is yet more enigmatic, since the realities of human affairs are not only difficult to measure, but are further confounded by sliding scales of expectations of what those realities ought to be.

It is difficult enough to ascertain the realities of specific events, to say nothing of characterizing complex, nationwide issues accurately over eleven years. While recognizing that statistics leave out a lot, for the purposes of this paper the trends of the realities of the various issues of the sixties are assumed to be more or less accurately represented by data available in *Statistical Abstracts of the United States.* For example, one way of quantitatively expressing our involvement in the war in Vietnam is the number of our troops over there; and the number of troops there from year to year is a way of charting the trend of our involvement. Other sources of data will be noted as used, and for the few issues (e.g., student unrest, ecology) for which no appropriate data could be found, apparent trends in events will have to do.

For a first approximation of public opinion, the figures published by the Gallup Organization[1] on "the most important problem facing America" are assumed to indicate the relative amount of public concern over each of several issues at single points in time. It is likely that, were each of the current issues given a separate questionnaire item, each would have a large majority agreeing that it was an important issue. The Gallup item provides perhaps a sharper discrimination among issues than in fact exists in reality, but it has the advantages of yielding clear discriminations *and* of having been asked consistently throughout the decade. Like it or not, no other trend data so well suited to a study of this type are available. There are other trend data that relate to individual issues, and these will be presented where appropriate.

Television and newspapers have been cited in almost all studies since 1960 as the two media most relied upon for news and information, with magazines and radio usually third and fourth. While books are not usually cited as important sources by cross-sectional samples of the nation's population, there is no doubt that these do influence to some extent the segment of the population involved in policy decisions. Also, as Kadushin, *et al.,*[2] suggest, there is a select assortment of magazines that may disproportionately influence at least the "intellectual elite" of the nation and perhaps the policymaking segment as well.

It would clearly be impossible to carry out a completely representative, content-analytic study of the full range of informational stimuli carried by

[1]The Gallup Opinion Index, Nos. 1-67, 1965-1970, Gallup International, Princeton, New Jersey.

[2]Charles Kadushin, Julie Hover, and Monique Tichy, "How and Where to Find Intellectual Elite in the United States," *Public Opinion Quarterly,* Vol. 35, 1971, pp. 1-18.

television and newspapers to the nationwide public during the years 1960 through 1970. The sheer volume of material *available* would overwhelm, to say nothing of the material no longer available (for example, the nightly network newscasts) or the problem of generalizing from the available (mostly local) material to the potential nationwide audience. Therefore, a strategy of indicators was used. Although news magazines are not cited as primary sources of information by most people, it seems likely that their content reflects the nationwide content of the prominent news media — television and newspapers. That is, if television and newspapers were presenting abundant material concerning ecology (or drugs, or whatever), the news magazines probably would be doing so also.

Three weekly news magazines — *Time, Newsweek,* and *U.S. News* — were analyzed by counting the numbers of articles appearing in each publication, during each year from 1960 through 1970, on a number of issues prominent during the sixties. No attention was paid to the actual amount of space, nor to the content of the material, nor to any bias or slant that might be involved. The tallies for these magazines were added together, thus providing a rough measure of *what* the news media were emphasizing, *when.*

The source of data for the content analysis of these publications was the *Readers' Guide to Periodical Literature.* Articles (but not book reviews) were tallied, by publication and by year, for the following issues (using *only* the topics listed under the headings):

VIETNAM: *Vietnam* . . . American participation . . . peace and mediation (except negotiation meetings) . . . politics and government . . . protests, demonstrations, etc., against . . . public opinion

RACE RELATIONS: *Negro* . . . militants . . . students . . . student demonstrations . . . student militants . . . in U.S. . . . . civil rights . . . culture . . . education . . . history . . . politics and suffrage . . . segregation . . . resistance to segregation . . . social conditions . . . *Race Relations* . . . in U.S. . . . . prejudice

INFLATION: *Inflation (financial)*

CRIME: *Crime and Criminals* . . . in U.S. . . . . prevention . . . procedure . . . criminal statistics . . . *Law Enforcement*

URBAN RIOTS (covering the general topic only — not specific cities, which were in some years listed separately): *United States* . . . riots

CAMPUS UNREST: *Student* . . . demonstrations . . . militants . . . movement . . . SDS . . . SNCC . . . opinion (all in U.S. only) . . . *Kent State* (in 1970 only)

ENVIRONMENT: *Ecology* . . . study and teaching . . . *Environment* . . . environmental movement . . . environmental policy . . . pollution . . . control . . . laws and legislation . . . *Air Pollution* . . . *Water Pollution*

DRUGS: *Drugs* . . . abuse . . . laws and legislation . . . *Hallucinogenic Drugs* . . . *LSD* . . . *Marijuana* . . . *Narcotics* . . . habit . . . addicts . . . control of . . . and youth

SEX: *Sex* . . . (psychology) . . . in literature . . . in moving pictures . . . in art and the arts . . . in the performing arts . . . instruction . . . and laws . . . relations . . . sexual behavior . . . sexual ethics

MASS MEDIA: *Mass Media* . . . *Television Broadcasting* . . . and children . . . censorship . . . moral aspects . . . news . . . in politics . . . laws and regulations . . . in U.S. . . . social aspects

POPULATION: *Population* . . . overpopulation . . . increase of . . . distribution of

POVERTY: *Poor* . . . in U.S. . . . *Poverty* . . . *Slums*

SMOKING: *Smoking* . . . *Cigarettes* . . . advertising

SCIENCE: *Research* . . . federal aid . . . In U.S. . . . *Science* . . . and civilization . . . social aspects . . . and state . . . *Technology* . . . technological change . . . and civilization

WOMEN'S RIGHTS: *Woman, Women* . . . equal rights . . . in U.S. . . . and men . . . social and moral questions . . . liberation movement . . . marches, rallies . . . suffrage

NEWS COVERAGE AND PUBLIC OPINION

The relative amount of public concern about each issue can be gauged in at least three ways. One measure is the highest yearly percentage attained by the issue. Another measure is the sum of the yearly percentages, a sort of aggregate importance indicator. A third measure is the average percentage attained by the issue during the years it showed up as one of the "most important issues," a rough measure of average intensity.

Since there is no obvious criterion by which to decide among the three ways of expressing the "importance" of an issue, they were ranked according to the average of the three bases for comparing them. These ranks are given in Table 1, along with the amount of news coverage and the concomitant ranks of the issues. Judging from the correlation between the two sets of ranks, news coverage and public opinion are strongly related on an over-all basis.

Table 2 shows, for the years 1964 through 1970, the number of articles on each of eight major issues in the weekly news magazines and the peak percentage for each year of each issue on the Gallup Poll item, "What is the most important problem facing America?" The table begins with 1964 because that is the first year for which the Gallup data are available on this item for any of the issues except race relations.

Of the issues, the Vietnam war, race relations, and inflation were the only ones invariably noted as "the most important problem," with the other issues

TABLE 1
Amount of Coverage Given by National News Magazines to
Various Issues During the 1960's, and Rank Scores of the
Issues as "Most Important Problem Facing America" During
That Period

Issue	Number of Articles	Coverage Rank	Importance Rank
Vietnam war	861	1	1
Race relations (and urban riots)	687	2	2
Campus unrest	267	3	4
Inflation	234	4	5
Television and mass media	218	5	12[a]
Crime	203	6	3
Drugs	173	7	9
Environment and pollution	109	8	6
Smoking	99	9	12[a]
Poverty	74	10	7
Sex (declining morality)	62	11	8
Women's rights	47	12	12[a]
Science and society	37	13	12[a]
Population	36	14	12[a]

Rank-order correlation between coverage and importance = .78 (p = .001).
[a]These items were never noted as "the most important problem" in the Gallup findings, so are ranked equally below the items that did.

mentioned in some years and not in others. If we construct a contingency table of the data in Table 2, breaking it at the approximate median of the number of articles, 25, and by whether or not the particular issue was rated during the year as "the most important problem," we find that media coverage and public opinion are strongly related. The chi-square for this table, 24.1 with one degree of freedom, has a p of less than .001, suggesting that the amount of media coverage for an issue during a given year is clearly related to whether or not it shows up as an important problem in the Gallup Poll.[3] In fact, four of the nine exceptions to this relationship can be easily explained away: it can be argued that inflation (accounting for three of the exceptions) was a pervasive enough problem, and had enough visibility of its own in the form of obviously rising prices, to make people aware of it independently of media coverage. The other explainable exception is that the first peak in coverage of drugs occurred when psychedelia and the flower children were in bloom, and, while newsworthy, drugs had not yet emerged as a serious problem.

The data thus far suggest a strong connection between media attention to an issue and the appearance of that issue as "the most important problem." But

[3]There is, of course, nothing magic about the number 25. The tallies of articles here only indicate the relative amount of media coverage of given issues in given years.

TABLE 2
Comparison of Number of Articles Found in Three Weekly
News Magazines, and Peak Percentage of People Saying
Issue was "One of the Most Important Problems Facing the
Country," by Issue and Year, 1964–1970

Year		Number of Articles	Peak Percentage		Number of Articles	Peak Percentage
1964	Vietnam War	49	50%	Inflation	12	8%
1965		160	37		11	6
1966		208	56		44	16
1967		160	40		12	8
1968		123	52		25	10
1969		99	40		69	9
1970		44	27		31	10
1964	Race Relations	43	60	Crime and	18	0
1965	(and Urban)	64	52	Lawlessness	35	5
1966	Riots)	73	25		21	0
1967		92	30		25	2
1968		75	25		35	29
1969		86	15		25	18
1970		29	13		22	8
1964	Campus	7	0	Drugs	1	0
1965	Unrest	22	0		10	0
1966		7	0		24	0
1967		17	0		30	0
1968		46	0		18	0
1969		109	5		36	0
1970		52	27		35	3
1964	Pollution,	1	0	Poverty	11	0
1965	Environment	11	0		4	4
1966		12	0		3	0
1967		14	0		7	0
1968		3	0		36	4
1969		15	0		6	0
1970		41	6		4	3

before attempting to relate media coverage and public opinion to the realities
of the events, two points concerning "public opinion" must be discussed. First,
we must recognize that when, for example, Table 2 shows that "drugs" in 1970
achieved a peak of 3 percent, this means that 3 percent of those surveyed chose
this as the issue about which they were most concerned. *In principle,* it is
entirely possible that a minority that small could be influenced by something
other than the level of media coverage. However, the relationships in the data
seem consistent enough with the explanation being posed to rule out this
alternative explanation of the findings. . . .

Looking at the trends in media attention shown in Table 2, it appears that
the patterns of media coverage did not have a one-to-one relationship to the

realities of any of the issues. Coverage of the Vietnam war, campus unrest, and urban riots[4] peaked a year or two earlier than these events reached their climaxes. Media coverage of drugs roughly paralleled the rise in drug use, except for the 1967 peak; and, except for the peak of coverage in 1966, the three news magazines attended to inflation somewhat in line with the situation. But coverage of race relations, crime, poverty, and pollution showed little if any relation to the actualities of their underlying issues, nor did coverage of the issues which never appeared as "most important" — smoking, science, population, mass media, and women's rights. Peaks in coverage appeared during years in which the situation in these areas was no different from other years, and in several cases coverage increased while the problem was showing improvement, or dropped while the problem was getting worse. . . .

CONCLUSIONS

This study investigated two relationships: news coverage vis-a-vis public opinion, and news coverage vis-a-vis reality. While the topics are broad, the methodology unproved, and the variables loosely defined, convincing connections emerged in the first relationship, and at the very least some questions were raised concerning the second.

---

[4]The coverage of "urban riots" is shown in Table 2 as combined with "race relations." The number of articles on "urban riots" in the news magazines for the years 1964 through 1970 were, respectively, 6, 6, 17, 41, 36, 15, and 3.

II   MEASURING
AGENDA-SETTING EFFECTS

Agenda-setting is a metaphoric description of the role that the news media play in the formation of public opinion. Stating a theoretical perspective as a metaphor is simultaneously a strength and a weakness. Its strength is the ability to stir creative insights among mass communication researchers. To date, some 200 empirical studies have been guided by this metaphor. But the diversity of this research has fragmented our efforts to build a comprehensive theory of the agenda-setting role of mass communication. As James Winter noted dispairingly in the 1981 *Mass Communication Review Yearbook,* the drive for total innovation has overwhelmed the scientific principle of careful replication. Even if the concept of agenda-setting has not always been parsimonious, unquestionably, it has been a fruitful concept. It has stimulated and guided the imagination of numerous scholars, who have created a meaningful set of theoretical constructs through empirical measurement of news media content and effects.

In the original study by McCombs and Shaw (chapter 2) the agenda-setting effect was measured by asking voters what they personally thought were the key issues of the presidential campaign. The answers to that survey question defined the public agenda. The opening selection in this section by Jack McLeod, Lee Becker, and John Byrnes expands this conceptualization and describes three different public agendas. The question used in the Chapel Hill study, "What are you most concerned about these days?," and the Gallup Poll's continuing question, "What is the most important problem facing this country?", are operational definitions of an *intrapersonal* public agenda. They provide psychological measures of agenda-setting. However, rather than asking people what they think, it is possible to use a more behavioral measure by asking people what they talk about with family, friends, and acquaintances. This yields a measure of an *interpersonal* public agenda. Finally, German scholar Elisabeth Noelle-Neumann notes in her book, *The Spiral of Silence,* people also have a picture in their mind about what others in the community regard as the major issues of the day. This is a *perceived community* public agenda.

Marc Benton and Jean Frazier further extend the measurement of the public agenda to three levels of awareness. At the first level is an agenda of issues. In most studies of agenda-setting this is a broad array of public affairs topics, such as the economy or foreign affairs. Of course, each of these broad topics can be broken down into a series of more specific issues. Within the general category of the economy are such specific issues as unemployment, budget deficits, and tax increases. At the third level is the specific information on these issues presented by the news media, for example, pledges not to raise taxes, proposals to eliminate various tax deductions, or changes in farm subsidies.

The basic agenda-setting hypothesis asserts that the issues and information presented on the media agenda become over time the issues and information on the public agenda. Of course, the news media do not create these issues out of whole cloth, and some critics of the agenda-setting approach have asserted that real world events, not the news media, set the public agenda. At best, argue these critics, the news media are the mirror that reflects these real world events. Of course, recall from Part I that Funkhouser's (chapter 4) examination of public opinion in the 1960s found that the public agenda and the press agenda showed much greater covergence with each other than either did with indicators of trends in the world outside.

Additional evidence of the agenda-setting role of the press independent of trends in the real world is provided by Margaret Gordon and Linda Heath's extensive analysis of crime news on the agendas of newspapers in Chicago, San Francisco, and Philadelphia. The data strongly support the agenda-setting hypothesis. In all three cities readers of the newspaper with the most crime news have a greater fear of crime than do readers of the other newspapers.

Deciding on appropriate operational definitions for the public and news media agendas is a major part of the measurement problem for scholars studying the agenda-setting process. The readings in this section sample a wide variety of agendas. But the heart of the agenda-setting idea is the assertion that the content of the media agenda determines, or, at least, substantially influences, the public agenda. This is a causal statement. Finding a significant correlation between the media agenda and the public agenda—as McCombs and Shaw did in the original agenda-setting study—supports the idea of agenda-setting, but it does not establish it as a causal model. Statements of causality require proof both of correlation and of time order. A cause not only must be related to its effect; the cause must precede the effect in time. McCombs and Shaw, as well as subsequent studies, established a correlation between the media agenda and the public agenda. Later studies have sought evidence of time order in a variety of ways.

Kim Smith used two different statistical techniques, cross-lagged correlations and Granger analysis, to directly test the idea that the media agenda is the cause and the public agenda, the effect. Content analyses of a local newspaper and public opinion surveys measured seven issues across an 8-year span.

The effort to determine cause and effect in agenda-setting research reached its apogee in a series of laboratory experiments conducted by Shanto Iyengar and his colleagues. A laboratory experiment can control subjects' exposure to news reports about an issue and can compare the perceived salience of these issues to issues not covered in the news. These experiments, which manipulated a series of TV newscasts viewed by the subjects, provide definitive causal evidence of the agenda-setting influence of the news. This evidence demonstrating the influence of TV news is especially impressive because many field studies have found that television is a weaker agenda-setter than newspapers.

This set of readings sketches a broad portrait of agenda-setting, which has emerged from two decades of empirical research. These readings also illustrate the imaginative ways that have been used to measure the impact of the news agenda on the public agenda.

5 Another Look at the Agenda-Setting Function of the Press*

Jack McLeod
Lee B. Becker
James E. Byrnes

The agenda-setting hypothesis holds that the media agenda is manifested in the ratings of importances or saliences of issues among audience members. As usually stated, the hypothesis does not specify the precise measurement of these saliences, and the measures of these saliences have varied in recent studies along the lines of the diverse origins of the concept. Park (1925) was most concerned with the effects of media presentation on the topics of conversation within a *community* served by the media; Lippmann (1922) was most concerned with the effects of the media presentation on the *individual's* view of reality. McCombs and his associates have followed Lippmann, using an *intra*personal concept rather than an *inter*personal one more in the Park tradition. McCombs and Shaw (1972), for example, operationalized the concept by asking respondents: "What are you *most* concerned about these days. That is, regardless of what politicians say, what are the two or three *main* things which you think the government *should* concentrate on doing something about?" This might be called "individual issue salience." On the other hand, the notion of the media setting the agenda for its audience seems to allow for a more general definition involving community or interpersonal interaction. A proper operationalization of this latter concept could involve asking respondents both what they talk about with other members of the community and what issues other community members are raising with them. This could be labeled "community issue salience."

Communication Research (Vol. 1, No. 2, pp. 131–165), copyright ©1974 by Sage Publications Inc. Reprinted by permission of Sage Publications Inc.

There is yet a third solution to this conceptual problem, however, which is a sort of compromise, lying midway between the *intra*personal and *inter*personal concepts discussed above. The agenda-setting hypothesis implies that the media can change the views of social reality of its individual audience members by indicating which issues are being discussed by the candidates, those that will be discussed by friends in the future, or those that will be used by other voters in their decisions about the candidates, and therefore be the key issues in the campaign. Clearly this "reality" concept, which we will call "perceived issue salience," is more interpersonal than that used by McCombs and his associates since the "reality" is tied to the interpersonal environment of the individual. While it is an empirical question as to which of these three conceptualizations eventually will be most useful in prediction to outcomes (such as voting and campaign activity in the political sphere), what seems most important at present is that researchers make clear the distinctions and their choice of variable for study. Ideally, multiple measures could be incorporated into the same investigation. Panel designs could be used to sort out the proper time ordering and answer the questions, does interpersonal discussion precede or follow the "reality" saliences, and at which point do the more interpersonal effects occur?

The researcher must also decide whether to measure saliences through responses elicited from open-ended questions or by using fixed-alternative questions developed from open-ended pretest questions. Each approach has different advantages and disadvantages as do the alternatives in the choice between obtaining rankings of issues or ratings on the basis of some underlying scale—e.g., ranging from extremely important to not at all important. Rankings result in statistical analysis problems while ratings do not control for individual differences in use of scales. The latter problem of individual difference variance might be controlled for by standardizing each individual's set of ratings. . . .

STUDY DESIGN

During September and the first two weeks of October 1972 personal interviews were conducted with 389 potential voters in Madison, Wisconsin, by students enrolled in a Communication Research Methods course at the University of Wisconsin. The systematic, probability sample was drawn from official voter registration lists for the city, which provide voter age, with substitutions within the same dwelling unit allowed when the original sample member was no longer at that address. Substitutions were anticipated because of the transitory nature of much of Madison's university-related population, and interviewers chose same-sex and approximate same-age respondents from within the living unit. The nonstudent areas of the city were oversampled to increase the size of the nonstudent sample. The interview schedule was part of a larger study of young voters and somewhat more than half of the respondents were less than 25 years of age. The younger and older voters are analyzed separately in all comparisons.

About halfway through the interview the respondents were handed a list of six general issues "which you may have heard or read about in the current presidential campaign." The respondents were asked to indicate "which issue has been most important so far?" The respondents then indicated the next most important issue until all six of the issues had been assigned a rank from one to six. The six issues, selected because of anticipated differences in their play in the two test newspapers, were: Defense Spending, Combating Crime, Honesty in Government, America's World Leadership, the Vietnam War, and the Tax Burden. The respondent's rankings of these six issues were considered measures of *perceived issue salience,* the salience conceptualized in our earlier discussion as being intermediate between an intrapersonal measure (individual issue salience) and an interpersonal discussion measure (community issue salience).

These same issue categories were used for a content analysis of both of Madison's daily newspapers, the liberal *Capital Times* and the conservative Wisconsin *State Journal.* All 38 Monday through Saturday issues of both newspapers were analyzed for the main campaign period, September 1 through October 14, preceding our field survey period by two weeks. In addition, a reconstructed week procedure was used to sample 36 issues from the March through August period, representing approximately one-fifth of the issues from that time span. Analysis was confined to the front and jump pages of the papers, except for the September-October period when the editorial page was included. Total number of inches for each issue were summed for a given page; included in the sums were headlines and pertinent pictures.

The content categories included material directly tied to the presidential campaign as well as news within these six issue areas that was not directly linked to the campaign. Some examples of items included within each category are:

Defense Spending: Congressional defense budget hearings; McGovern calling for "cutting the fat" from defense spending.

Combating Crime: Release of FBI crime statistics; Nixon speech warning of dangers of drug peddlers.

Honesty in Government: Agnew denial of the Administration's apparent involvement in Watergate; McGovern attacks on the Administration's handling of the ITT case and the wheat sales.

America's World Leadership: Detente with Russia; Nixon visit to China.

The Vietnam War: Stories from the battlefields; troop withdrawal and peace developments.

Tax Burden: Property tax relief; proposals by the candidates to relieve the tax load of the middle class.

The audience interview schedule also included questions used to measure various control variables: party preference, strength of partisanship, medium most relied on for politics, campaign interest, interpersonal political communication, and four items related to gratifications sought from political news in newspapers. Respondents also were asked their presidential voting preference.

During the week following election night of 1972, telephone interviews were conducted with 356 of the previously interviewed respondents. Questions from this round provided possible "effect" variables: direction of presidential vote, change of interest in the campaign, vote change, and campaign knowledge. A final effect criterion, vote turnout on election day, was obtained from a postelection check of the city clerks' voting records.

RESULTS

Media Content Agenda

The late campaign content analysis results, presented in Table 1, show rather striking differences between our test newspapers, the liberal *Capital Times* and the conservative *State Journal*. The Honesty in Government issue illustrates this difference most clearly. The *Capital Times* devoted almost as much space to this issue on the three pages studied (48.7%) as it did to all of our other five issues combined; in contrast, the *State Journal* showed much less attention (16.4%) to the events of this period that began to link the Watergate burglary and other illegal activities to the inner rooms of the White House. The discrepancy was even stronger for the front page considered separately (55.6% to 11.9%).

Table 1 also indicates that the two test newspapers showed remarkable consistency in the proportion of space given each of the six issues across the front, jump, and editorial pages. This gives support to our initial assumption that the ideological differences in editorial viewpoint would carry over to produce differing content agendas on the news pages, although the fact that the liberal paper subscribes to the Washington *Post* news wire and the opposition paper does not, may account for some of the greater attention given Watergate and related matters.

While the findings of Table 1 provide encouragement for going ahead with the study of the effects of a differential newspaper agenda on the audience, three questions about the methodological adequacy of the content analysis should be answered: (1) How representative a sample of the entire newspaper is our selection of the front, jump and editorial pages? (2) How complete is the

TABLE 1
Content Agenda from September 1 to October 14 as Presented
on Major Pages of the *Capital Times* (lib) and the Wisconsin
State Journal (con) (in percentages)

Issue	Front Page	Jump Page	Edit Page	Total
Capital Times (lib)				
Vietnam War	31.8	42.3	37.9	37.1
Honesty in government	55.6	43.2	45.2	48.7
America's world leadership	1.6	5.1	6.8	4.0
Combating crime	–	–	3.6	0.7
Tax burden	9.6	6.5	3.9	7.3
Defense spending	1.4	2.9	2.6	2.2
Total	100.0	100.0	100.0	100.0
No. of column inches	2,331	2,185	1,062	5,578
State Journal (con)				
Vietnam War	59.7	57.8	42.6	56.5
Honesty in government	11.9	17.3	27.7	16.4
America's world leadership	5.9	7.7	15.0	7.9
Combating crime	4.3	3.6	6.6	4.3
Tax burden	12.3	8.8	8.1	10.3
Defense spending	5.9	4.8	–	4.6
Total	100.0	100.0	100.0	100.0
No. of column inches	1,248	1,082	399	2,723

Note. The unit of analysis for the newspaper agendas is the column inch. In this and the following tables, the Capital Times will be referred to as the liberal (lib) paper while the Wisconsin State Journal will be referred to as the conservative (con) paper. Both papers are published in Madison, Wisconsin.

coverage of the six issues used? (3) How generalizable is the September 1 to October 14 period to the entire campaign period in terms of the attention devoted to various issues?

A check on the adequacy of using only selected pages to represent the entire newspaper was provided by analyzing the total content of a subsample of newspapers. While the front and jump pages account for only one-fourth of the news hole of each paper, the two pages represent 67.0% and 54.7% total content devoted to the six issues in the *Capital Times* and *State Journal*, respectively. More importantly, analysis of the subsample reveals no serious revision of the relative attention to each of our six issues. Confining our analysis to the main campaign pages does slightly overestimate the attention to the two main categories, Honesty and Vietnam, but it does so rather evenly for the two papers. The sampling appears to have created no serious distortion of the total agenda content.

The completeness of agenda issues analyzed was checked by separately coding all issue material specifically attributed to the campaign but not covered by our six issues. Only two issues emerged with any appreciable frequency: welfare and economic issues not subsumed by the tax burden and defense spending. All these "other" issues combined made up only about ten percent of issue-oriented material, thereby indicating that our six issues chosen were a fairly complete sample of issue material in the campaign.

Finally, the question of adequacy of using the September-October period is part of the larger problem of establishing an adequate time lag between the content agenda shift and the point at which we would expect that shift to be manifested in the salience ratings of the audience. Our use of the late campaign period entailed an average lag of two weeks. Concern over the appropriateness of this lag led to sampling the content of the March to August campaign period. If large differences within each newspaper were shown for the various time periods, it would be appropriate to analyze the agenda for salience comparisons separately, by time periods.

Table 2 shows the content agendas of the two papers broken down into three time periods using the mean column inches per day for comparison. Since the late campaign period analysis shows comparability of the news and editorial pages, the sample of the entire campaign period was confined to the front and jump pages. It is clear that the heavier Honesty in Government play in the *Capital Times* noted for the late campaign is consistent with the same imbalance earlier in the campaign. In terms of column inches, for the whole campaign the liberal paper devoted five times as much space to Honesty issues (e.g., the ITT scandal) as did the conservative paper. Differences in play for the other five issues appear quite consistent across the three time intervals. The time lag problem, then, becomes less important because of the consistency in play across time by the two papers.

TABLE 2
Content Agenda as Presented by the *Capital Times* (lib) and
the Wisconsin *State Journal* (con) During the Spring, Summer,
Fall of 1972; Average Column Inches Per Day

Issue	March 6-June 17		June 18-August 31		September 1-October 14		Total	
	Lib	Con	Lib	Con	Lib	Con	Lib	Con
Vietnam War	58.1	50.2	41.5	28.3	43.9	36.1	49.7	40.0
Honesty in government	39.8	10.5	46.5	4.7	58.9	8.8	45.8	8.2
America's world leadership	9.8	19.2	3.9	5.8	4.0	4.1	6.6	11.7
Combating crime	0.0	7.5	13.7	5.2	0.0	2.4	4.7	5.3
Tax burden	3.6	7.1	4.1	0.0	9.6	6.5	4.9	4.6
Defense spending	1.2	0.7	4.4	3.8	2.5	3.3	2.5	2.3
Total	112.4	95.1	114.1	47.8	118.8	61.3	114.3	72.0

Note. Entries are mean number of column inches per day. Entries in the first two columns are based on samples of 18 days each. Entries in the third column are based on the full population of days. Entries in the final column are based on the estimates from the first three columns.

Despite virtually identical news holes, the two newspapers show a striking difference in the average amount of space given the six issues during each of the three time periods. While the *Capital Times* shows a slight increase in space from early to late in the campaign (112.4 to 118.8 column inches per day), the *State Journal's* attention to the six issues reveals a sharp drop (95.1 to 47.8 inches) that coincides with the Watergate burglary. The conservative paper's campaign coverage increases only slightly during the late campaign period (61.3 inches). The discrepancy in total column inches makes the proportions devoted to various issues as used in Table 1 somewhat misleading. Consequently, the average number of column inches is the best indicator of content agenda to be used for our comparisons with audience saliences. In terms of the column inch criterion, Table 2 shows that Honesty in Government and the Vietnam War are stronger on the liberal newspaper's agenda and America's World Leadership and Combating Crime are more strongly emphasized by the conservative newspaper, while Tax Burden and Defense Spending divide about equally between the two papers.

Audience-Perceived Saliences

The overwhelming dominance of the Vietnam War in the perceived saliences of the audience is shown in Table 3. Almost two-thirds of the younger and older readers of each newspaper picked the Vietnam War as the most salient among the six issues, a proportion that seems considerably higher than would have been expected from the amount of attention given to it in the press during the campaign. In sharp contrast, Honesty in Government, the second most emphasized issue overall, was accorded below average (average = 2.50) rankings by all groups except the older readers of the liberal newspaper. The

TABLE 3
Perceived Issue Salience: Mean Rankings of Six Issues by Age
and Newspaper Read Most for Politics

	Younger Adult Sample		Older Adult Sample	
Issue	*Lib*	*Con*	*Lib*	*Con*
Vietnam War	4.47	4.47	4.38	4.25
Honesty in government	1.98	1.95	2.61	1.98
America's world leadership	1.24	1.17	1.28	1.18
Combating crime	1.22	1.44	1.21	1.52
Tax burden	2.90	2.80	2.84	3.35
Defense spending	3.19	3.17	2.68	2.72
(*n*)	(68)	(89)	(59)	(77)

Note. For computation of the means presented in this table, the issue chosen as the most important was assigned the value five, and assignment of values continued this way so that the least important issue was assigned the value zero.

two issues least emphasized in media content, Tax Burden and Defense Spending, received above average rankings among all comparison groups. Overall, there is little in Table 3 to justify any presumption of a blanket newspaper agenda-setting effect.

Media Agenda-Audience Salience Relationships

While Tables 2 and 3 provide much of the basic data relevant to the agenda-setting hypothesis, a series of steps was required to test the hypothesis more specifically. First, a scale of political exposure to the two test newspapers was developed in the form of a four-point scale: readers who depended most on the liberal paper for their political information from newspapers *and* did not read the conservative paper (4); readers who depended most on the liberal paper but also read the conservative paper (3); readers who depended most on the conservative paper but also read the liberal paper (2); and readers who depended most on the conservative paper *and* did not read the liberal paper (1). Thus, a newspaper agenda scale was formed running from consistent exposure to the liberal paper's agenda to consistent exposure to the conservative paper's agenda through the two "predominant but mixed" positions. Respondents who did not report reading either of the two papers were eliminated from the analysis.

Second, it was necessary to develop an index of perceived issue saliences that would range from rankings with maximal agreement with the liberal paper's content agenda to maximal agreement with that of the conservative newspaper. This required judging each campaign issue as to its predominance in the content of one or the other paper. As is shown in Table 2, Honesty in Government and the Vietnam War received considerably heavier play in the liberal paper while America's World Leadership and Combating Crime predominated in the conservative paper. Tax Burden and Defense Spending were rather evenly divided in the two papers and, consequently, were dropped from further analysis. The index of perceived issue salience was then formed by adding each person's rankings of the two dominant issues of the liberal paper and subtracting from that the sum of the person's rankings of the two issues that received more attention from the conservative paper.

The most straightforward test of the agenda-setting hypothesis, the zero-order correlation between the content agenda and perceived issue salience index (Table 4), provides support only among the older sample (+.162). Results for the younger respondents are in the right direction (+.051), but at a level well short of statistical significance. Since political party preference might be expected to be related to both choice of a partisan newspaper and to the ordering of the salience of issues, it is necessary to control for this variable. As shown by the partial correlation comparisons in the first row of Table 4,

TABLE 4
Relationship Between Newspaper Content Agenda and
Perceived Issue Saliences: Zero-Order and Partialed by Party
Preference for Total Samples and Within Levels of Possible
Contingent Orientations

Contingent Orientations	Younger Adult Sample			Older Adult Sample		
	Zero Order	Partial	(n)	Zero Order	Partial	(n)
Total samples	+.051	+.031	(157)	+.162[a]	+.120[b]	(136)
Partisanship						
Strong	−.054	−.077	(97)	+.186[a]	+.135	(81)
Weak	+.218[a]	+.202[b]	(60)	+.119	+.106	(54)
Difference	+.272[a]	+.279[a]		−.067	−.029	
Importance of newspapers						
Most important	+.127	+.082	(79)	+.254[a]	+.195[a]	(77)
Lesser importance	−.039	−.041	(78)	+.041	+.025	(58)
Difference	+.166	+.122		+.213	+.170	
Campaign interest						
Very interested	−.340	−.341	(30)	+.035	+.020	(24)
Less interested	+.138[b]	+.108	(127)	+.219[a]	+.193[a]	(111)
Difference	+.478[a]	+.449[a]		+.184	+.173	
Interpersonal discussion						
High	+.057	+.030	(127)	+.176[a]	+.127	(100)
Low	+.028	+.037	(30)	+.062	+.057	(35)
Difference	−.029	+.007		−.114	−.070	

Note. Zero-order correlations shown here are between the individual's reliance on test newspapers and the perceived issue saliences scaled for actual newspaper content. In the partials, party direction is pulled out. A positive correlation is in the predicted direction. Two types of significance tests were employed: the difference of a correlation from zero and the difference between two correlations. All correlations are Pearsonian.
[a]$p < .05$, one-tailed.
[b]$p < .10$, one-tailed.

party preference reduces but does not eliminate the basic agenda-setting correlation.

At least as important as the basic test of agenda-setting is the study of contingent orientations under which the hypothesis holds in greater or lesser strength. The first of these orientations shown in Table 4 is partisanship in terms of the strength of the party orientation regardless of party choice. McCombs and Shaw (1972) have argued that the content agenda should have maximal effect on those whose political allegiances are weakest, the uncommitted voters. We would thereby expect that our weak partisans (consistent independents and party leaners) would exhibit stronger agenda-setting correlations than would the strong partisans (those who identify with a political party). This prediction is upheld in Table 4 among our younger voters where the weak partisans show significant agenda-setting coefficients even after party preference is controlled (+.202), while no relationship is found for the strongly partisan young voters. For respondents over 25, however, the partitioning by partisanship does not produce the predicted differences.

The older respondents in our sample are somewhat more dependent upon the newspapers for political information, although the majority of both age groupings pick the press rather than television, friends, or peers as sources of such news (Table 4). We can expect that dependence on an information source should increase the influence of that source; therefore, we can hypothesize that newspaper agenda-setting should be strongest among those who consider newspapers to be their most important source of political information. Table 4 indicates some support for the hypothesis and, indeed, suggests the contingent condition such that only when the newspaper is the top source of political information is there a political agenda-setting effect. Since most of those attributing lesser importance to newspapers picked television as their most important source, their perceived issue saliences should be more dependent upon the content agenda of the television medium.

We can also hypothesize that agenda-setting should be strongest among the least interested, using the same reasoning as for the partisanship expectation — that the lesser involved would bring less structured "personal agendas" to the campaign. McCombs and Weaver (1973), however, found an agenda-setting effect only among the highly interested voters. Our results are consistent with the expectation that the less interested would exhibit the greater effects. The highly interested older voters show essentially no agenda-setting impact, while the relationship among the highly interested younger voters actually is negative.

Previous studies have indicated contradictory results regarding the contingent effects of interpersonal discussion on agenda-setting. Table 4 shows no impact on the younger adults, but among older adults a slight tendency for greater agenda-setting relationships among those discussing the campaign with their friends most frequently.

Another set of potential contingent orientations involves the gratifications readers seek from their newspapers. Respondents indicated the extent to which each of four gratifications was a reason for reading a newspaper. The gratifications were selected from among those used by Blumler and McQuail (1969). Table 5 indicates that the partitioning of the first of these, "to keep up with latest events," generates a substantial difference in agenda-setting coefficients among older adults. As anticipated, the small number of older voters who do not use newspapers to "keep up" are very likely to be sensitive to the content agenda (+.478 partial); however, the same comparison for the younger group does not reach significance (+.099 partial).

The second gratification, "to help me make decisions," implies a rational mode of newspaper use that examines information in depth sufficient to nullify effects of mere repetition. This reasoning is given some support by the

TABLE 5
Relationship Between Newspaper Content Agenda and
Perceived Issue Saliences: Zero-Order and Partialed by Party
Preference within Levels of Various Newspaper Gratifications

Reasons for Reading a Newspaper	Younger Adult Sample			Older Adult Sample		
	Zero Order	Partial	(n)	Zero Order	Partial	(n)
To keep up with events						
High	+.051	+.004	(105)	+.108	+.062	(109)
Low	+.050	+.099	(51)	+.495[a]	+.478[a]	(26)
Difference	−.001	+.095		+.387[a]	+.416[a]	
To help make decisions						
High	−.014	−.034	(111)	+.123	+.046	(83)
Low	+.229[b]	+.211[b]	(46)	+.233[a]	+.217[b]	(52)
Difference	+.243[b]	+.245[b]		+.110	+.171	
For interpersonal discussions						
High	−.055	−.077	(111)	+.037	+.001	(96)
Low	+.246[a]	+.222[b]	(46)	+.445[a]	+.432[a]	(39)
Difference	+.301[a]	+.299[a]		+.408[a]	+.431[a]	
Because I agree with editorials						
High	−.175	−.200	(65)	+.303[a]	+.200[b]	(65)
Low	+.218[a]	+.201[a]	(92)	−.007	−.008	(70)
Difference	−.393	−.401		+.310[a]	+.208	

Note. Zero-order correlations shown here are between the individual's reliance on test newspapers and the perceived issue saliences scaled for actual newspaper content. In the partials, party direction is pulled out. A positive correlation is in the predicted direction. Ns differ because of missing data for some of the items. Difference of a correlation from zero and difference between two correlations tests were used. All correlations are Pearsonian.
[a]$p < .05$, one-tailed.
[b]$p < .10$, one-tailed.

finding in both age level comparisons that the low decision makers tend to show agenda-setting relationships.

Using the newspaper to "give me something to talk about with other people" clearly operates as a contingent condition such that respondents endorsing this gratification show no agenda-setting effect. Those not using newspapers for this reason show strong content agenda-issue salience correlations. The particularly strong differences for older adults on this gratification in Table 5 seem to be contrary to the findings for these respondents for campaign discussion with friends shown previously in Table 4, where the *high* discussants showed some indication of agenda-setting. We should note, however, that campaign discussion is tied to a distinct time frame and area of content while the gratification is not. Campaign discussion is also a function of other people's activity or could reflect a personal characteristic of easy communication, while "having something to talk about" is one person's activity and possibly reflects an inadequacy of communication style. At any rate, the communicatory utility gratification and discussion in the campaign are virtually uncorrelated among our study respondents.

The final gratification, using a newspaper "because I agree with its editorial stands," presents a clear reversal between the age groups in Table 5. While agenda-setting relationships are shown among the nonendorsers of this gratification for the young, it is those accepting this reinforcement item who show such effects among the older adults. Here and elsewhere in our data there are hints that agenda-setting is combined with an element of partisanship and selectivity in the older group that is lacking among younger respondents.

Subsequent Effects of Agenda-Setting

The importance of agenda-setting as a communication process is enhanced to the extent that it has consequences beyond altering the salience perceptions of the audience. In Table 6, the relationships of reliance on a given newspaper and perceived issue salience to vote choice are presented. Candidate choice was measured two times, first in the September-October campaign interview synchronous with our media and salience questions and later in the postelection telephone interview. In the September campaign scaling of vote choice, "don't know" and "probably won't vote" occupies the intermediate position between voting intentions for Nixon and McGovern. In the postelection analysis, the middle position represents actual nonvoting. Since party affiliation plays an overwhelming role in predicting voting choice (+ .691 for young and + .705 for older groups in the first analysis, + .658 and + .656 in the postelection comparison) and is also moderately associated with newspaper choice and issue salience, it is necessary to partial for party affiliation in all comparisons.

Table 6 shows that those voters who saw Honesty and Vietnam as important issues relative to Crime and World Leadership are less likely to prefer Nixon in September-October and to vote for Nixon than are other voters. This holds at both time intervals for the older adults and to a lesser extent for the younger respondents even after controlling for party preference. The results also show a direct link between reading of the liberal paper and a non-Nixon candidate preference during the September-October period that is explainable neither by party preference nor by the indirect link of newspaper reliance to perceived issue salience.

Comparison of the election day voting results with the corresponding coefficients for the September-October data in Table 6 gives a rough indication of how the given independent variable may have operated *during* the late campaign period. As mentioned earlier, the predictive power of party preference declines slightly for the election day voting, possibly indicating that its strong influence peaked prior to the late campaign. Newspaper relied on most

TABLE 6
Relationships Between Newspaper Relied On and Perceived
Issue Saliences and Candidate Choice Early in the Campaign
and on Election Day Controlling for Party Preference

| | Younger Adult Sample | | Older Adult Sample | |
| | Newspaper | Perceived | Newspaper | Perceived |
Candidate Choice	Relied On	Saliences	Relied On	Saliences
September–October				
Zero order	+.238[a]	+.180[b]	+.348[a]	+.318[a]
Partial	+.170[b]	+.131[c]	+.208[a]	+.287[a]
(n)	(157)	(157)	(134)	(134)
Election day				
Zero order	+.208[a]	+.222[a]	+.279[b]	+.360[a]
Partial	+.130[c]	+.187[b]	+.119	+.337[a]
(n)	(144)	(144)	(118)	(118)

Note. Zero-order correlations shown here are between the individual's reliance on test newspapers and the voter's choice of a candidate and perceived issue saliences scaled for actual newspaper content and voter choice. Candidate choice was scaled so that preference for Nixon was scored 1; no preference, won't vote, or don't know was scored 2; and preference for McGovern was scored 3. Candidate choice was ascertained in the September–October period and again during the week following the election. All correlations are Pearsonian; a positive correlation is in the predicted direction. First order partials have party preference pulled out. Significance tests are for the difference of a correlation from zero.
[a]$p < .01$, one-tailed.
[b]$p < .05$, one-tailed.
[c]$p < .10$, one-tailed.

also declines in predicting vote late in the campaign while the perceived salience measure gains in predictive power. These results are compatible with the causal sequence formulation that perceived saliences lead to voting preferences rather than the reverse. It should be recalled, however, that the election day perceived salience measures required for full cross-lagged analysis and a better test of this causal formulation are not available.

Subsequent analyses not shown in Table 6 reinforce the presumption of late campaign shifting being associated with perceived issue saliences. Republicans who saw Honesty and Vietnam as being important in the campaign relative to Crime and World Leadership were somewhat more likely than other Republicans to report changing their voting choice in the last few weeks of the campaign and to become more interested late in the campaign. They also were more likely to abstain on election day and were slightly less knowledgeable about campaign outcomes. Because of small sample size, however, these relationships were not statistically significant. Among Democrats, those with relatively high Honesty-Vietnam saliences were more likely than others to vote on election day (p < .05), but no differences were found for perceived change, change in interest, or election knowledge.

REFERENCES

BLUMLER, J. and D. McQUAIL (1969) Television in Politics: Its Uses and Influence. Chicago: Univ. of Chicago Press.

LIPPMANN, W. (1922) Public Opinion. New York: Macmillan.

McCOMBS, M. E. and D. L. SHAW (1972) "The agenda setting function of the media." Public Opinion Q. 36 (Summer): 176–187.

McCOMBS, M. E. and D. WEAVER (1973) "Voters' need for orientation and use of mass media." Presented to the International Communication Association, Montreal.

PARK, R. E. (1925) The City. Chicago: Univ. of Chicago Press.

The Agenda-Setting Function of the Mass Media at Three Levels of "Information Holding"*

6

Marc Benton
P. Jean Frazier

This study had two broad purposes. The first was to extend the examination of the agenda-setting function of the mass media to include various levels of peoples' information holding. The second was to examine how people held the information which they were receiving from the media. Both of these purposes were carried out regarding economic issues.

Issues were conceptualized as involving information at three distinct levels: Level 1 includes general issue names. The names of major issues such as "the economy," "the political system," "government inefficiency," and "overpopulation" are level 1 information. Level 2 consists of subissues, including problems, causes, and proposed solutions. Examples of these types of information are problems such as "high food prices," "inflation," and "unemployment"; causes like "Arab oil prices," and "bad weather conditions"; and proposed solutions "tax rebate," and "gas rationing." Level 3 contains specific information about subissues, including pro and con rationales for proposed solutions ("oil tax would be inflationary," "people are unlikely to spend the rebate on consumer goods") and people or groups connected to the proposed solutions (President Ford, Republican Congressmen, State Legislators).

Levels 2 and 3 appear to be different levels of information from Level 1 information and from each other. Palmgreen, Kline and Clark (1974) refer to these types of information when they suggest the need to distinguish important

Communication Research (Vol. 3, No. 3, pp 261-274), copyright©1976 by Sage Publications Inc. Reprinted by permission of Sage Publications Inc.

aspects of "information-holding"—proposals, actors and actor-proposal link-ages—but in their paper, information at these two levels is grouped together. With the three-level conceptualization of information, both information presented in the media and information held by people can be examined. The first objective in the present study was to test the hypothesized agenda-setting function of the media at information Levels 2 and 3. Previous agenda-setting research has focused exclusively on what is identified here as the first level of information—issue names. The usual procedure has been to examine the correlation between the amount of space or time devoted to a few issues in the media and the percentage of respondents who name the issues as ones of importance. For this second objective, the study focused on: (1) factors differentiating people in terms of the amount of information held at the different levels, and (2) relationships among the different kinds of information held by people and the factors leading to differences in patterns of information-holding.

Specific research questions relating to the two objectives are as follows:

Level I

Agenda-Setting

Do TV, newspaper and news magazines present the same issue—news agenda to the public?

Is the amount of mass media coverage of a general issue correlated with the salience of that issue for the public?

Information Holding

Are respondents aware of the *general issue* as a major problem?

What are the characteristics of respondents who hold information?

Level II

Agenda-Setting

Do TV, newspapers and news magazines present the same agenda to the public?

Is the amount of mass media coverage of specific proposals correlated with the public's awareness of each subissue?

Do persons who utilize one medium more than another report information that correlates with what has been presented via that medium about specific and proposed solutions to a greater degree than with that presented via another medium?

Information Holding

Do respondents mention specific *problems, causes,* and *proposed solutions* to problems associated with the general issue?

What are the characteristics of respondents who hold information?

If respondents mention specific problems, do they also then mention causes and solutions? What types of respondents consistently hold all three types of information?

Level III

Agenda-Setting

Do different types of media present the same agenda to the public in terms of specific information about subissues?

Is the amount of mass media coverage of rationales for proposed solutions correlated with the public's awareness of these types of specific information?

Do persons who utilize one medium more than another report information that correlates with what has been presented via that medium about rationales?

Information Holding

Do respondents mention pro–con *rationales* for proposals mentioned at this level? Are respondents aware of *both* pro and con arguments for alternative proposals?

If respondents mention specific rationales, do they also then link "actors" with the proposed solutions?

What are the characteristics of people who hold information at the level?

STUDY DESIGN

"The economy" was selected as the issue for study. During January and February, 1975, "the economy" was an issue of major importance in the United States, and was receiving a great deal of attention in the mass media. An issue generating such a quantity of information was essential for the purposes of the study, in order to examine the effect of the media in setting peoples' agenda at Levels 2 and 3, since large amounts of information generally would not appear at these levels unless the issue was of major consequence.

The study design included a content analysis of media coverage of economic issues and a survey of residents in the city of Minneapolis, Minnesota. Data for the content analysis were obtained during the period January 15–February 9,

1975, and the survey was conducted during the period January 29–February 9, 1975.

Content Analysis.   Media coverage data for the content analysis were obtained from the three available national network television stations, the two Minneapolis metropolitan daily newspapers, and *Time* and *Newsweek* magazines. National and local news programs on television, as well as political presentations regarding the economy, were tape-recorded for later coding. Both the print and broadcast material were coded with an intercoder reliability coefficient above .81.

The content analysis code was based on the conceptualization described above, and generated data concerning the types of economic information at each of the three levels of information holding: (1) the general issue, (2) problems, causes, and proposals, and (3) persons and groups making proposals, rationales given for proposals, and pro versus con positions taken on proposals. Other agenda setting research has coded primarily the amount of space or time, or number of stories devoted to major issues or problems. In this study, we coded the time (TV) or space (print media) of much more specific information within the major issue of "the economy," the categories at Levels 2 and 3.

Survey.   A multistage probability sample of Minneapolis households was obtained through random sampling of census tracts and households within census tracts. Each interviewer then utilized a randomized respondent selection key to determine the individual to be personally interviewed within each household. Of the total 209 households and individuals randomly selected to be interviewed, 111 interviews were obtained, indicating that 53% of the interviews were completed.

The interview schedule basically utilized the "content-free" technique developed by Edelstein (1973). Specific questions focused on subissues of the economic problem: causes, proposed solutions, prominent people or groups associated with proposals, rationales, and pro versus con positions. These questions were content-free in the sense that respondents were allowed to define their own content for these sections for the interview schedule. Measures were also taken of amount of media behavior, respondent's position on the proposed amount of interpersonal communication about the economy, and a series of demographic variables.

ANALYSIS

Agenda Setting.   The data analysis concerning agenda-setting concentrates on Levels 2 and 3. Data concerning agenda-setting for Level 1 (issue names) were not collected because previous agenda-setting studies have consistently found a high correlation between media and public agendas at this level. Data collected in this study, however, do give some indication of agenda setting taking place at this level. Media coverage of economic issues during the study data collection period was extensive. Similarly, 54% of the respondents mentioned an economic problem as being one of the major problems facing the United States today. Thus, the heavy media coverage of the economy is clearly reflected among our respondents.

The correlations between newspapers and television, and newspapers and news magazines for the amount of coverage regarding Level 2 data were .71 and .72 respectively ($p < .01$). The relationship between television and news magazines was a nonsignificant .43. Other agenda setting studies have found high intercorrelations among media at Level 1. To indicate the kinds of proposals discussed in the media and mentioned by respondents, Table 1 shows the extent of media coverage and proportion of respondents mentioning various proposed solutions. Overall, the correlation between the agenda for all media and all respondents at agenda setting Level 2 (coverage of proposed economic solutions) was .65 ($p < .02$). Table 2 (columns 1 and 3) presents the correlations between the Level 2 agenda presented via each type of medium and the agenda for those respondents who named that medium as their most important source of economic information. These data indicate that newspa-

TABLE 1
Proposed Solutions to Economic Problems in Television, Newspapers, and Among Survey Respondents

	Media		
Proposed Solutions	Newspapers	TV	Survey
Tax Rebate	271.5[1]	183.0[2]	43[3]
Oil Tax	261.5	521.0	17
Gas Rationing	173.5	56.0	14
Food Stamps	101.5	176.0	5
Moratorium on Government Spending	98.5	44.0	6
Need to Raise Social Security	54.5	5.5	1
Need for National Health Insurance	41.0	0	0
Need for Housing and Housing Slump	39.0	0	1
Government Jobs	38.5	106.5	8
Nuclear Power as an Alternative to Oil	32.5	9.5	1
Relax Schedule on Auto Pollution Standards	29.0	7.0	0
State Income Tax Cut	22.5	24.5	1
State Gas Tax	21.5	2.0	3

1. These figures are the sums of column length of story × percent of tabulations.
2. These figures are the sums of column amount of story time × percent of story tabulations.
3. These figures are the percentages of usable responses listing a proposed solution: they are not additive.

TABLE 2
Correlations (Pearson r) for Agenda-Setting at Level 2: Media
Coverage of Economic Proposals with Respondent's Agenda,
by Medium Utilized for Economic Information

Newspaper Agenda With Newspaper Reader's Agenda	Newspaper Agenda With TV Oriented Viewer's Agenda	TV Agenda With TV Viewer's Agenda	TV Agenda With Newspaper Reader's Agenda
r = .81	r = .62	r = .27	r = .16
n = 13	n = 13	n = 13	n = 13
p < .01	p < .05	n.s	n.s.

pers appear to be setting the agenda for newspaper-oriented respondents. However, there was only a low correlation between the TV agenda and public agenda among TV-oriented respondents. In order to determine the source of television viewers' agenda, cross-media correlations were examined. Columns 2 and 4 of Table 2 show correlations between the newspaper agenda and TV viewers' agenda, and between the television agenda and newspaper readers' agenda, controlling for the substantial correlation between the newspaper and television agendas. These data show that TV-oriented respondents *also* appear to have their Level 2 agenda set by newspapers. Thus, the level 2 proposal agenda for both groups of respondents seems to have been set by newspapers, and television appears to have little agenda setting input for either group.

We will next look at the agenda setting hypothesis regarding Level 3 information: rationales for the three proposals mentioned most frequently. Although the correlations were not statistically significant because of the small number of rationales given, they are consistently positive and high (see Table 3). Thus, the media do appear to be setting the public agenda concerning rationales for the proposed solutions — Level 3. To parallel the analysis of data at Level 2, respondents were again divided into TV-oriented and newspaper-oriented. "Tax rebate," the most frequently mentioned proposal, was utilized to examine more closely the agenda setting function of specific media. We found that the agenda setting relationship for rationales — Level 3 — is similar to that found for proposed solutions — Level 2. The newspaper agenda is

TABLE 3
Correlations (Pearson r) for Agenda-Setting at Level 3: Media
Coverage of Proposal Rationales with Respondent Rationales
for the Top Three Proposals

Proposal	r	N	P-value
Tax Rebate and Tax Cut	.62	8	p < .10
Oil Tariff and Tax	.59	7	n.s.
Gas Rationing	.48	5	n.s.

strongly correlated with newspaper-oriented respondents' agenda ($r = .68; p <$ .10), but again, the TV agenda is uncorrelated with viewers' agenda ($r = .08$; n.s.).

To determine if television viewers' agenda is being set by newspapers at Level 3, as occurred at Level 2, cross-media partial correlations were again examined. Essentially the same relationship held at Level 3 as at Level 2 — newspapers appear to set the agenda for both groups of respondents ($r = .59$; n.s.), and television does not appear to be having agenda-setting input for either group ($r = -.42$; n.s.).

To summarize the agenda setting findings in this research, agenda setting was found at all three levels of information holding: general issue, proposed solutions for the issue mentioned, and rationales for proposed solutions. Consistently, newspapers were found to be responsible for the agenda setting taking place at Levels 2 and 3, *even* when respondents indicated that their most important source of information about the economy was television. In some of the previous research on agenda setting, television has been found to perform a substantial role in setting the public agenda at Level 1 (e.g., McCombs and Shaw, 1972), while other research has found little or no relationship between TV agenda and viewers' agenda (e.g., Tipton, Haney, and Baseheart, 1975). In the present study, television was found to play only a minor, insignificant role in setting the public agenda at Levels 2 and 3 — levels involving more in-depth knowledge about the general economic issue. These data indicate differential media roles when the agenda setting hypothesis is extended to other important levels of information holding.

INFORMATION-HOLDING

In examining information holding, the unit of analysis shifts from the group (i.e. "public") level to the individual level. Two basic questions are examined in this section. First, what factors affect how much information at the various levels people hold? Second, what factors affect the ways people structure information?

Ninety-six percent of the respondents mentioned pro-con rationales for proposed economic solutions, as well as prominent people or groups arguing for or against the proposal, indicating that respondents almost universally reached Level 3 of information holding. Since the economic situation studied here affects nearly everyone, it is not surprising that such a high percentage reached the third level of information holding concerning economic issues. The specific characteristics of our sample also may contribute to the relatively high level of information holding.

We first looked for factors affecting the amount of information held by the respondents. There was no consistent pattern of differences in amount of information held by respondents who varied in either their mass media behaviors or interpersonal discussions about the economy. This is a somewhat surprising result, since studies dealing with public affairs information and media use (e.g., Wade and Schramm, 1969), as well as research on the knowledge gap (e.g., Tichenor, Donohue, and Olien, 1970) has found print media use related to the amount of knowledge about topics of public interest.

However, two other variables were related to the amount of information which respondents held about proposals, rationales, and prominent people or groups. As would be expected (and as Edelstein, 1973, had also found previously), higher education respondents consistently held more information at both Levels 2 and 3 than did lower education respondents. Education is significantly correlated with 6 of the 7 types of information at Levels 2 and 3 although the average correlation is surprisingly low, .23.

A second variable showing a relationship to amount of information was the pro-con position of the respondent on the subissue mentioned. As Table 4 shows, there is consistency of amount of information according to the respondent's position on an issue. Respondents in favor of a proposal gave more reasons in support of the proposal than opposed to it, and listed more people in favor of it than in opposition to it. The opposite held for those respondents opposing a proposal, although due to small N the results are not statistically significant.

TABLE 4
Mean Number of Pro-Con Rationales, and Pro-Con Prominent
People/Groups by Respondent's Position

	Pro-Issue Respondents		
	Pro	Con	t-value
Number of Rationales	1.53	1.17	t = 2.624
	N = 57	N = 54	p < .01
Number of People/Groups	1.12	.44	t = 4.043
	N = 87	N = 57	p < .01
	Con-Issue Respondents		
	Pro	Con	t-value
Number of Rationales	1.42	1.79	t = 1.240
	N = 19	N = 19	n.s.
Number of People/Groups	.68	.79	t = 0.548
	N = 19	N = 19	n.s.

DISCUSSION

A major purpose of this study was to determine if the agenda setting function of the mass media, fairly well established empirically in terms of general issue-names, also appeared to hold at two subissue levels of information. Our findings indicate that newspapers appeared to be setting the agenda for all respondents at information Levels 2 and 3, and that television did not appear to have much impact on the public agenda at either Level 2 or 3, even for television-oriented respondents. When the unit of analysis is shifted to the individual information level in the analysis of information holding, however, communication variables were generally not related to the amount of information held by respondents, although education and the respondent's position on the proposal were.

It seems clear at this point that any future agenda setting studies should deal with information at several levels, and that further conceptualization and more sophisticated measures of information holding, perhaps along the lines Palmgreen, Kline, and Clarke (1974) have suggested, are needed. Studying the message discrimination behaviors of people at these 3 levels of information would seem to be a logical next step.

REFERENCES

EDELSTEIN, A. S. (1973) "Decision making and mass communication: a conceptual and methodological approach to public opinion," pp. 81–119 in Clarke (ed.) New Models for Mass Communication Research. Beverly Hills: Sage.

McCOMBS, M. and D.L. SHAW (1972) "The agenda setting function of the mass media." Public Opinion Q. 36: 176–188.

PALMGREEN, P., F. G. KLINE, and P. CLARKE (1974) "Message discrimination and information holding about political affairs: a comparison of local and national issues." Paper delivered to The International Communication Association, New Orleans, Louisiana.

TICHENOR, P. J., G. A. DONOHUE, and C. N. OLIEN (1970) "Mass media flow and differential growth in knowledge." Public Opinion Q. 34: 159–171.

TIPTON, L., R. D. HANEY, and J. BASEHEART (1975) "Media agenda setting in city and state election campaigns." Journalism Q. 52: 15–23.

WADE, S. and W. SCHRAMM (1969) "The mass media as sources of public affairs, science and health knowledge." Public Opinion Q. 33: 197–209.

7 The News Business, Crime, and Fear*

Margaret T. Gordon
Linda Heath

The consequences of the current use of crime as easy, competitive news include the police control of crime information, the lack of diversity in newspapers which routinely monitor the competition's crime coverage, and the expansion of crime news which results from monitoring the competition and using crime to attract readers. Whether such consequences should be viewed as costs depends on the effects of such factors on the readers' perceptions of crime. Specifically, two types of effects on readers will be discussed as "costs": inappropriate ranking of crime in the readers' agendas of serious national problems, and unwarranted levels of fear of crime among the readers.

Following the logic of the agenda-setting research of Shaw and McCombs (1977), we used data from interviews with residents of our three target cities to assess the degree to which newspapers convey a priority to crime by their treatment of crime news. Respondents were asked what they saw as the most serious problem facing their communities. As the table shows, crime was frequently mentioned by readers of all papers as the most serious community problem. From the table we can also see that readers of the newspaper with the highest percentage of nonadvertising space devoted to violent crime within each city are more likely to say crime is the most important neighborhood problem than are readers of the other papers within those cities. In two of the cities, Chicago and Philadelphia, the newspaper with the highest percentage of newshole devoted to crime also contained the most lead stories devoted to

*Reprinted from *Reactions to Crime* (Dan A. Lewis, editor) Sage, 1981, by permission of the authors.

TABLE 1

	Average Percentage Newshole Devoted to Violent Crime	Percentage Lead Stories Devoted to Crime	Percentage Readers Ranking Crime as Most Important Neighborhood Problem	Fear[†] Score
*Chicago Sun-Times	2.03	21.4	88.9	− .01
Chicago Tribune	1.86	17.3	81.0	− .18
Chicago Daily News	1.61	15.0	87.5	**
Chicago non-readers				.23
*Philadelphia Daily News	3.69	31.2	72.5	.17
Philadelphia Evening Bulletin	2.27	17.4	61.5	− .04
Philadelphia Inquirer	1.77	11.2	54.5	.09
Philadelphia non-readers				− .23
*San Francisco Chronical	2.27	22.6	81.2	− .13
San Francisco Examiner	2.45	17.8	85.6	.24
San Francisco non-readers				− .05

[†]High score indicates greater fear level.
*indicates city circulation war winner
**there were too few readers of the Chicago Daily News in our sample to allow reliable estimates for these statistical analyses.

crime. In San Francisco, the one city that represents an exception to this pattern, the crime prioritizing effect seems only to follow the percentage of newshole rather than the percentage of lead stories devoted to crime.

A second way in which crime coverage can translate into costs is if such presentation leads to unwarranted levels of fear of crime among readers. Violent crime is pervasive in our nation's large cities, and previous research has shown fear of crime is even more pervasive (Biderman, 1972; Furstenberg, 1972; Hindelang et al., 1978; Figgie, 1980; and Skogan and Maxfield, 1981). Such fear is often out of proportion to the actual danger posed by crime (e.g., Hindelang et al., 1978; Gordon et al., 1980) with women, the elderly, blacks, and the poor carrying the heaviest burden of fear (Biderman, 1972; Furstenberg, 1972; Riger et al., 1981). Because most people do not have direct experience with the serious violent crimes that they most fear, the role of the media in generating such fear becomes particularly important.

Since previous research has shown that sex and income are especially associated with fear of crime levels (Clemente and Kleiman, 1977; Stinchcombe et al., 1980; Riger and Gordon, 1981; Gordon et al., 1980), we conducted a three-way analysis of variance within each city with Sex, Income, and Paper Readership as the independent variables, and Fear Score as the dependent variable.

Concurring with previous research, we found significant main effects for Sex on Fear of Crime in all three cities: Chicago, $F(1, 171) = 3.98, p < .05$;

Philadelphia, $F(1, 186) = 6.35, p < .05$; San Francisco, $F(1, 250) = 22.86$, $p < .001$, with women always exhibiting higher levels of fear than men. Similarly, we found marginally significant main effects for Income in all three cities: Chicago, $F(5, 171) = 2.05, p = .07$; Philadelphia, $F(5, 186) = 2.02, p = .08$; San Francisco, $F(5, 250) = 2.06, p = .07$, with people with lower incomes showing more fear of crime than people with higher incomes. (This finding is qualified by the fact that in Chicago and Philadelphia the relationship was curvilinear, with the wealthiest category also showing a high level of fear of crime.) The Income and Sex analyses are not the focus of this chapter, but rather serve to factor out the well-documented effects of Sex and Income from Newspaper Readership effects on fear of crime.

The analysis of variance also revealed main effects for Newspaper Readership in each city: Chicago, $F(2, 171) = 3.82, p < .05$; Philadelphia, $F(3, 186) = 2.55, p = .057$; San Francisco, $F(2, 250) = 5.87, p < .01$). The table shows the mean deviation scores after controlling for Income and Sex effects from a Multiple Classification Analysis, indicating that *in all three cities, readers of the newspaper that devotes the largest proportion of its newshole to crime exhibit higher levels of fear of crime than do readers of other papers in those cities.* The relationship between reading no newspaper and fear of crime is not as clear-cut. In Chicago, residents who read no newspaper exhibit more fear of crime than do readers of either of the newspapers analyzed. In Philadelphia, residents who read no newspaper exhibit less fear of crime than do readers of any of the city's newspapers, and in San Francisco, nonreaders exhibit more fear than do readers of one of the papers and less fear than readers of the other paper. Note that these fear scores are mean deviations *after* controlling for Sex and Income effects. These differences could, however, be due to differences in local television or radio news coverage to which nonreaders might turn for news, or to other intracity dynamics (such as actual crime rate or the amount of neighborhood gossip about crime) which may impact differentially on nonreaders.

The fact that a large proportion of newshole devoted to violent crime is associated with high levels of fear of crime and enhanced perception of crime as a major neighborhood problem indicates that there are indeed costs associated with the use of crime as easy and competitive news. Whether the large proportion of newshole is the result of many short crime stories (as in the Philadelphia *Daily News*), a few long crime stories (as in the Chicago *Sun Times*), or many long crime stories (as in the San Francisco *Examiner*), the net result is high fear of crime among readers and high ranking of crime in terms of neighborhood problems.

REFERENCES

BIDERMAN, A. [Ed.] (1972) Crime and Justice: A Symposium. New York: Nailburg.
CLEMENTE, F. and M. B. KLEIMAN (1977) "Fear of crime in the U.S.: A multivariate

analysis." Social Forces 56:519–531.

FIGGIE (1980) Report on Fear of Crime: America Afraid. Willoughby, OH: A-T-O.

FURSTENBERG, F. (1972) "Fear of crime and its effect on citizen behavior," in A. Biderman (ed.) Crime and Justice: A Symposium. New York: Nailburg.

GORDON, M. T., S. RIGER, R. K. LEBAILLY and L. HEATH (1980) "Crime, women and the quality of urban life." Signs 5:S133–S160.

HINDELANG, M. J., M. R. GOTTFREDSON and J. GAROFALO (1978) Victims of Personal Crime: An Empirical Foundation for a Theory of Personal Victimization. Cambridge, MA: Ballinger.

RIGER, S. and M. T. GORDON (1981) "The fear of rape: A study in social control." J. of Social Issues. (forthcoming)

RIGER, S. and R. K. LEBAILLY (1981) "Coping with urban crime: Women's use of precautionary behaviors." Amer. J. of Community Psychology. (forthcoming)

SHAW, D. and M. E. McCOMBS (1977) The Emergence of American Political Issues: The Agenda-Setting Function of the Press. St. Paul, MN: West.

SKOGAN, W. G. and M. MAXFIELD (1981) Coping with Crime: Victimization, Fear, and Reactions to Crime. Beverly Hills, CA: Sage.

STINCHCOMBE, A. L., R. ADAMS, C. HEIMER, K. SCHEPPELE, T. SMITH and G. TAYLOR (1980) Crime and Punishment: Changing Attitudes in America. San Francisco: Jossey Bass.

8

Newspaper Coverage and Public Concern About Community Issues*

Kim A. Smith

At the community level . . . the evidence suggests that media coverage of an issue causes an increase in the number of people concerned about an issue. At the same time, the amount of coverage media devote to an issue is influenced by the public. Translated into general systems terms, feedback loops should exist between media coverage and public concern about issues over time. Based on the above discussion, it might be expected that these feedback loops will take two different forms.[1]

Amplification. In amplifying feedback loops, increases (or decreases) in an input variable cause increases (or decreases) in an output variable, which in turn feeds back to cause further changes in the input variable, and so on. By this process, cumulative changes in the input and output variables build up into larger ones over time.

Control. In control feedback loops, increases (or decreases) in the input variable lead to the opposite change in the output variable. As this pattern of interaction between the input and output variables continues over time, a distinct oscillatory path emerges.

It might be expected that amplifying feedback loops will be most frequent in earlier stages of community controversies, before solutions begin to be worked out among the various factions and media report on the rising conflict. Control feedback loops would seem most likely at later stages in the

---

*Reprinted from *Journalism Monographs* (No. 101, 1987) by permission of the editor.

controversy when the media begin to report on agreements among the conflicting factions, resulting in decreased public concern.[2]

TIME LAGS

On the basis of current evidence, it is not yet clear how long the lag might be between media emphasis on an issue and audience response. Panel studies have found agenda-setting effects with lag lengths ranging from two days to nine months.[3] A study by Stone and McCombs suggests that it takes about four months of cumulative media coverage on an issue before it registers on the public agenda, with diminishing effects thereafter.[4] But the lag lengths in most of these studies were necessarily set by the researchers' timing of the fieldwork periods. As Chaffee has observed, lag periods which are too long or too short to "capture" effects of media and public opinion may account for the fuzzy results concerning their direction in some studies.[5] However, an advantage of time-series analysis is that time lags of varying lengths can be measured.

HYPOTHESES

The evidence suggests the following general hypotheses about the newspaper coverage and public issue concern relationship:

1. Over time newspaper coverage and public concern about issues will exert a mutual influence on one another;
2. The mutual interaction between newspaper coverage and public concern about issues will be characterized by lags of unspecified lengths;
3. The feedback loops between newspaper coverage and public concern about issues will be amplifying and controlling in nature.

Unfortunately, sparse evidence exists on which to base *a priori* specification of models predicting the nature of the newspaper coverage and public issue concern relationship for specific community issues. The evidence presented above hints, however, that lag lengths, the mix of controlling and amplifying feedback loops, as well as the primary direction of effect will vary by issue. The intent of this research is to provide a basis for more rigorous theoretical modeling of media-public opinion influence in future research.

MEASURING PUBLIC ISSUE CONCERNS

A test of the mutual effects model posited here requires measurement of variables at equal intervals over an extended period of time. This study was able to make use of a unique series of 22 surveys which were conducted three times a year from 1974 through 1981 by the Urban Studies Center at the University of Louisville. The purpose of these surveys was to provide citizen feedback to local government decision-makers on a variety of community issues.[6]

Each of the 22 surveys was based on a probability sample with quotas, varying in size from 400 to 472 respondents, age fifteen or older.[7] Each sample was stratified by age, race and sex, based on census results and population projections supplied by the Kentucky State Data Center. Adjustments were made to the quota matrix when updated population information became available. As a result of these adjustments, the samples gradually became older, comprised of higher percentages of blacks and women, more suburban and had higher levels of family income over the eight-year period.[8]

The questionnaires for each survey were administered by professional interviewers after an extensive training session. Interviewers were given a list of randomly selected starting addresses drawn from city and county directories, along with their individual quota matrices. They were instructed to begin their searches for eligible respondents at the first address on their list, moving to the next residential address on the left until one was located and interviewed. The process then began again at the next address on their list. In practice, 90 percent of the interviews in the surveys were completed after contacting three households or less, an indication of a low refusal rate. A random sample of at least 20 percent of the interviews from each survey was verified by phone by the fieldwork supervisors.

As Sudman has pointed out, requiring interviewers to follow randomly selected travel patterns eliminates the tendency for interviewers to secure only the most accessible (usually high socioeconomic status) respondents.[9] Sudman has demonstrated that a probability sample with quotas is equivalent to a cluster sample with call-backs.[10] As with cluster samples, the sampling method used in these surveys does somewhat inflate variance estimates, increasing the probability of rejecting true null hypotheses (Type I error) in statistical analyses of the data.

In fact, the sampling design used in these surveys produced accurate results, as indicated by measured demographic variables. Over the 22 surveys, the percentages of those who owned their own homes and who had achieved at least high school education remained stable, consistent with the 1970 and 1980 census results for the Louisville area. The percent of each sample earning more than $15,000 tended to increase steadily over the 22 surveys. This sampling method did, however, tend to overestimate average household size, which is a result of an eligible respondent more likely being home at larger households than smaller ones.

As McLeod, Becker and Byrnes have pointed out, public concern about community issues can be measured in three conceptually distinct ways:[11] 1) respondents can be asked to name issues of importance to them personally *(intrapersonal)*; 2) they can be asked to name issues most often discussed with other people *(interpersonal)*; or 3) they can be asked to list the issues *perceived* as important to the social system which is the unit of analysis (community, nation, etc.).

Respondents in each survey in the series were asked in open-ended questions to name the three most important problems facing their neighborhoods and the community as a whole, measures similar to the intrapersonal and perceived salience concepts of public issue concern. A preliminary analysis of the data indicated that respondents tended to discriminate between issues at the different levels.[12] However, because the hypotheses in this study are formulated at the macro-level of the community, the issues nominated for the community as a whole were analyzed. The wording of this question was:

"What do you think are our community's (i.e. Louisville and Jefferson County's) most important problems and needs?"

Use of this type of open-ended question has some advantages for measuring the importance of community issues among the public. As Edelstein points out, the most important problems approach allows the respondents to define problems they find important rather than imposing categories on them defined by the researcher.[13] Particularly in urban communities, researcher-defined categories of problems are not likely to be inclusive enough to include those salient to citizens of distinct neighborhoods and varying demographic groupings.

Interviewers were instructed to probe for up to three responses. Coding categories from these responses were developed from the results of the first few surveys. Analysis of responses categorized as "other" in subsequent surveys showed that it was unnecessary to add categories to the original list. These categories were:

Sanitation. References to street cleaning, garbage collection and other sanitation services.

Housing. References to the quality and supply of housing.

Public Recreation. References to parks, playgrounds and other public facilities.

Health Care. References to private or public health problems, emergency medical services, doctors, hospitals and the Public Health Department.

Crime. References to local police departments, police conduct, and victim and victimless crime.

Education. References to public elementary, secondary and post-secondary education, including state and federal programs affecting the local school system.

Road Maintenance. References to street construction, widening, repair, and completion of roadway projects.

Drainage. References to drainage, sewers, and related problems such as standing water, flooding and water in basements.

Fire Protection. References to fire protection services and incidents of fire.

Zoning. References to zoning cases, code enforcement for housing and commercial buildings, compliance issues, and zoning board decisions.

The Environment. References to air, water, noise and other forms of pollution.

Community Spirit. References to activities or lack of them that would contribute to community understanding and spirit.

Economic Development. References to new businesses in the community, the need to develop more jobs and problems of joblessness.

Courts. References to judge's conduct, court administration and other general activity.

Human Relations. References to minority and gender discrimination issues and programs to remedy associated problems.

The Needy. References to the disadvantaged, handicapped, and mentally ill, including related social service programs.

Mass Transit. References to the public bus system or other public transportation.

Local Government. References to the efficiency, effectiveness and intentions of local governments, including the performance of elected and appointed officials.

Taxation. References to all local tax matters.

Other. All topics, including nonlocal ones, not fitting any of the above categories.

Table 1 shows the ranking of community problems aggregated over the 22 surveys.

As Table 1 shows, crime and education were by far the dominant concerns of respondents during the eight-year period of the surveys, accounting for 40 percent of the aggregated responses. Road maintenance, economic development, the environment and local government also ranked among the top issues, accounting for another one-third of all responses. Citizen concern about most of these issues does not appear limited to the Louisville area. Palmgreen and Stipak both report similar rankings of the same community issues in other areas of the country.[14]

MEASURING THE MEDIA'S AGENDA

Louisville is a media-rich community. The newspaper industry is dominated by the morning *Courier-Journal* and the afternoon *Louisville Times,* which have

TABLE 1
Aggregated Mentions of Community Issues in the 22 Surveys

Ranking	Issue[a]	Number of Mentions	Percent of Mentions
1	Crime	3,431	20.9
2	Education	3,151	19.2
3	Road Maintenance	1,704	10.4
4	Economic Development	1,591	9.7
5	The Environment	1,138	6.9
6	Local Government	970	5.9
7	Housing	623	3.8
8	Public Recreation	609	3.7
9	Sanitation	570	3.5
10	Drainage	530	3.2
11	Mass Transit	408	2.5
12	The Needy	395	2.4
13	Taxation	325	2.0
14	Community Spirit	314	1.9
15	Zoning	209	1.3
16	Courts	160	1.0
17	Human Rights	158	1.0
18	Heath Care	95	.6
19	Fire Protection	41	.3
	Total	16,422	100%

[a]The "other" category was excluded from this analysis

a combined daily circulation of over 330,000. Several weekly and bi-weekly suburban newspapers also serve the community, as well as the oldest black-oriented newspaper in the nation. Three network-affiliated television stations, an independent and a public station broadcast to the community. Separate cable systems serve the city and the suburban areas in Jefferson County. About 30 radio stations offering a complete spectrum of formats are located in the area.

Ideally in such situations, separate indices of the electronic and print media's agendas should be constructed. This was not possible in this study. Consequently, the *Louisville Times* agenda on community issues was measured as an indicator of general media emphasis on them during the eight-year-period of this study.[15] Previous studies have normally found high intercorrelations between the print and electronic media's emphasis on issues during election campaigns.[16] Some evidence, as described earlier, also exists that the agenda of local news broadcasts are influenced by that of newspapers.[17]

A simple random sample of 236 editions (29 per year) of the *Louisville Times* (substituting the *Courier Journal* for Sunday editions) was drawn from those issued during the years 1974 through 1981. Staff members from the Urban Studies Center assigned all stories from the front and "metro" pages to the same categories used to code the public opinion question, if the main emphasis of the story pertained to the Louisville area.[18] All other stories on these pages were classified as "other." Three checks of intercoder reliability conducted during the coding resulted in acceptable levels of agreement each time (+.85).

These procedures resulted in a final sample of 2,369 articles. Table 2 shows the aggregate results for the eight years:

As with the public's agenda, education and crime were the top two issues on the media's agenda, accounting for over 17 percent of the stories on the front and metro pages. Another 20 percent of the stories on these pages were devoted to local government, economic development, public recreation, health care, the environment, the needy, courts and community spirit. Ryan and Owen report similar results from a content analysis of eight major urban newspapers' coverage of social issues.[19]

The Spearman's rho correlation between the aggregated rankings for the media and public agendas is .65 ($p < .05$). A comparison of Tables 1 and 2 will show that the major differences between the two agendas involve issues with which people would likely have personal experience: road maintenance, health care, the courts, drainage and mass transit. This rank-order correlation,

TABLE 2
Aggregated Article Count of *Louisville Times* Sample from
1974–1981

Rank[a]	Issue	Number of Articles	Percent of Articles
1	Education	254	10.7
2	Crime	154	6.5
3	Local Environment	90	3.8
4	Economic Development	85	3.6
5	Public Recreation	68	2.9
6	Health Care	64	2.7
7	The Environment	55	2.3
8	The Needy	38	1.6
9	Courts	35	1.5
10	Community Spirit	33	1.5
11	Inflation	28	1.2
11	Housing	28	1.2
13	Local Elections	24	1.0
14	Roads	20	.9
15	Fire Protection	19	.8
16	Sanitation	16	.7
17	Taxation	14	.6
18	Human Relations	13	.6
18	Drainage	13	.6
18	Mass Transit	13	.6
21	Zoning	12	.5
	Other	1,293	54.6
	Total	2,369	100%

[a]The "other" category was excluded from these rankings

however, only indicates that problems high on the media's agenda tended to be ranked high among the public over the eight year-period. As Becker has cautioned, these results do not indicate agenda-setting effects on individuals, but rather influences between media coverage and public concern for issues at the macro-level of the community.[20]

The most frequent method of analyzing data in agenda-setting studies has been to create an "official" agenda of issues and then examine the cross-lagged correlations between media and public agendas at two points in time. However, use of this method would have obscured the fact that each of the seven issues has a different temporal history, as will be described shortly. An issue-by-issue analysis allows an examination of differences in the causal relationship between newspaper coverage and public concern among them. A separate analysis of each issue was therefore performed.

THE ANALYSIS

The first step in the analysis was to identify the "cross-correlation function" between newspaper coverage and public concern for each issue over time.[21] Using the Pearson product-moment formula, the cross-correlations were calculated between the two series at the T-0 point, the positive lags (i.e., with media coverage leading public issue concern by 4, 8 and 12 months) and at the negative lags (i.e., with public issue concern leading media coverage by lags of 4, 8 and 12 months). The cross-correlations at the positive lags do not necessarily equal those at the negative lags.[22]

If, as hypothesized, newspaper coverage and public issue concerns influence each other over time, significant cross-correlations should be found at both negative and positive lags. A primarily newspaper coverage influence pattern would be evidenced by significant correlations at only the positive lags (newspaper coverage leading public issue concern). A primarily public concern influence pattern, on the other hand, would have significant correlations at only the negative lags (public issue concern leading newspaper coverage). A spurious effects relationship between newspaper coverage and public concern, due to a third variable acting on both series, would be indicated by correlations across all positive and negative lags. If the two series are unrelated, the cross-correlations at all positive and negative lags would be insignificant. Table 3 shows the results of this analysis for the seven issues.[23]

The patterns of cross-correlations for the education, economic development and crime issues indicate mutual influence. Significant correlations are evident for education at the -4 month lag ($r = .38$) and at T-0 ($r = .47$), as well as at the $+4$ ($r = .48$) and $+8$ ($r = .45$) month lags. For economic development, significant correlations appear at the -12 month lag ($r = -.37$), the -8

TABLE 3
Cross-Lag Correlations Between Newspaper Coverage and
Public Concern for Seven Issues
N = 22 Observations

| | P.O. → N_p | | | Lag Length[a] (in months) | N_p → P.O. | | |
	-12	-8	-4	0	+4	+8	+12
Education	.19	.26	.38[b]	.47[b]	.48[b]	.45[b]	.18
Economic Development	-.37[b]	-.46[b]	.00	-.24	.02	.38[b]	.22
Crime	-.41[b]	-.13	-.23	-.04	.38[b]	.13	.08
The Environment	-.21	.03	.14	.03	.31	.42[b]	-.16
Local Government	-.04	.05	.20	-.07	-.08	.26	.24
Health Care	.57[b]	-.07	-.13	-.16	-.27	.12	-.09
Public Recreation	.39[b]	.30	-.23	-.05	-.04	-.03	-.19

[a]Cross-correlations at the positive lags are for newspaper coverage leading public concern by the specified number of months. Cross-correlations at the negative lags are for public concern leading newspaper coverage by the specified number of months. The T-0 column represents public concern prior to or early in the following four-month period of newspaper coverage.
[b]Significant at $p < .05$.

month lag ($r = -.46$) and the +8 lag ($r = .38$). The crime issue has significant correlations at the -12 month lag ($r = -.41$) and the +4 month lag ($r = .38$).

A one-way effect of newspaper coverage on public concern is indicated by the pattern of correlations for the environment and local government issues. A significant correlation appears at only the +8 lag ($r = .42$) for the environment series. A similar pattern is evident across the cross-correlations for local government, although the largest correlations at +8 months ($r = .26$) and +12 months ($r = .24$) are not significant.

A one-way effect of public concern on newspaper coverage is suggested by the pattern of cross-correlations for the health care and public recreation issues. A large significant correlation is evident at the -12 month lag ($r = .57$) for health care, while the only significant correlation for public recreation is also at the -12 month lag ($r = .39$).

MULTIVARIATE ANALYSES

The results of the cross-correlation analysis, then, offer mixed support for the hypothesis that newspaper coverage and public concern about issues mutually influence each other. However, it is necessary to use multivariate methods at this point to take into account the interdependencies that exist among each set of lagged variables for the seven issues. A frequently used multivariate test of causality (at least among economists and political scientists) is based on the concept of "Granger causality."[24] Granger has suggested that a variable X causes variable Y, if Y is better predicted from the past histories (i.e., the lagged values) of Y and X together than the past history of Y alone. The reverse case would hold true if Y causes X. Mutual influence is indicated when both Y and X are better predicted by their past histories and those of each other than their past histories alone.[25]

Granger causality is tested by regressing the public opinion series for each issue on its set of lagged values, followed by the block of lagged values of the media series. The media series for each issue is likewise regressed on its set of lagged values, followed by the lagged values of the public opinion series. An F-test is used to determine if the additional variance accounted for by the block of lagged values serving as the independent variables in each equation is significant.[26] Table 4 shows the results of the Granger analysis for the seven issues.

Consistent with the results of the cross-correlation analysis, substantial amounts of variance are accounted for when both public concern and newspaper coverage for education, economic development and crime are treated as dependent variables in the regression models. Moreover, the lagged values of each other appear to add considerably (although not always significantly) to the variance accounted for beyond that of the past histories of both newspaper coverage and public concern for these issues. Comparing the size of these increases in variance, however, it appears that only in the case of education do newspaper coverage and public concern have an equal influence on each other. Past values of public concern have considerably greater influence on media coverage for economic development than the reverse case. Past values of media coverage of crime, on the other hand, have greater influence on public concern than the reverse case.

For the environment and local government issues, the cross-correlation analysis suggested that media coverage had a one-way effect on public concern. In the case of the environment, public concern is considerably better predicted by its past values and those of media coverage than when newspaper coverage is treated as the dependent variable. Furthermore, the percentage increase in variance accounted for in public concern by lagged values of newspaper coverage is significantly greater than in the reverse case. For local government, a considerably larger amount of variance is accounted for in public opinion than in newspaper coverage. Yet the percentage increase in variance accounted for by adding lagged values of each other is about the same in both regression models, suggesting some mutual influence between newspaper coverage and public concern.

Finally, the cross-correlation analysis indicated that public concern about health care and public recreation had a one-way effect on newspaper coverage. For health care, somewhat more variance is accounted for in newspaper coverage than in public opinion. Lagged values of public opinion also account for a much larger amount of variance in newspaper coverage than do lagged

TABLE 4
Regression Analysis to Assess Causal Influence Between
Newspaper Coverage and Public Concern for Seven Issues
N = 22 Observations[a,b]

		Dependent Variable	
		Public Concern	Newspaper Coverage
Education	Lagged Y_{t-n}	.189	.145
	Lagged Y_{t-n} + X_{t-n}	.322	.278
	% increase	13.3	13.3
Economic Development	Lagged Y_{t-n}	.720	.042
	Lagged Y_{t-n} + X_{t-n}	.816	.397
	% increase	9.6	35.5[c]
Crime	Lagged Y_{t-n}	.036	.483
	Lagged Y_{t-n} + X_{t-n}	.217	.543
	% increase	18.1	6.0
The Environment	Lagged Y_{t-n}	.448	.118
	Lagged Y_{t-n} + X_{t-n}	.746	.198
	% increase	29.8[c]	8.0
Local Government	Lagged Y_{t-n}	.624	.081
	Lagged Y_{t-n} + X_{t-n}	.727	.168
	% increase	10.3	8.7
Health Care	Lagged Y_{t-n}	.103	.071
	Lagged Y_{t-n} + X_{t-n}	.220	.337
	% increase	11.7	26.6
Public Recreation	Lagged Y_{t-n}	.259	.049
	Lagged Y_{t-n} + X_{t-n}	.368	.185
	% increase	10.9	13.6

[a]One observtion is lost each time a variable is lagged. Thus this regression analysis was run on 19 observations.
[b]The first row of figures for each issue shows the variance accounted for by the block of lagged values (at 4, 8 and 12 months) of the dependent variable (Y_{t-n}). The second row of figures shows the variance accounted for by the block of lagged values of Y_{t-n} plus the lagged values (at 4, 8 and 12 months) of the independent variable (X_{t-n}). The third row shows the percentage increase in variance accounted for by the addition of X_{t-n} to the equation. Thus the left-hand column tests the causal impact of newspaper coverage on public concern, while the right-hand column tests the causal impact of public concern on newspaper coverage.
[c]Percent increase significant at $p < .05$.

values of newspaper coverage in public opinion. On the other hand, more variance is accounted for in public concern for public recreation than newspaper coverage of this issue. However, the percentage increase in variance accounted for by lagged values of each other in public concern and newspaper coverage is about the same, suggesting some degree of mutual influence.

The results of the Granger analysis further suggest, therefore, that public concern about education, economic development and crime tend to mutually influence each other. The results for local government and public recreation also indicated feedback effects between public concern and newspaper coverage.

NOTES

1. Heise, *op. cit.* Heise also argues that it is possible for unstable feedback loops to occur in systems. In such situations, the changes produced by the interaction of input and output variables become larger and larger with each cycle, until the structure of the social system is destroyed. It seems unlikely that unstable feedback loops would characterize media coverage-public concern systems, given that there is a finite number of people who can become concerned about an issue.

2. See Olien, Donohue and Tichenor, "Media and Stages of Social Conflict," *op. cit.*

3. Tipton, *et al., op. cit.*; Sohn, *op. cit.,* Watt *et al., op. cit.*

4. Stone and McCombs, *op. cit.*

5. Steven H. Chaffee, "Longitudinal Designs for Communication Research: Cross-Lagged Correlation," paper presented to the Association for Education in Journalism. Carbondale, Ill., August 1972.

6. This survey series was designed by Mr. Paul Schulte, executive vice president of the Southern Research Corporation in Louisville, Kentucky. For more information on this series, see Stanley A. Murrell and Paul Schulte, "A Procedure for Systematic Citizen Input to Community Decision-making," *American Journal of Community Psychology,* 8:19–30 (1980).

7. Twenty-five surveys were actually conducted by the Urban Studies Center in this series. Only the first 22 surveys are analyzed here, however, because the last three were irregularly scheduled.

8. For more detail on the samples, see Murrell and Schulte, *op. cit.*

9. Seymour Sudman, *Reducing the Cost of Surveys* (New York: Longman, 1964).

10. Sudman, *op. cit.*

11. Jack M. McLeod, Lee B. Becker and James E. Byrnes, "Another Look at the Agenda-Setting Function of the Press," *Communication Research,* 1:131–165 (April 1974).

12. Murrell and Schulte, *op. cit.*

13. Alex Edelstein, *The Uses of Communication in Decision-making: A Comparative Study of Yugoslavia and the United States* (New York: Praeger, 1974).

14. Palmgreen, *op. cit.*; Brian Stipak, "Attitudes and Belief Systems Concerning Urban Services," *Public Opinion Quarterly,* 41:41–55 (1977).

15. The *Louisville Times* agenda was measured rather than the more widely read *Courier-Journal* because of its particular emphasis on community public affairs.

16. Maxwell E. McCombs, "Newspaper Versus Television: Mass Communication Effects Across Time," in Shaw and McCombs, *op. cit.*; Weaver, Graber, McCombs and Eyal, *op. cit.*

17. McCombs, *op. cit.,* pp. 89–106; Weaver, Graber, McCombs and Eyal, *op. cit.*

18. The size of each article in column inches was also measured. In this analysis, the article count was used rather than the size of articles, because it was felt that the former was a more direct reflection of the paper's emphasis on the topic than the latter. In practice, however, the two measures were highly correlated.

19. Michael Ryan and Dorothea Owen, "A Content Analysis of Metropolitan Newspaper Coverage of Social Issues," *Journalism Quarterly,* 53:634–640 (Winter 1976).

20. Becker, *op. cit.*

21. An overview of time-series analysis is presented by Robert Krull and Albert S. Paulson, "Time Series Analysis in Communication Research," in Paul M. Hirsch, Peter V. Miller and F. Gerald Kline, eds., *Strategies for Communication Research* (Beverly Hills: Sage Publications, 1977), pp. 187–204. A more detailed discussion of the time-series analysis can be found in Richard McCleary and Richard A. Hay, Jr., *Applied Time Series Analysis for the Social Sciences* (Beverly Hills: Sage Publications, 1980). A more advanced text on the topic is G.E.P. Box and G.M. Jenkins, *Time Series Analysis: Forecasting and Control* (San Francisco: Holden-Day, 1970).

22. For further explanation of these procedures see Krull and Paulson, *op. cit.* or McCleary and Hay, *op. cit.*

23. The cross-correlations for each set of time series were calculated on the "raw" series. It is possible, however, that the right combination of trends (steady increases or decreases) and/or

seasonal cycles in the time series could result in spurious cross-correlations. Because the education, economic development, local government and environment public opinion series, as well as the crime and education media series, exhibited autocorrelations at the first lag above .30, the results shown in Table 4 could be spurious.

To determine if this was the case, all of the series were differenced one degree and, if after an inspection of the resultant residuals correlogram, autocorrelation at the first lag was still present, a first-order autoregressive parameter was fit (see McCleary and Hay, *op. cit.* for details on this procedure). Then the cross-correlations for the residuals for each issue were calculated. (See G. William Schwert, "Tests of Causality: The Message in the Innovations," in Karl Brunner and Allan H. Meltzer, eds., *Three Aspects of Policy and Decision-Making* (New York: North-Holland, 1979). As the table below shows, the cross-correlations between the white noise series were changed in magnitude by this procedure. However, only in the case of crime would the inference concerning causal direction be changed, keeping in mind that the T-0 point represents public concern prior to or early in the following four month period of media coverage.

	-12	-8	-4	Lag (in months) 0	4	8	12
Education	.20	-.35	.08	-.30	.38	.18	-.18
Economic Development	-.06	.40	.10	-.25	-.55	-.47	-.19
Crime	.03	.11	.07	.49	.03	.07	-.04
The Environment	.11	-.10	.07	-.03	-.34	.22	.04
Local Government	-.01	-.14	.14	.13	-.50	.04	.40
Health Care	-.23	.14	-.01	-.41	.16	.15	-.17
Public Recreation	-.24	.19	.21	-.31	-.02	.12	.24

24. An excellent discussion of the concept of Granger causality is contained in the papers in Karl Brunner and Allan L. Meltzer, *op. cit.* See also the papers in Christopher A. Sims, ed., *New Methods in Business Cycle Research: Proceedings from a Conference* (Minneapolis: The Federal Reserve Bank of Minneapolis, 1977).

25. For an example of two tests of Granger causality, see John R. Freeman, "Granger Causality and the Time Series Analysis of Political Relationships," *American Journal of Political Science,* 27:325–405 (May 1983); see also, Ralph A. Catalano, David Dooley, and Robert Jackson, "Selecting a Time-Series Strategy," *Psychological Bulletin,* 94:506–523 (1983).

26. A problem with using ordinary least squares regression in time-series analysis is that the error terms of the final models are likely to be autocorrelated to varying degrees, resulting in biased estimations. This problem can be further compounded when lagged values of the dependent variable are included in the model. To the extent that this is the case, the contribution of lagged values of the dependent variable will be overestimated and those of the independent variable will be underestimated. An examination of the correlogram of the residuals from each model, however, showed that only for the crime model was autocorrelation a problem (p. = .33 at the first lag). Thus, for this model, the impact of previous levels of public concern are probably somewhat exaggerated and the impact of media coverage underestimated. See Douglass A. Hibbs, Jr., "Problems of Statistical Estimation and Causal Inference in Time-Series Regression Models," in Herbert L. Costner, ed., *Sociological Methodology: 1973-1974* (San Francisco: Jossey-Bass, Inc., 1974), pp. 252-308.

9

Experimental Demonstrations of the "Not-So-Minimal" Consequences of Television News Programs*

Shanto Iyengar
Mark E. Peters
Donald R. Kinder

In sum, we will: (1) provide authoritative experimental evidence on the degree to which the priorities of the evening newscasts affect the public's agenda; (2) examine whether network news' priorities also affect the importance the public attaches to various standards in its presidential evaluations; and (3) further exploit the virtues of experimentation by exploring individual cognitive processes that might underlie agenda setting.

Overview

Residents of the New Haven, Connecticut area participated in one of two experiments, each of which spanned six consecutive days. The first experiment was designed to assess the feasibility of our approach and took place in November 1980, shortly after the presidential election. Experiment 2, a more elaborate and expanded replication of Experiment 1, took place in late February 1981.

In both experiments, participants came to two converted Yale University offices to take part in a study of television newscasts. On the first day, participants completed a questionnaire that covered a wide range of political topics, including the importance of various national problems. Over the next four days participants viewed what were represented to be videotape recordings of the preceding evening's network newscast. Unknown to the partici-

*Reprinted from *American Political Science Review* (1982, Vol. 76, pp. 848–858) by permission of the American Political Science Association.

pants, portions of the newscasts had been altered to provide sustained coverage of a certain national problem. On the final day of the experiment (24 hours after the last broadcast), participants completed a second questionnaire that again included the measures of problem importance.

Experiment 1 focused on alleged weaknesses in U.S. defense capability and employed two conditions. One group of participants ($N = 13$) saw several stories about inadequacies in American defense preparedness (four stories totalling eighteen minutes over four days). Participants in the control group saw newscasts with no defense-related stories ($N = 15$). In Experiment 2, we expanded the test of agenda setting and examined three problems, requiring three conditions. In one group ($N = 15$), participants viewed newscasts emphasizing (as in Experiment 1) inadequacies in U.S. defense preparedness (five stories, seventeen minutes). The second group ($N = 14$) saw newscasts emphasizing pollution of the environment (five stories, fifteen minutes). The third group ($N = 15$) saw newscasts with steady coverage of inflation (eight stories, twenty-one minutes). Each condition in Experiment 2 was characterized not only by a concentration of stories on the appropriate target problem, but also by deliberate omission of stories dealing with the two other problems under examination.

Participants

Participants in both experiments responded by telephone to classified advertisements promising payment ($20) in return for taking part in research on television. As hoped, this procedure produced a heterogeneous pool of participants, roughly representative of the New Haven population. Participants ranged in age from nineteen to sixty-three, averaging twenty-six in Experiment 1 and thirty-five in Experiment 2. They were drawn primarily from blue collar and clerical occupations. Approximately 30 percent were temporarily out of work or unemployed. Blacks made up 25 percent and women, 54 percent of the participants in Experiment 1 and 10 percent and 61 percent, respectively, in Experiment 2.

Participants were first scheduled for one of several daily sessions. Each of these sessions, with between five and ten individuals, was then randomly assigned to one of the two conditions in Experiment 1, or one of the three conditions in Experiment 2. Random assignment was successful. Participants in the defense condition in Experiment 1 did not differ at all in their demographic characteristics, in their political orientations, or in their political involvement from their counterparts in the control condition, according to day 1 assessments. The sole exception to this pattern—the control group had a significantly larger proportion of black participants (38 vs. 15 percent, $p <$ .05)—is innocuous, since race is unrelated to the dependent variables. And in Experiment 2, across many demographic and attitudinal pretreatment comparisons, only two statistically significant differences emerged: participants in the defense condition reported watching television news somewhat more often ($p < .05$), and participants in the pollution condition were somewhat less Democratic ($p < .03$). To correct for this, party identification has been included as a control variable, where appropriate, in the analyses reported below.

Manipulating the Networks' Agenda

On the evening before each day's session, the evening national newscast of either ABC or NBC was recorded. For each of the conditions being prepared, this broadcast was then copied, but with condition-inappropriate stories deleted and condition-appropriate stories inserted. Inserted stories were actual news stories previously broadcast by ABC or NBC that were acquired from the Vanderbilt Television News Archive. In practice, the actual newscast was left substantially intact except for the insertion of a news story from the VTNA pool, with a condition-irrelevant story normally deleted in compensation. All insertions and deletions were made in the middle portion of the newscast and were spread evenly across experimental days. In Experiment 1 the first newscast was left unaltered in order to allay any suspicions on the part of the participants, and for the next three days a single news story describing inadequacies in U.S. military preparedness was inserted into the broadcasts. Similar procedures were followed in Experiment 2, except that we added material to all four newscasts.

RESULTS

Setting the Public Agenda

We measured problem importance with four questions that appeared in both the pretreatment and posttreatment questionnaires. For each of eight national problems, participants rated the problem's importance, the need for more government action, their personal concern, and the extent to which they discussed each with friends. Because responses were strongly intercorrelated across the four items, we formed simple additive indices for each problem. In principle, each ranges from four (low importance) to twenty (high importance).

The agenda setting hypothesis demands that viewers adjust their beliefs about the importance of problems in response to the amount of coverage problems receive in the media. In our experiments, the hypothesis was tested by computing adjusted (or residualized) change scores for the importance indices and then making comparisons across conditions. Adjusted change scores measure the extent to which pretest responses underpredict or overpredict (using OLS regression) posttest responses. Participants whose posttest scores exceeded that predicted by their pretest scores received positive scores on the adjusted change measure; those whose posttest scores fell short of that predicted received negative scores.

Table 1 presents the adjusted change scores for each of the eight problems inquired about in Experiment 1. In keeping with the agenda-setting hypothesis, for defense preparedness *but for no other problem,* the experimental treatment exerted a statistically significant effect ($p < .05$). Participants whose news programs were dotted with stories alleging the vulnerability of U.S. defense capability grew more concerned about defense over the experiment's six days. The effect is significant substantively as well as statistically. On the first day of the experiment, viewers in the experimental group ranked defense sixth out of eight problems, behind inflation, pollution, unemployment, energy, and civil rights. After exposure to the newscasts, however, defense ranked second, trailing only inflation. (Among viewers in the control group, meanwhile, the relative position of defense remained stable.)

Experiment 2 contributes further support to classical agenda setting. As in Experiment 1, participants were randomly assigned to a condition—this time to one of three conditions, corresponding to an emphasis upon defense preparedness, pollution, or inflation. Changes in the importance of defense, pollution, and inflation are shown in Table 2. There the classical agenda setting hypothesis is supported in two of three comparisons. Participants exposed to a steady stream of news about defense or about pollution came to believe that defense or pollution were more consequential problems. In each case, the shifts surpassed statistical significance. No agenda setting effects were found for inflation, however. With the special clarity of hindsight, we attribute this single failure to the very great importance participants assigned to inflation before the experiment. Where twenty represents the maximum

TABLE 1
Adjusted Change Scores for Problem Importance: Experiment 1

	Condition	
Problem	*Defense*	*Control*
Defense*	.90	− .79
Inflation	− .49	.23
Energy	− .40	.22
Drug addiction	− .19	− .48
Corruption	− .67	.05
Pollution	− .58	.60
Unemployment	.28	.54
Civil rights	− .27	− .27

*$p < .05$, one-tailed t-test.

TABLE 2
Adjusted Change Scores for Problem Importance: Experiment 2

Problem	Condition		
	Pollution	Inflation	Defense
Pollution	1.53**	−.71	−.23
Inflation	−.11	.11	−.06
Defense	−.44	−.34	.76*

*$p < .05$.
**$p < .01$.

score, participants began Experiment 2 with an average importance score for inflation of 18.5!

As in Experiment 1, the impact of the media agenda could also be discerned in changes in the rank ordering of problems. Among participants in the defense condition, defense moved from sixth to fourth, whereas pollution rose from fifth to second among viewers in that treatment group. Within the pooled control groups, in the meantime, the importance ranks of the two problems did not budge.

Taken together, the evidence from the two experiments strongly supports the classical agenda setting hypothesis. With a single and, we think, forgivable exception, viewers exposed to news devoted to a particular problem become more convinced of its importance. Network news programs seem to possess a powerful capacity to shape the public's agenda.

Priming and Presidential Evaluations

Next we take up the question of whether the media's agenda also alters the standards people use in evaluating their president. This requires measures of ratings of presidential performance in the designated problem areas – national defense in Experiment 1, defense, pollution, and inflation in Experiment 2 – as well as measures of overall appraisal of the president. For the first, participants rated Carter's performance from "very good" to "very poor" on each of eight problems including "maintaining a strong military," "protecting the environment from pollution," and "managing the economy." We measured overall evaluation of President Carter in three ways: a single five-point rating of Carter's "*overall performance* as president"; an additive index based on three separate ratings of Carter's *competence;* and an additive index based on three separate ratings of Carter's *integrity*.

In both Experiments 1 and 2, within each condition, we then correlated judgments of President Carter's performance on a particular problem with rating of his overall performance, his competence, and his integrity. (In fact these are partial correlations. Given the powerful effects of partisanship on political evaluations of the kind under examination here, we thought it prudent to partial out the effects of party identification. Party identification was measured in both experiments by the standard seven-point measure, collapsed for the purpose of analysis into three categories.)

At the outset, we expected these partial correlations to conform to two predictions. First, when evaluating the president, participants will weigh evidence partly as a function of the agenda set by their news programs. Participants exposed to stories that question U.S. defense capability will take Carter's performance on defense into greater account in evaluating Carter overall than will participants whose attention is directed elsewhere; that is, the partial correlations should vary according to the broadcasts' preoccupations, in keeping with the priming hypothesis. Second, the priming effect will follow a semantic gradient. Specifically, priming is expected to be most pronounced in judgments of Carter's overall performance as president, somewhat less apparent in judgments of his competence, a personal trait relevant to performance; and to be least discernible in judgments of his integrity, a personal trait irrelevant to performance.

Experiment 1 treated our two predictions unevenly. As Table 3 indicates, the first prediction is corroborated in two of three comparisons. Steady coverage of defense did strengthen the relationship between judgments of Carter's defense performance and evaluations of his overall job performance, and between judgments of Carter's defense performance and integrity, as predicted. However, the relationship reverses on judgments of Carter's competence. And as for our second prediction, Experiment 1 provides only the faintest encouragement.

More encouraging is the evidence provided by Experiment 2. As Table 4 indicates, our first prediction is upheld in eight of nine comparisons, usually handsomely, and as predicted, the effects are most striking for evaluations of Carter's overall performance, intermediate (and somewhat irregular) for judgments of his competence, and fade away altogether for judgments of his integrity.

TABLE 3
Correlations between Overall Evaluations of Carter and Judgments of Carter's Performance on Defense as a Function of News Coverage: Experiment 1

	Coverage emphasizes defense	Coverage neglects defense
Carter's overall performance	.59	.38
Carter's competence	.03	.58
Carter's integrity	.31	.11

Table entries are first-order Pearson partial correlations, with party identification held constant.

TABLE 4
Correlations between Overall Evaluations of Carter and Judg-
ments of Carter's Performance on Specific Problems as a
Function of News Coverage: Experiment 2

	Coverage emphasizes defense	Coverage neglects defense
Carter's overall performance	.88	.53
Carter's competence	.79	.58
Carter's integrity	.13	− .17

	Coverage emphasizes pollution	Coverage neglects pollution
Carter's overall performance	.63	.42
Carter's competence	.47	.56
Carter's integrity	.33	.15

	Coverage emphasizes inflation	Coverage neglects inflation
Carter's overall performance	.63	.39
Carter's competence	.71	.38
Carter's integrity	.07	.08

Table entries are first-order Pearson partial correlations, with party identification held constant.

In sum, Experiments 1 and 2 furnish considerable, if imperfect, evidence for priming. The media's agenda does seem to alter the standards people use in evaluating the president. Although the patterns are not as regular as we would like, priming also appears to follow the anticipated pattern. A president's overall reputation, and, to a lesser extent, his apparent competence, both depend on the presentations of network news programs.

CONCLUSION

Fifty years and much inconclusive empirical fussing later, our experiments decisively sustain Lippmann's suspicion that media provide compelling descriptions of a public world that people cannot directly experience. We have shown that by ignoring some problems and attending to others, television news programs profoundly affect which problems viewers take seriously. This is so especially among the politically naive, who seem unable to challenge the pictures and narrations that appear on their television sets. We have also discovered another pathway of media influence: priming. Problems prominently positioned in television broadcasts loom large in evaluations of presidential performance.

III THE AGENDA-SETTING PROCESS

Every theory has a history. Ideas unfold. Hypotheses are tested. The theory becomes established. More testing occurs. Often the theory is refined, and sometimes even discarded. Knowledge advances.

Some theories have rather elaborate histories that read like lengthy Russian novels. The physical sciences provide the best-known examples of such theories. Sir Isaac Newton's encounter with an apple led first to a creative scientific breakthrough. Extensive testing of Newton's ideas next produced new theories about the physical universe. Later, Einstein and others modified and in part rejected some of these theories.

On a less grand scale, leading communication theories often undergo a similar cycle of generation and rejuvenation. So it is with agenda-setting. The first two parts of this anthology contain readings on the initial conception and measurement of the agenda-setting hypothesis.

Agenda-setting research today has entered a phase that may prove crucial to its endurance. The readings in this section attempt to elaborate the basic notion that media in general affect the public's issue priorities in general. The question now has become: When do specific media have specific kinds of effects, if indeed they have any effect at all?

This question is best viewed as a natural and positive part of the evolutionary nature of mass communication research. Reflecting on the call by Oscar Gandy, Jr. to go "beyond agenda-setting" (excerpts of which are in Part VI), Maxwell E. McCombs has commented: "Scholars receive no greater compliment than to have significant new work build upon their research."

Elsewhere he noted, "No one contends that agenda-setting is an influence process operating at all times and all places in all people." The identification of particular times, places, and people requires further research into the agenda-setting process. The chapters that follow examine more precisely the patterns of interaction between the media and public agendas.

Each of the readings attempts to identify "contingent conditions" for agenda-setting. That is, they enumerate the conditions under which agenda-setting effects are either enhanced or diminished. As James P. Winter explains:

> Especially in survey research, where there are numerous uncontrolled variables, it is not sufficient to simply indicate that relationships occurred. It is important to determine the robustness of relationships, and one way to do that is to look at their contingent conditions.

One contingent condition examined in recent research is duration of exposure. In "Agenda-Setting for the Civil Rights Issue," James P. Winter and Chaim H. Eyal find that the period of time over which media cover an issue is important for determining its place on the public's agenda. The agenda-setting effect of civil rights stories in *The New York Times* was greatest after about 1 month of coverage, and did not increase as stories accumulated over time. Of course, the time frame for agenda-setting may vary across issues, with certain issues catching on faster than others.

Geographic proximity is a second factor that influences the agenda-setting process. The article by Philip Palmgreen and Peter Clarke demonstrates that agenda-setting is more likely to occur for national problems than local ones. Local issues, covered by local media, were the least susceptible to an agenda-setting influence. Similarly, L. Erwin Atwood, Ardyth B. Sohn, and Harold Sohn find that although a small town's newspaper can contribute to a "community discussion" of non-local news, it has no significant impact on local issue priorities.

One of the most controversial contingent conditions for agenda-setting is the type of medium involved. Agenda-setting effects have been demonstrated for newspapers, television, and radio. However, most studies that compare different media find that newspapers are most likely to produce issue salience.

Significant disagreement exists as to the underlying explanation for the superiority of print as an agenda-setting medium. Some communication researchers attribute the phenomenon to the ability of newspapers to cover news events in greater detail than their broadcast counterparts. Others contend that the impact of print is itself contingent on other factors. For example, the reading by Palmgreen and Clarke suggests that newspaper impact is greatest only for local issues. Other studies report that newspaper influence may be less superior in covering events over time, especially for heavy television watchers. In fact, some researchers find that television surpasses newspapers as an agenda-setter for dramatic, highly pictorial events.

Print and broadcast media can have mutually reinforcing effects. Klaus Schoenbach's article shows that television contributes to agenda-setting by "spotlighting" issues that are covered more thoroughly by newspapers. (Schoenbach's article is noteworthy also because it finds several contingent conditions operating in an international setting.) Later in this section, David B. Hill's article demonstrates that prior exposure to newspaper stories enhances the agenda-setting impact of television.

Hill's research identifies yet another contingent condition for agenda-setting: audience attributes. He finds that certain groups of people—viewers with higher educational levels and greater "news awareness"—are especially susceptible to agenda-setting influences. This elaborates the notion by David Weaver that "need for orientation" (i.e., an "inherent curiosity about the environment") is an important predictor of agenda-setting. Other audience attributes found to be associated with agenda-setting are age, amount of political information, and degree of interpersonal communication about issues covered by the media.

Hill further suggests that the divergent findings of the agenda-setting literature may in part be due to the use of different research methodologies. His "cross-sectional" approach seems less likely to identify strong agenda-setting effects than longitudinal research designs. Moreover, the timing of a study may influence its findings. Palmgreen and Clarke report that agenda-setting studies conducted during election periods may produce different results than those done in non-campaign periods.

Indeed, the remainder of this anthology is testimony to the many fruitful branches that have grown from the original theoretical conception of a media agenda-setting influence.

10 Agenda-Setting for the Civil Rights Issue*

James P. Winter
Chaim H. Eyal

In the nine years since McCombs and Shaw (1972) published the results of their research on mass media agenda-setting, communications researchers have employed a plethora of conceptual and operational definitions in their attempts to "replicate" McCombs and Shaw's 1972 findings. The majority of those replications have compared the importance assigned to issues and personalities in the media (*media agenda*) with subsequent public salience of those issues and personalities (*public agenda*). Agenda-setting research has involved the construction of media and public measures, with extensive content analyses used to determine the former, while survey techniques have assessed the latter.

An extensive review of more than 50 agenda-setting and related studies recently indicated several conceptual and methodological problems associated with research in this area. One of these problems concerns the varied and haphazard selection of time periods and related temporal variables under study (Eyal et al., 1981).

Since most of these studies measure and compare the media and public agendas over time, the temporal variable would appear to be crucial. However, as we will see from a review, this has not been the case in the literature. The question of the appropriate "time frame" for analysis has received little systematic attention; in fact it has only recently been elaborated (Eyal et al., 1981; Eyal, 1980). One of the time frame components identified is the optimal

*Reprinted from *Public Opinion Quarterly* (1981, Vol. 45, pp. 376–383) by permission of The University of Chicago Press.

effect span or peak association between media and public emphasis of an issue. Those studies that have to some degree broached the questions of time frame suggest that the optimal effect span between aggregate media attention and public priority is between two and five months, and that the impact is a cumulative one, with exposure over time leading to enhanced public salience (McCombs et al., 1975). As McCombs and Masel-Walters (1976) indicated: "It appears that the cumulative effects of from three to four months of day-to-day news play result in some issues rising high on the agenda and others disappearing from public view" (p. 7).

In a nonelection study of university students, Stone (1975) examined *Time* and *Newsweek* for six months before and three months after the dates of his fieldwork. Accumulating the media duration backward from the interviews, he found a monotonic increase in correlations between media and public agendas, especially up to two months prior to interviewing. Cumulative media content from a full seven months prior to the interviews provided the highest zero-order correlations with students' agendas, on several issues.

Despite this indication, some researchers have found agenda-setting effects using as little as one week's media content from immediately prior to the interview period (Mullins, 1977; Becker and McCombs, 1977). Indeed, in a study comparing national television and Gallup Poll data over an eight-year period, Zucker (1978) found that the media emphasis on the *month immediately prior* to the interview period was a better predictor of public opinion than was earlier media content. However, Zucker's study was designed to focus on the causal order in agenda setting, and on types of issues and their duration of exposure in the media rather than the optimal effect span.

A second important variable that has only recently been considered is the nature of the individual issues examined. McCombs (1981) described four approaches to agenda-setting research: using either aggregate or individual public agenda data, in conjunction with either a set of issues or a single issue. But perhaps the variable nature of issues precludes treating them in the aggregate, another problem that may explain inconsistent findings. With a few recent exceptions (Zucker, 1978; Stroman, 1978; Erbring et al., 1980; Winter et al., 1980) agenda-setting researchers have aggregated diverse issues, and expected wholesale transferral of issue saliences from media to public. The problems associated with treating issues in the aggregate have been elaborated in these recent studies, and will not be reiterated here. Two studies also demonstrated that aggregating diverse issues led to null results which were replaced by strong agenda-setting effects when issues were subsequently regrouped or examined individually (Eyal, 1980; Winter et al., 1980).

A problem associated with the aggregate treatment of issues is that the issues themselves have been used as the unit of analysis, with rank-order correlations computed between media and public emphasis. This usually restricts the sample size to about seven issues or cases, requiring quite high correlations for statistical significance. This problem also has been discussed elsewhere (Winter et al., 1980) and will not be further elaborated here, but it calls for new methodological approaches which will allow for an increase in sample size, and subsequently in statistical power. One such approach was used by Erbring et al. (1980), whose cross-sectional study contained individual-level data and used respondents as the unit of analysis. The authors themselves pointed out the limitations of this approach, and suggested that longitudinal, time-series analyses be conducted in future research. The present study does this by combining an extensive content analysis of the media with the examination of a single issue on the public agenda, using public opinion poll data taken at numerous points in time.

Although the present study has been designed to overcome the limitations outlined above, it is not without shortcomings. The most important one is that although issues are not aggregated in the manner of past research, the nature of the public opinion data used means that the public agenda is in aggregate form. We are thus unable to identify the important social context, demographic and media use characteristics of the public that are termed "contingent conditions." These variables constitute an important element of agenda-setting theory, but it is felt that the present study makes a significant contribution despite their absence.

METHOD

The public agenda was determined from 27 Gallup polls conducted between 1954 and 1976, which asked the question, "What is the most important issue facing the American people today?" Responses can be classified as the *perceived community agenda* on the part of the public (DeGeorge, 1981). The public agenda consisted of the percentage of respondents who replied to the question with a response categorized as "civil rights," a percentage that ranged from 0 to 52 over the 22 years. The unit of analysis in the study is the poll, or the time-points represented by each of the 27 polls. Hence, the sample size is 27.

The media agenda consisted of the number of front-page stories on civil rights in the *New York Times,* in each of the six months prior to each poll. As the *Times* is considered the most prestigious national newspaper, it was thought that *Times* coverage would be indicative of national media coverage on this issue, and that it would be an adequate estimate of media content for comparison with national opinion polls.

There are limiting factors given this imprecise if relatively workable approach. Foremost among these is our ability to truly generalize from *Times* coverage to media content across the nation. However, there are several reasons why the *Times* was selected as an estimate of national media coverage.

It is *the* elite U.S. newspaper. Breen (1968:546) found that 10 top newspapers, including the *Times,* provided the same basic account of two days of Detroit race riots in 1967. Given the predominance of the wire services (Crouse, 1972), it is reasonable to assume that the nonprestige press gives comparable coverage to important issues. This idea receives further support from what Breed (1955:279) termed the "arterial effect," the observation that news flows downward from the elite dailies. Crouse (1972:73) also indicated, with respect to the 1972 presidential election, that front-page coverage in the *Times* meant prominent coverage in "every other paper in America." Finally, Brown (1971:223) has asserted that the *Times* is a model from which the television networks derive their news judgments.

It is thought that the above limitations will tend to impede the ability to detect an agenda-setting effect, and will thus be conservative errors. At the same time it will be valuable to determine whether effects can be detected using these aggregate measures and a single issue in a nonelection study.

RESULTS

Zero-order correlations (Pearson's *r*) between the public agenda as measured in the Gallup polls, and each of the preceding six months' *Times* content indicated a slight monotonic *descent* moving back in time to four months prior to the interviews (from $r = .706$ to $r = .654$) followed by a dramatic drop in the fifth and sixth months prior to the polls (.530 and .384 respectively). All of the zero-order correlations were significant at the $p < .05$ level.

Next, the cumulative impact of the independent variables[1] was examined. The cumulative effect of the first two months prior to the public agenda measures (.84) was about as high as or higher than all other combinations of cumulative correlations. The correlations for each individual month were then examined while controlling for all of the preceding months in an attempt to establish whether the higher correlations for the two months immediately prior to interviews were the result of "cumulative" or "recency" effects. If partialing out the prior months significantly reduced the zero-order correlations then this would be evidence of cumulative media effects over time. If, on the other hand, partialing out prior months had no effect on the high zero-order correlation in the first month prior to polling, then this would be evidence that recent media content is more influential: hence a "recency" effect.

---

[1] By "independent variables" we mean media content in each of the six months prior to polling. Obviously it is possible from the data reported herein that the impact was in the opposite direction, i.e., public opinion influenced media content. Research using panels, time series analysis, and cross-lagged comparisons has indicated that this is not the case (c.f. Stone, 1975; Shaw and McCombs, 1977; Zucker, 1978).

TABLE 1
Zero and Partial Order r's Between Media and Public Agendas
Controlling for Prior Months

	1st Month Prior	2nd Month Prior	3rd Month Prior	4th Month Prior	5th Month Prior
Zero-order	.71	.70	.68	.65	.53
Partials	.71	.43	.28	.48	.40

Partialing out prior months had no effect on the correlation between public agenda and media agenda in the first month prior to interviewing ($r = .71$). This was not the case, however, for each of the other four months for which partialing was possible, all of which were significantly reduced. The indication is that for the first month prior there is a "recency effect" that is not as highly related to previous months, while for the other months there is a cumulative effect which of course is related to media agenda in previous months.

The next question was whether including all six months in a regression model would significantly improve our prediction of the dependent variable over the inclusion of two months only, or whether in fact one even had to go beyond including one month prior to interviewing. The zero- and partial-order correlations suggest that one month would be sufficient. For example, the fifth-order partial correlation between first month prior and public agenda ($r = .71$) does not appear to be dramatically improved by including the second month prior to form a two-month cumulative variable, and then partialing out all other months ($r = .77$).

Entering the public agenda variable into a multiple regression with all six months yielded an explained variance of .797, compared with $r^2 = .707$[2] for the first two months only. An F-test revealed that the difference in explained variance was not significant at the $p < .05$ level.[3] Thus, as expected from the partial correlations, going back beyond two months prior to interviewing for the media agenda did not significantly improve the prediction of the public agenda. Is going back only one month enough? Apparently not. The variance explained by the first month alone is .498, which is significantly improved by the addition of the second month ($r^2 = .707$, $F = 17.4$, $p < .01$).

So, for the civil rights issues it has not been necessary to extend the media agenda beyond two months prior to interviewing in order to predict public salience. Of course, as has been indicated several times in the literature, the time frame will vary with individual issues. Economic issues or political ones

---

[2]High interrelationships among the independent variables suggested the possibility of multicollinearity. By examining the correlation matrix, the ability to explain one independent variable from the others, and the standard errors associated with the b coefficients, the authors concluded that multicollinearity was not a problem in the analysis.

[3]For the appropriate formula, see Kerlinger and Pedhazur (1973:70).

such as Watergate may take months before they become a part of the public agenda, while we are virtually all aware of acts of political terrorism, for example, in a short period of time.

DISCUSSION

This study has provided further evidence of a strong agenda-setting effect despite the use of an aggregate public agenda and the *New York Times* front page as a national media indicator. More important, it indicates that at least for the civil rights issues, *the optimal effect span is the four- to six-week period immediately prior to fieldwork.* While content analyzing the media one month prior to this results in a significant improvement in prediction, there is little reason for gathering data from any farther back in time than that. These findings contradict those reported by Stone (1975) and support those reported by Zucker (1978), by suggesting that it is *recent* media emphasis rather than cumulative effects over time that leads to public salience.

REFERENCES

Becker, Lee B., and Maxwell E. McCombs 1977 "U.S. primary politics and public opinion: the role of the prss in determining voter reactions." Paper presented to the Political Communication Division of ICA. Berlin, W. Germany.

Breed, Warren 1955 "Newspaper opinion leaders and the process of standardization." Journalism Quarterly 32:277-84, 328.

Breen, M. A. 1968 "Ten leading newspapers rated for coverage of 1967 Detroit riots." Journalism Quarterly 45:544-46.

Brown, Les 1971 Television. New York: Harcourt Brace Jovanovich, Inc.

Crouse, Timothy 1972 The Boys on the bus. New York: Random House.

DeGeorge, William F. 1981 "Conceptualization and measurement of audience agenda in agenda-setting research." In G. Cleveland Wilhoit and Harold de Bock (eds.), Mass Communication Review Yearbook, Vol. 2. Beverly Hills: Sage.

Erbring, Lutz, Edie N. Goldenberg, and Arthur H. Miller 1980 "Front-page news and real-world cues: a new look at agenda-setting by the media. American Journal of Political Science 24:16-49.

Eyal, Chaim, H. 1980 "Time frame in agenda-setting research: a study of the conceptual and methodological factors affecting the time frame context of the agenda-setting process." Unpublished doctoral dissertation, Syracuse University.

Eyal, Chaim H., J. P. Winter, and W. F. DeGeorge 1981 "The concept of time frame in agenda-setting." In G. Cleveland Wilhoit and Harold de Bock (eds.), Mass Communication Review Yearbook, Vol. 2, Beverly Hills: Sage.

Funkhouser, G. Ray 1973 "The issues of the sixties: an exploratory study in the dynamics of public opinion." Public Opinion Quarterly 37:62-75.

Kerlinger, Fred, and E. J. Pedhazur 1973 Multiple Regression in Behavior Research. New York: Holt, Rinehart and Winston.

McCombs, M. E. 1981 "The agenda-setting approach." In Dan D. Nimmo and Keith R. Sanders (eds.), The Handbook of Political Communication. Beverly Hills: Sage.

McCombs, M. E., L. B. Becker, and D. H. Weaver 1975 "Measuring the cumulative agenda-setting influence of the mass media." Paper presented to the Mass Communications Division, Speech Communication Association Annual Convention, Houston.

McCombs, M. E., and Lynne Masel-Walters 1976 "Agenda-setting: a new perspective on mass communication." Mass Communication Review 3:2.

McCombs, M. E., and Donald Shaw 1972 "The agenda-setting function of the mass media." Public Opinion Quarterly 36:176–87.

Mullins, L. E. 1977 "Agenda-setting and the young voter." In D. Shaw and M. McCombs (eds.), The Emergence of American Political Issues: The Agenda-Setting Function of the Press. New York: West.

Myers, Sandra L. 1978 "A selected, annotated bibliography of articles on political communication." Political Communication Review 3:27–48.

Shaw, D. L., and M. E. McCombs 1977 The Emergence of American Political Issues: The Agenda-Setting Function of the Press. New York: West.

Stone, Gerald 1975 "Cumulative effects of the media." Paper presented at the Syracuse University Conference on Agenda-Setting, Syracuse, N.Y.

Stroman, Carolyn 1978 "Race, public opinion, and print media coverage." Unpublished doctoral dissertation, Syracuse University.

Winter, James P., Chaim H. Eyal, and Ann H. Rogers 1980 "Issues-specific agenda-setting: inflation, unemployment and national unity in Canada, 1977–1978." Paper presented to the Mass Communication Division, International Communication Association Annual Conference, Acapulco, Mexico.

Zucker, H. G. 1978 "The variable nature of news media influence." In B. D. Ruben (ed.), Communication Yearbook 2. New Brunswick, N.J.: Transaction Books.

11 Agenda-Setting With Local and National Issues*

Philip Palmgreen
Peter Clarke

An object of much recent research has been the identification of variables which mediate the agenda-setting function of the mass media. As McCombs (1976a: 2) states in his recent review of the agenda-setting literature, "No one contends that agenda-setting is an influence process operating at all times and all places in all people." In his review, McCombs identifies a number of "contingent conditions" which have been shown by research to affect agenda-setting. These include the individual's need for orientation, frequency of interpersonal discussion, level of media exposure, and voting decision state (decided versus undecided).

As this list illustrates, most of the mediating variables which have been identified thus far are at the psychological or individual level. Little attention, however, has been directed toward various *systemic* factors which might enhance, mitigate, or modify agenda-setting processes. Of particular relevance here might be the political system level (local-state-national) involved. Yet the great majority of agenda-setting studies have been concerned only with national issues, and then mostly within the limited context of political campaigns.

LOCAL VERSUS NATIONAL COMPARISONS

Although a comparison of agenda-setting processes across political system levels would certainly appear desirable, such comparisons are not easily made.

Communication Research (Vol. 4, No. 4, pp. 435–452), copyright © 1977 by Sage Publications Inc. Reprinted by permission of Sage Publications Inc.

Simply comparing studies which employ national issues with others focusing on local issues can be highly misleading, since any differences observed may be due to differences in samples of respondents, media systems, and operationalization of variables. In particular, agenda-setting studies are likely to employ different content analysis procedures, issue classification systems, analytical schemes, and methods of measuring the public issue agenda (e.g., interpersonal versus intrapersonal). Thus, the Cohen (1975) study, the only previous study of agenda-setting which employed local issues, cannot be juxtaposed with the myriad national investigations to provide direct local versus national comparisons.

The present study attempted to remedy these and similar comparison problems by randomly assigning respondents in the same city (Toledo, Ohio) to either local or national issue "conditions," and by employing the same measurement and analytical procedures in both samples.

METHODOLOGY

Data was gathered in Toledo over a three-day period in early December 1973 as part of a broad study of political communication and information holding. The selection of Toledo was based on two major criteria. First, its status as a major metropolitan area (population 379,104 in 1970) assured it of a large number of local issues or problems in the political arena at any particular point in time. Second, Toledo has a well-developed mass media system for covering both local and national political issues.

Personal interviews were obtained via professional interviewers from a modified random sample (sex and age quotas were imposed) of 400 residents of the city of Toledo (18 years of age and older). Every other household within randomly selected block clusters was alternately assigned either the local or national version of the questionnaire. This resulted (after removal of certain unusable questionnaires) in local ($n = 189$) and national ($n = 184$) samples which were closely matched on a range of demographic and communication variables such as age, sex, race, length of residence, voter registration, and newspaper and television use. In addition, the demographic characteristics of both samples conformed closely to 1970 U.S. Census figures.

Measuring the Public Agenda. Respondents were asked to name "any problems facing people in this country [or Toledo, depending upon whether the respondent was assigned to either the local or national condition] which you think the government in Washington [Toledo city government] should work to help solve." The respondent was then asked to choose that problem which he considered to be "most important." The interview proceeded to focus on this problem.

Measuring the Media Agenda.   A content analysis of Toledo newspaper and television coverage of nominated problems was carried out for the two weeks immediately prior to the gathering of interviews. A comprehensive listing first was made of all issues nominated by respondents at both political levels. After some collapsing into categories, this resulted in a total of 55 issues nominated at the local level and 33 at the national. Certain issues were nominated at both the local and national levels (e.g., "energy crisis," "crime"), resulting in a total of 73 separate issues nominated. Content analysis category descriptions were devised for each of these issues. In most cases where an issue was nominated at both local and national levels (e.g., "crime," "energy crisis"), both Toledo and non-Toledo (state, national) media content was included in arriving at the media coverage level for that issue. For example, all stories about crime, whether they concerned crime in Toledo or crime in other areas of the United States, were included in calculating the total media coverage level for "crime." This coverage level was then assigned to respondents in both the local and national political focus samples. An exception to this policy was made in those cases where the respondent specifically focused on either a local or national aspect of an issue (e.g., "education," where most local respondents were concerned specifically with improving the Toledo school system). In such cases, only local Toledo content was employed in the coverage index for local respondents, while both Toledo and non-Toledo content was used in the index for national respondents.

Newspaper coverage was indexed by enumerating the total number of "stories" relating to each issue category (some stories related to more than one issue) which appeared in the Toledo *Blade* for the period November 19–30, 1973. Coverage indices for the three major television networks for the same period were based on an analysis of summaries of the evening news contained in *Television News Index and Abstracts,* published by the Vanderbilt Television News Archives of Vanderbilt University. Since the evening news was broadcast during this period in the same time slot by all three networks, an average television coverage index was calculated. Local television news coverage was based on an analysis of transcripts of the 6:00 p.m. and 11:00 p.m. newscasts of the three major Toledo television stations. Again, an average index was calculated. An index of total mass media coverage was arrived at by summing the indices for the *Blade,* the national networks, and the local stations.

RESULTS

There are rather striking differences in the number and kinds of issues which people singled out for attention at the local and national levels of government. At the national level, only 33 issues were mentioned, with the energy crisis (62 mentions) and corruption in government (45 mentions) dominating the agenda. The only other issues receiving significant attention were inflation (18 mentions) and welfare-poverty (13 mentions).

This high level of consensus is somewhat less in evidence at the local level. There, 55 different issues were nominated, headed by crime (39 mentions), housing (16), welfare-poverty (12), the local educational system (10), and urban renewal (9). Local aspects of the energy crisis also received some attention (9 mentions). Although several other issues received such dual mention at both the local and national levels (e.g., crime, unemployment, drugs), the agenda on the whole are characterized by very dissimilar kinds of issues, reflecting, it would appear, a rather acute public awareness of the differing scope and functions of local and national government.

Table 1 provides a medium-by-medium comparison of issue coverage levels. The greater "newshole" available to newspapers is apparent at the local and national levels. Overall, issues most frequently nominated by national respondents received dramatically heavier mass media coverage than local issues. National issues received twice as much coverage on the average ($\overline{X}_N = 34.7$ stories) than did local issues ($\overline{X}_L = 17.1$). When each issue is weighted by the number of respondents nominating that issue, the average coverage level is 152.3 stories for national respondents and 61.6 for local respondents. Of national respondents, 58% nominated issues which received attention in at least 187 newspaper and television stories in the two weeks prior to interviewing. By comparison, 57% of local respondents nominated issues receiving coverage levels of only 16 stories or less.

The energy crisis, perceived chiefly as a national level issue, received the greatest share of media coverage (273 stories). Continued fascination with the Watergate scandal accounted for the great majority of the 190 stories related to "corruption in government." Apparently reflecting this overwhelming media

TABLE 1
Coverage (number of stories) by Medium of Local and National
Issues

Issue Level	Medium		
	Newspapers	Local Television*	National Network Television
Local	606	210	126
(55 issues)	(347)**	(113)**	(18)**
National	745	244	157
(33 issues)	(596)***	(211)***	(152)***

*6:00 p.m. and 11;)) p.m. coverages are summed in this index.

**Coverage levels with stories concerned with "corruption in government" and the "energy crisis" (issues perceived chiefly as national issues) removed.

***Coverage levels with stories concerned with "crime" (an issue perceived chiefly as a local issue) removed.

emphasis, these two issues were nominated as "most important" by 107 of the 184 national respondents. By contrast, these issues received only 10 nominations at the local level. At the local level, only the ubiquitous issue of crime (187 stories, 39 nominations) commanded coverage or nomination levels approaching those of the dominant national issues (except for local aspects of the energy crisis).

Agenda-Setting. These findings thus are consistent with the generally recognized tendency of the media to give greater play to national issues. It was hypothesized that this tendency, in conjunction with the directly observable character of many local political problems and the nature of local interpersonal political networks, would result in a weaker media agenda-setting influence at the local issue level. This hypothesis received strong support in this study, as evidenced by the respective local and national correlations between total media coverage levels for each issue and the proportion of respondents at each political level who nominated each issue as "most important." The correlation (Pearson r) at the local level is a modest .53 ($n = 55$ issues), while at the national level ($n = 33$ issues) it is a relatively strong .82 (difference between r's significant at .01).

Newspapers Versus Television. It was hypothesized that when agenda-setting is broken down by individual medium, the newspaper would prove to be a stronger agenda-setter than television, and that this superiority would be even stronger with regard to local issues. This hypothesis received only partial support, and, as the data in Table 2 reveal, there is a need to specify which *type* of television coverage is under consideration, since large differences emerge in the relative influence of local television news and national network coverage.

As expected, newspapers (The *Blade*) exerted the strongest influence on respondents' local issue priorities, followed by local television news. As one would expect, national network television coverage had no significant impact on local public issue salience.

At the national level, however, national network television is clearly superior to the *Blade* in setting the public agenda. The strong correlation (.92)

TABLE 2
Correlations (Pearson *r*) Between Issue Coverage and Salience of Issues—by News Medium and by Local and National Levels

	Medium		
Issue Level	*Newspapers*	*Local Television*	*National Network Television*
Local	.65*	.50*	.13
National	.70*	.85*	.92*

*$p < .001$.

between network news coverage and the public hierarchy of issue salience is all the more impressive in view of the large number of issue categories (33) on which the correlation is based (since inflation due to issue aggregation is minimized). In any case, the results clearly are not in line with those of previous studies indicating a superiority of newspapers over television in setting national issue agendas. This discrepancy is further underlined by the strong agenda-setting influence of *local* television news ($r = .85$). This latter influence may be traced to the liberal coverage of issues defined as "national" (by respondents) provided by the Toledo stations in their "local" news telecasts.

A major reason for the discrepancy between this and prior studies may be that previous studies have been conducted during national campaigns, while this investigation took place in a non-campaign setting. McClure and Patterson's (1974b: 24–25) study of the 1972 presidential campaign indicated that "if coverage of events like the Watergate incident and the peace talks is eliminated, [national] television news gave more coverage to campaign activity— rallies, polls, strategies—than to issues." Fully one-third of the campaign coverage was devoted to such stories. Thus, in the supposedly issue-oriented atmosphere of a campaign, extensive television coverage of these issues paradoxically was lacking. During non-campaign periods, however, in the absence of the magnetic attraction of campaign hoopla, broadcast journalists appear to devote more attention to the substantive issues of the day. This seems to be particularly true of the time period spanned by the content analysis phase of this study. Both the energy crisis and Watergate, the two issues most frequently nominated by national respondents, received heavy amounts of network (and "local" TV) coverage during this period. It appears reasonable to hypothesize that during periods when television coverage of issues is relatively lacking (e.g., during campaigns), the agenda-setting influence of this news source will be correspondingly diminished. When the magnitude of the issue "stimulus" is relatively strong, the agenda-setting impact of television will be proportionately greater. Newspapers, on the other hand, with much greater "newshole" and thus much greater flexibility in their ability to cover both issues and non-issue related events simultaneously, should show greater stability in agenda-setting influence over time.

The Media as Sources of Issue Information.   The relative agenda-setting influence of television versus newspapers found in this study are consistent with other data concerning the relative strengths of the various media as sources of issue information at the local and national issue levels. Table 3 shows the percentages of respondents naming each of four media as carrying "the most information that is useful" concerning each respondent's self-nominated "most important issue." At the national level, 52.2% of those naming such a medium said television (no distinction was made between

TABLE 3
Percentages of Respondents Naming Each Medium as Carrying
the Most Information about Issues

	Medium			
Issue Level	Newspapers	Television	Magazines	Radio
Local*	45.4%	45.4%	3.1%	6.1%
National*	32.6%	52.2%	11.6%	3.6%

*Local n = 130, national n = 138. Fifty-one local and 43 national respondents felt no mass medium offered useful information.

network and local TV) carried the most useful information. Newspapers were far behind, with only 32.6%. At the local level, newspapers and television shared the leadership position, with both preferred by 45.4% of the local respondents. It may be assumed that respondents here meant *local* TV news coverage, which displayed local agenda-setting power close to that of newspapers.

Of perhaps a more valid nature are data (see Table 4) indicating the number of respondents who could actually recall having "seen, read, or heard" anything concerning their "most important" issues in the Toledo media in the two weeks prior to the interview. These message discrimination data show television (again, no distinction between network and local TV) once again as the primary source of information about national issues, with 51.9% of respondents able to recall at least one message from that medium. Newspapers are second with 42.1%. On the other hand, newspapers provided the most information about local issues — 31.7% discriminated messages from that source compared to 23.8% for television.

It should be noted that message discrimination measures are indices of "effective" issue coverage by the various media, once audience members' information selection processes have had an opportunity to operate. The *presence* of issue information in media channels cannot induce agenda-setting effects unless audience members are *exposed* to that information. The concept of "effective coverage" is particularly important with regard to the relative

TABLE 4
Percentages* of Respondents Discriminating One or More Messages From Each Medium

	Medium			
Issue Level	Newspapers	Television	Magazines	Radio
Local	31.7%	23.8%	0.5%	5.8%
National	42.1%	51.9%	7.3%	11.5%

*Percentages do not total to 100% since respondents could cite more than one source for each recalled message.

impact of newspapers and television at the national level. On the basis of sheer coverage levels, we would expect newspapers to be the dominant agenda-setter at the national level (see Table 1). Apparently, however, television is more "efficient" in disseminating its messages, as the data in Tables 3 and 4 indicate. This greater efficiency is translated into the relatively stronger agenda-setting effect of television for national issues.

DISCUSSION

The results of this study indicate, then, that the media play very different agenda-setting roles depending on whether the issues under study are of local or national political origin. First, the agenda-setting impact of the media as a whole vis-à-vis other information sources is generally weaker at the local level. Squaring the agenda-setting correlations found at each political level reveals that the media agenda (all media combined) accounted for a sizable 67% of the variance in the public agenda at the national level, while "explaining" only 28% of the variation in local issue salience. While the latter percentage still is indicative of considerable media influence at the local level, the impact of alternative sources of information (e.g., interpersonal channels, personal observation) is strongly indicated.

Second, the *relative* agenda-setting influence of newspapers and television appears to depend on the political level involved. Newspapers, network television, and local television news programs have very different informational roles to play at each level. These differences are reflected in agenda-setting terms.

The results here also strongly suggest the need to consider still another political context variable in making intermedia comparisons: campaign versus noncampaign periods. It seems highly plausible that the discrepancy between the findings of this study and earlier inquiries into the relative agenda-setting powers of newspapers and television is due to the noncampaign context of this investigation. Comparative studies which employ the same methodology in exploring agenda-setting during campaign and noncampaign periods are needed.

As McCombs (1976a: 4) has observed, "Public issues can be arrayed along numerous dimensions: local versus national, the personally-close versus the distant, emotional vs. abstract, etc. It is not likely that the agenda-setting function of the mass media is concerned equally with all types of issues *ceteris paribus*. The salience of some types of issues on personal agenda are likely to show significant media influence while others show little or no such influence. Furthermore, interactions between types of issues and other agenda-setting variables are highly likely." The wisdom of these observations is amply demonstrated by the findings of this study. Certainly the agenda-setting function, which emerged initially in a form hauntingly reminiscent of the old "hypodermic needle" model of media effects, has been shown by recent research to be a highly complex phenomenon contingent on a variety of conditions. Type of issue would seem to be one condition deserving special research attention.

REFERENCES

COHEN, D. (1975) "A report on a non-election agenda-setting study." Paper presented to the Association for Education in Journalism, Ottawa, Canada.

McCLURE, R. D. and T. E. PATTERSON (1974a) "Agenda-setting: comparison of newspaper and television network news." Paper presented to the Conference on the Agenda-setting Function of Mass Communications. Syracuse University, New York. McCOMBS, M. (1976a) "Agenda-setting research: a bibliographic essay." Pol. Communication Rev. 1: 1-7.

12 Daily Newspaper Contributions to Community Discussion*

L. Erwin Atwood
Ardyth B. Sohn
Harold Sohn

Long before Cohen wrote his oft-quoted phrase on the press' presumed ability to influence what the public thinks about, Park wrote that the newspaper had taken over the job of the town gossip in providing topics for public discussion. The extent to which the newspaper can substitute for the town gossip is, of course, limited by the norms of the industry and the laws of privacy and libel, but there is little reason to believe that any item in the newspaper is exempt from becoming a topic on the community conversation agenda. People do talk to each other, but the literature examining the relationships between what they read about in the newspaper and what they talk about day-to-day is meager. Several studies have shown that the wire services set the agenda for what the newspapers print. To what extent does the newspaper set the agenda for community discussion?

Data were gathered during mid-July 1975 from 150 residents of a small Southern Illinois city (population about 8,000). The sample was a two-stage design to provide a representation of the community. At the first level, blocks within the city limits were chosen at random, and within each block two dwelling units were randomly selected. Interviewers were instructed to interview females and males at a ratio of 8 to 7, respectively. Respondents under 25 years of age were over-sampled since only 15% of the population was in the 20-34 age group, a group among whom newspaper reading is low. Each respondent who subscribed to a daily newspaper was asked what he/she remembered reading in the paper during the preceding day. Up to four

---

*Reprinted from *Journalism Quarterly* (1978, Vol. 55, pp. 570–576) by permission of the editor.

119

responses were recorded. All respondents were asked what they had been talking about with friends and family. Five such discussion questions were asked focusing on local, regional, state, national and international events. Again, up to four responses were recorded for each question.

Each issue of the local daily newspaper for a two-month period preceding the final day of interviewing was content analyzed. A set of 41 categories was used to code 3,415 non-advertising items in 51 issues of the paper. The categories were also used to classify the respondents' responses to the one reading and five discussion questions. Double classifications were used when called for by the content of the story.

The importance of the content category for the newspaper's agenda was defined as frequency of publication of stories whose content fit specified categories. The importance of the content category for the reading and discussion agenda was determined by classifying the open-ended responses by content category. The respondents' answers were summed across the four potential responses for the reading and for each of the five discussion levels. These frequencies were then summed across all individuals to provide a total frequency for each category. This procedure provided seven variables for analysis — newspaper agenda, reading agenda and the five conversational agendas.

Rank difference (tau) and partial correlations were computed between newspaper agenda, the reading agenda and the community discussion agenda for 1) all respondents, 2) respondents under 35 years of age, 3) respondents 35 years of age and older, 4) women and 5) men.

Much agenda-setting research has concentrated on analysis of aggregate data which permits comparisons of audience agenda with media agenda. However, aggregate data analysis obscures individual differences among audience members that could lead to a better understanding of audience-media relationships. This report considers both types of data. Aggregate comparisons are made between reported community newspaper reading agenda and conversation agenda and between conversation agenda and newspaper agenda in terms of correlations across 41 content categories. Comparisons are also made at the individual level between what respondents said they read and what they talked about for each of the 41 content categories.

RESULTS

The classification procedure permitted coding of a newspaper story into more than one category (*e.g.,* a story about financing local schools could be classified as both taxes and education); the total number of classifications was 4,648, a total of 1,233 secondary listings. The zero-order rank correlation between newspaper content and reported reading is significant for all sub-groups in the sample (e.g., men and women, older and younger respondents).

When all respondents are considered as a group, the zero-order correlations between content of the newspaper and reported discussion across the 41 categories are significant for all five levels of proximity (Table 1). The correlations between content reported read and topics of conversation are significant only for local and national levels. When the effects of reading are held constant, the partial correlations between newspaper content and reported discussion are nonsignificant at both local and national levels. This suggests that what these respondents say they have been talking about at the local and national levels is, in part, dependent upon what they have been reading in the local newspaper.

National and local stories constituted the two largest proportions of content in the paper, 41% and 26% respectively. The significant partial correlations between newspaper content and discussion at state and international levels suggests the contribution of other sources of information to discussion of people and events at those levels.

Age Groups. Substantial differences appear between the two age groups. For the under-35 readers, the zero-order correlations are significant for all newspaper content-discussion levels except for local news. There is a significant correlation between what the younger readers reported reading and what they reported talking about at the local level. There are also significant read-talk correlations at the regional and national levels but not at the state and international levels. When the effects of reading are held constant at the regional and national levels, the partial correlations between newspaper content and community discussion are not statistically significant, suggesting an agenda-setting effect of reading the newspaper.

For the over-35 readers, only the correlation between newspaper content and regional topics of conversation was not significant. Significant correlations appear between reported newspaper reading and reported discussion at the local, state and international levels. When the effect of reading is held constant, the partials between newspaper content and community discussion are not statistically significant. Again this seems to suggest that the content of community discussion at local, state and international events is influenced by what is read in the local daily newspaper.

Women and Men. There are significant zero-order correlations, for women readers, between newspaper content and discussion of local, regional and state events. The correlations between reported reading and discussion of these areas are also significant. When the effects of reading are held constant, the partial correlations for local and regional news are non-significant again

TABLE 1
Correlations Between Newspaper Content, Reading, and Five
Categories of Community Discussion

Content Categories	Newspaper Content Tau	Reading Partial	Tau
All Respondents ($N = 150$)			
Local	.25*	.15	.28**
Regional	.23*	.19	.13
State	.32*	.23*	.17
National	.27*	.19	.23*
International	.28**	.26*	.11
Reading	.44**		
Uncer 35 Years ($N = 55$)			
Local	.18	.07	.24*
Regional	.31**	.19	.30**
State	.35**	.35**	.09
National	.26*	.12	.32**
International	.23*	.18	.15
Reading	.52**		
Over 35 Yearss ($N = 95$)			
Local	.28**	.18	.29**
Regional	.19	.17	.08
State	.28**	.18	.29**
National	.25*	.19	.19
International	.25*	.18	.23*
Reading	.41**		
Women ($N = 86$)			
Local	.24*	.14	.32**
Regional	.21*	.15	.21*
State	.33*	.25*	.29**
National	.15	.10	.17
International	.19	.17	.09
Reading	.36**		
Men ($N = 64$)			
Local	.26*	.13	.31**
Regional	.31**	.28**	.14
State	.27*	.22*	.17
National	.35**	.22*	.34**
International	.20	.13	.17
Reading	.51**		

*$p < .05$
**$p < .01$

suggesting an agenda-setting effect of reading local and regional news but not state news.

For men, all correlations between newspaper content and reported discussion are significant except for international events, but only the correlations between reported reading and local and national topics discussed are significant. When the effects of reading are held constant, only the partial correlation for local news discussion and newspaper content is non-significant. It appears that the local daily newspaper is an independent source of information only at the local level for men, and that other sources of information contribute important items to what men discuss at regional, state and national levels.

Individual Correlations. To test the reading-talking relationships for the 41 categories across the 115 readers of the local daily newspaper, phi coefficients were computed for each category. These outcomes bear on two questions, one a potential methodological problem and the other a substantive question about agenda-setting.

Since the respondents were first asked what they had been reading about and then were asked what they had been talking about, there is the possibility that the responses to the conversation questions were a function of the responses to the reading questions, a response-response outcome. If the outcomes indicate no significant correlations, or no more than a chance number of significant correlations, it seems reasonable to assume that the respondents' answers to the conversation questions were responses to the conversation questions rather than a function of the responses to the reading questions. At the same time, this may be interpreted as an indication there was no measured agenda-setting for individual items. However, if a substantial number of correlations are significant, both the methodological problem and the substantive question of individual effects will be tenable interpretations of the outcomes. Only by removing the order effect potential from the interviewing process can the question be clearly tested.

Only three of the 41 phi coefficients were statistically significant, local mining ($r = .41$, p $< .01$), national defense ($r = .51, p < .01$), and business economics ($r = .27, p < .05$). Since two significant outcomes would be expected by chance alone, the data appear to provide little evidence of either the potential order effect of the questions or agenda-setting.

Content Categories. The use of broad categories raises the question as to whether the material in any category that people are reading is the same material as they are talking about. The voters could be reading about election law reform, travel schedules and changes in the polling places. At the same time they could be talking about a name-calling incident. All might be coded into one broad category—politics. In this situation there would be a correspondence between categories read and talked about, but the relationship would be spurious and a function of the breadth of the category and not of correspondence between what people were reading and talking about.

To provide some information about this potential problem, one of the categories, coal mining, was examined in detail. The site of the study is a coal-mining community. Five months prior to data collection, plans had been announced to sink two new coal mines near the community. Respondents were asked if they anticipated changes in the community due to activity of the mining industry. If the respondents answered "yes" to that question, they were asked what changes they expected. Up to four answers were recorded. All stories about the new mines were analyzed for changes they indicated the community could expect. Fifteen content categories for the anticipated changes were developed.[20] More than three-fourths of the respondents (118 or 79%) said they expected changes in the community. Twenty-seven persons (18%) said they did not expect changes, and five (3%) said they did not know whether or not there would be changes. In all, there were 247 different responses.

The correlation between the changes in the community that the newspaper stories indicated could be expected and the readers' anticipations of community changes were .72 (p .05). Whether the newspaper was setting the community expectations or reflecting them, is course, open to question. There is little question but that the newspaper and its readers share similar expectations regarding community changes as they related to the coal industry. For each of the 247 responses given, the respondents were asked if they regarded the change as "good" or "bad." Only 15 responses were perceived as negative. The newspaper's content also was nearly all positive in terms of the anticipated changes.

In view of the high correlation between the expected changes reported by the newspaper and those reported by the readers, it appears that the general content classification is a useful method of categorizing media content and community discussion topics for agenda-setting research.

SUMMARY

The outcomes support the hypotheses that there will be significant correlations between content of the local daily newspaper and what people in the community report reading and talking about. In view of the non-significant partial correlations between newspaper content and discussion of local news, it appears that the findings also support the third hypothesis.

At the risk of reifying audience behavior, the aggregate data correlations suggest there is something we can call "community discussion," and that discussion is influenced by the content of the local newspaper. While the newspaper may partially set the public discussion agenda, it clearly is not the only source of information for topics of conversation. Overall, the correlations are rather low. In addition to the information provided by the mass media, the interpersonal communication channels apparently provide a variety of items that are unlikely to be reported in the media.

While we feel these findings demonstrate agenda-setting by the newspaper, we cannot tell, from these data, whether the outcomes would be best interpreted as media "effects" or "uses and gratifications." It seems likely that both processes would operate in day-to-day media use. A person would ordinarily have some purpose in mind in picking up the newspaper, if only to "see" what is in the paper today. Once the individual begins scanning the paper there is then the opportunity for unanticipated content to intrude into the individual's frame of reference creating a "direct effect." Separating the two processes in on-going conditions of media use may be one of the more difficult problems facing agenda-setting research.

.

13 Agenda-Setting Effects of Print and Television in West Germany*

Klaus Schoenbach

Agenda-setting — the idea that mass media can define issues as important — has become one of the most fruitful areas of mass communication research in the United States. The results of the following study, the first agenda-setting study in West Germany, replicate but also modify the evidence found in the United States.

The data for this study stem from a panel survey of the West German electorate. The panel was part of a study assessing the role of the mass media in the first direct elections to the European Parliament — the legislative body of the European Community. The first panel wave started in April 1979 — shortly before the beginning of the election campaign in Germany on May 1. A representative sample of 813 West Germans who were 18 years and older was interviewed. The second wave was fielded on June 1 and finished on June 9, one day before the election in Germany. There were 578 respondents still in the sample. The third wave started 1 week after election day, on June 18, and was in field until July 5, 1979. The 459 persons interviewed in all three waves are the basis of our analysis. A comparison between these respondents and those who were interviewed only once or twice showed no significant differences as to age, gender, education, political participation, or attitudes toward the European community.

Many American agenda-setting studies have simply counted how often respondents called specific issues important, and thus constructed a "top

---

*Paper presented at the International Communication Association in 1982. Reprinted by permission of the author.

seven" list of the problems of a country, region, or community. This rank order has been compared to the one in the media — for instance the seven issues with the largest coverage or the best placement. Such a research design can hardly be used to describe the impact of press and broadcasting on the agenda of single individuals. It can only show the similarity between media coverage and the agenda of a community as a whole. In *our* agenda-setting analysis, however, the individual change in the agenda of every single respondent is related to his or her individual media use. Changes in personal agendas were assessed by comparing the interviewee's answers in April 1979 (in the first panel wave) and at the end of June/beginning of July 1979 (in the third panel survey), thus comprising the whole length of both election campaign and election day coverage of the media. Fourteen domestic and foreign policy issues had been presented on a card to the respondents who had been asked the question: "Would you please tell me for each issue whether it is very important for you personally, fairly important, or not too important?"

According to the terminology of McLeod, Becker, and Byrnes (1974), this question taps the "intrapersonal" agenda, the one that is important for the respondent personally, and it describes it issue by issue. How strongly was it changed or confirmed by media use?

RESULTS

During the European election campaign 1979, between 25% and 50% of all respondents changed the degree of importance assigned to any one of the 19 domestic and foreign policy issues used in our study.

There were resistant and less resistant issues: Relatively few respondents changed their opinions about the relevance of unemployment, pensions, and law and order. Unstable, on the other hand, were issues like the construction of nuclear power plants, reduction of working hours, all the European issues, the *Ostpolitik,* the abolishment of the death penalty, and the reunification of Germany. So, the most stable issues were the ones expressing "materialistic" value orientations. Changes, however, more often appeared in the post-materialistic area. A second possible categorization is the one Harold Zucker (1978) introduced: our post-materialistic issues are also "unobtrusive" problems visible for most of the people only via the mass media.

Amazingly, the average personal relevance of almost all the issues *decreased* during the time period observed: a sign for being fed up, for desensitization through too much political information during the election campaign? Apparently, however, this was not an effect of "videomalaise" or "mediamalaise". On the contrary, almost all the significant effects of media behavior reversed this pattern: People who regularly watched TV, read newspapers, or recalled media coverage about the European election, kept or increased the initial importance they had assigned to the issues.

The post-materialistic, unobtrusive issues — which were more unstable — tended to be the most influenced by media use.

There is a clear-cut hierarchy of media exposure effects. Having been exposed to the coverage of the European election is apparently more effective than routinized, habitual media use. So for instance, reading news magazines regularly does not make a difference in changing or confirming the relevance of an issue. But having perceived specific information about a political topic in a news magazine does make a difference. In our study, the frequency with which respondents had read something about the European elections in news magazines and seen election coverage on TV news (measured in the last panel wave), shows the most significant effects on the intrapersonal agenda. The frequency with which information about Europe was attended to in local newspapers and on television in general, holds the second position. Habitual media behavior, as mentioned before, is not very successful in changing attitudes towards political issues. Having read prestige newspapers regularly shows the most effects, that is: for 3 out of 14 issues.

A first systematic investigation of the agenda-setting effects of West German media use showed that some of the results of American research in this area are applicable to West Germany as well, if we modify them according to the specific situation of this European country. We found evidence for the greater sensitivity of unobtrusive issues, and we could prove the "spotlighting effect" of TV news. But evidently the latter result cannot be explained by a division of labor between newspapers and TV news alone. It points toward a more general law: Not only print media but also TV programs with greater information capacity are able to transmit issue relevance earlier than TV news. So the difference in channel capacities seems to be crucial, not necessarily the one between print and broadcasting. Still print media, in general, seem to be somewhat more powerful agenda-setters than television. Routinized media behavior is significantly less capable to explain changes in issue importance than media use for specific information. Because recalling a medium's coverage of a particular topic is certainly facilitated by regular exposure to it, but also requires a minimum amount of attention, our results show the combined impact of exposure and interest as hypothesized by the transactional approach to mass communication effects.

14 Political Issues and Voter Need for Orientation*

David H. Weaver

A desire of knowledge is the natural feeling of mankind. . . .
— Dr. Samuel Johnson

It seems obvious that if mass communication is to have a direct agenda-setting impact on voters, voters must first be exposed to the message. Although this exposure may at times be accidental or incidental (especially in the case of broadcast media, billboards, and 72-point banner headlines), much of it is undoubtedly purposive, planned behavior. Therefore, one of the first questions to be addressed in the search for psychological explanations for agenda-setting is: Why do some voters expose themselves to certain mass media messages more than do other voters?

Although there is no single satisfactory answer, or set of answers, to this question, there are studies which shed some light in this area. In general, these studies indicate that three major factors (among many minor factors) play an important part in determining the messages to which a person will attend and how much of these messages he or she will perceive.

These factors are the degree of (1) *interest* in the message content; (2) *uncertainty* about the subject of the message; and (3) *effort required* to attend to the message (including the perceived likelihood that a reliable source of information is available). Obviously these are not final explanations because we may still ask why some people are more interested in, or more uncertain

*Reprinted by permission of the publisher from *The Emergence of American Political Issues* (Donald Shaw and Maxwell McCombs, editors) West Publishing Company, 1977.

about, certain messages than are others, but these are starting points in the search for psychological explanations of agenda-setting.

McCombs and Weaver have incorporated the first and second of these psychological factors in their concept of need for orientation.[1] This concept assumes that each person feels some need to be familiar with his surroundings, both his physical and mental environment. According to Tolman's concept of cognitive mapping, each individual will strive to map his world, to fill in enough detail to orient himself, to intellectually find his way around.[2]

The importance of a need for orientation and the use of mass communication in fulfilling this need is documented in other studies. Westley and Barrow[3] and McCombs,[4] found that different levels of need for orientation accounted for the varying "effectiveness" of newspaper editorial endorsements in selected California political contests. Mueller,[5] who studied a Los Angeles junior college board election (with 133 candidates) where the usual orienting cues of party affiliation and incumbency were unavailable, found that four cues, including endorsement by the Los Angeles *Times,* were used by voters for orientation and accounted for the majority of differences in votes.

In short, McCombs and Weaver suggest that increased need for orientation leads to increased mass media use, which in turn leads to increased agenda-setting effects by media. As an individual strives to map political (or other) issues through the use of mass media, he is more susceptible (at least in many situations) to the agenda-setting effects of the media.

A Typology of Orientational Need

McCombs and Weaver use two factors to define need for orientation: (1) relevance of information and (2) degree of uncertainty concerning the subject of the message. Because the news media (newspapers and television in particular) permeate nearly every aspect of American life and are readily available to most citizens, the third factor suggested by studies of information seeking (degree of effort required to attend to the message) was taken as a given. Political information is certainly not hard to obtain, so the typology constructed depicts different levels of need for orientation by the differing amounts of relevance and uncertainty, as the following shows:

In this typology it is asserted that low relevance (regardless of degree of uncertainty) results in a low need for orientation (Group III), that high relevance and low uncertainty result in a moderate need for orientation (Group II), and that high relevance and high uncertainty result in a high need for orientation (Group I).

McCombs and Weaver also suggest that persons with a high need for orientation about political matters (Group I) are more susceptible to mass media agenda-setting influence with regard to national political news issues than are Group II respondents (those with a moderate need for orientation),

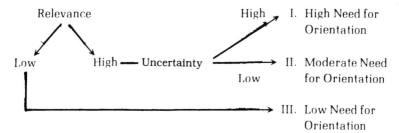

FIGURE 1. Antecedents of need for orientation.

and Group II respondents are more susceptible to agenda-setting than Group III respondents (those with a low need for orientation).

Recent Follow-Up Findings

Complete data from the Charlotte study show that even when relevance and uncertainty are measured in a number of ways, differing levels of need for orientation are related systematically to frequency of use of mass media and to the strength of the agenda-setting effect. In addition, these data lend support to the predictive and explanatory value of simultaneously considering several factors such as relevance and uncertainty.

To measure relevance of politics to Charlotte voters, five scales were used (three in June and two in October). To measure each respondent's degree of uncertainty about politics, four scales were used (two in June and two in October).[6] In general, measures of relevance were gauges of political involvement (political interest, amount of political discussion or participation, and sense of effectiveness and commitment). Political uncertainty was measured by the degree of professed political party affiliation and firmness of choice of political candidate.

Need for Orientation and Media Use

Use of political involvement to measure relevance of politics is obvious. Use of party identification plus certainty of voting choice to measure political uncertainty is based on the frequent finding that party identification is a major determinant of the vote and, therefore, is a major orienting cue for voters. In the absence of strong party identification and support of friends and family, the independent voter is deprived of a convenient orienting cue and thus has a high degree of uncertainty as he faces the task of choosing a candidate.

As Table 1 indicates, the prediction that Group I (those with a high need for orientation) will have a greater proportion of frequent media users than Group II (moderate need) is supported in 16 of 20 comparisons.[7] The prediction that

TABLE 1
Need for Orientation and Frequent Use of Mass Media

Need For Orientation						Uncertainty Scales
Hi	I 79.8%*	I 65.6%	I 68.3%	I 68.0%	I 67.3%	
Mod	II 62.5	II 64.3	II 74.2	II 73.1	II 76.2	(W)
Lo	III 47.4	III 60.8	III 57.0	III 56.8	III 58.7	
	I 72.3	I 60.7	I 74.3	I 69.2	I 72.7	
	II 69.2	II 64.6	II 66.1	II 65.3	II 61.8	(X)
	III 46.2	III 57.6	III 54.0	III 54.1	III 56.4	
	I 84.8	I 70.0	I 72.4	I 71.0	I 75.0	
	II 66.0	II 61.6	II 68.2	II 65.0	II 62.5	(Y)
	III 46.2	III 57.9	III 54.0	III 54.5	III 56.7	
	I 81.0	I 80.0	I 78.9	I 74.2	I 68.4	
	II 69.4	II 54.5	II 68.4	II 63.2	II 68.0	(Z)
	III 43.1	III 59.3	III 53.2	III 53.8	III 57.8	
Relevance Scales	(A)	(B)	(C)	(D)	(E)	

*Indicates that 79.8 percent of the respondents in Group I (those with a high need for orientation) were frequent users of mass media (newspapers, television, and news magazines) for political information; 62.5 percent of the respondents in Group II (those with a moderate need for orientation) were frequent users of mass media; and 47.4 percent of the respondents in Group III (those with a low need for orientation) were frequent users of mass media.

Note. Two measures are needed to define an individual's level of need for orientation: a measure of relevance and a measure of uncertainty. To strengthen the analysis in this table a number of different measures are used to operationalize the two concepts defining need for orientation.

Specifically, the five measures of relevance are: (A) the political interest index; (B) political discussion index; (C) political participation index; (D) political efficacy scale; and (E) sense of citizen duty scale.

The four measures of uncertainty are: (W) strength of politicaly party affiliation; (X) congruity of friends' perceived vote intention; (Y) congruity of family's perceived vote intention; and (Z) degree of certainty about choice of a presidential candidate to vote for.

Group II will have a larger proportion of frequent media users than Group III (low orientational need) is supported in 19 of 20 comparisons and the prediction that Group I will have a larger proportion of frequent media users than Group III is supported in all 20 comparisons. Overall, 55 of 60 possible comparisons among the three groups (91.7%) support the prediction that higher levels of need for orientation are associated with higher levels of mass media use.

Need for Orientation and Agenda-Setting

Need for orientation also is related to the agenda-setting effect of mass media, although less strongly and less systematically than to frequency of media use.

Table 2 presents the rank-order correlation coefficients between the agendas of the various groups and the "official" agenda of the *Observer* for June.

Although these correlations with the *Observer* are not especially strong, Group I's agenda is more similar to the *Observer* agenda than is Group II's agenda in three of six comparisons, and Group II's agenda more closely resembles the newspaper agenda than Group III's agenda in five of six comparisons. In addition, Group I's agenda is more similar to the newspaper agenda than Group III's in all six comparisons. In short, 14 of the 18 possible comparisons among the three groups (77.8%) support the positive relationship between need for orientation and susceptibility to the agenda-setting effect of newspapers.

Table 3 presents the rank-order correlation coefficients between the agendas of the various groups and the combined agenda of ABC, CBS, and NBC nightly national news broadcasts in June.[8] Although these correlations are generally not as strong as those involving the *Observer* agenda, they also indicate a positive relationship between need for orientation and the agenda-setting effect of television.

Group I's agenda is more closely related to the combined television agenda in three of six comparisons with group II; Group II's agenda more closely resembles the combined television agenda than Group III's in five of six

TABLE 2
Need for Orientation and Newspaper Agenda-Setting
(June 1972)

Need for Orientation				Uncertainty Scales
Hi	I .51*	I .29	I .35	
Mod	II .33	II .37	II .58	(W)
Lo	III .25	III .25	III .19	
	I .41	I .58	I .41	
	II .35	II .26	II .47	(Z)
	III .15	III .37	III .21	
Relevance Scales	(A)	(B)	(D)	

*Indicates that the agenda of national issues consiered most important by Group I respondents (those with a high need for orientation) was correlated .51 (Kendall's tau) with the "official agenda" of national issues from the Charlotte Observer in June, 1972; that the agenda of Group II respondents (those with a moderate need for orientation) was correlated .33 with the newspaper agenda for June; and that the agenda of Group III respondents (those with a low need for orientation) was correlated .25 with the newspaper agenda for June.

Note. Two measures are needed to define an individual's level of need for orientation: a measure of relevance and a measure of uncertainty. To sgrengthen the analysis in this table a number of different measures are used to operationalize the two concepts defining need for orientation.

See Table 1 for the list of specific indicators.

TABLE 3
Need for Orientation and Television Agenda-Setting
(June 1972)

Need for Orientation				Uncertainty Scales
Hi	I .25*	I .24	I .29	
Mod	II .26	II .31	II .39	(W)
Lo	III .19	III 0	III .14	
	I .35	I .39	I .55	
	II .19	II .05	II .41	(Z)
	III 0	III .10	III .05	
Relevance Scales	(A)	(B)	(D)	

*Indicates that the agenda of national issues consiered most important by Group I respondents (those with a high need for orientation) was correlated .25 (Kendall's tau) with the "official agenda" of issues from ABC, CBS, and NBC nightly news television broadcasts in June 1972; that the agenda of Group II respondents (those with a moderate need for orientation) was correlated .26 with the combined TV agenda; and that the agenda of Group III respondents (those with a low need for orientation) was correlated .19 with the combined TV agenda.

Note. Two measures are needed to define an individual's level of need for orientation: a measure of relevance and a measure of uncertainty. To sgrengthen the analysis in this table a number of different measures are used to operationalize the two concepts defining need for orientation.

See Table 1 for the list of specific indicators.

comparisons; and Group I's agenda is more similar to the television agenda than the agenda of Group III in all six comparisons. Overall, 14 of 18 comparisons (77.8%) support the prediction that voters with a higher need for orientation will be more susceptible to the agenda-setting effect of television than those with a lower need for orientation.

Closer to Election Time

Table 4 illustrates the rank-order correlations between the agendas of the different voter groups and the *Observer* for October, as the campaign came to a close. In October, 8 of 12 comparisons (66.7%) support a positive relationship between need for orientation and a newspaper agenda-setting effect.

Less support for a positive relationship between need for orientation and a television agenda-setting effect is presented in Table 5.[9] For television in October, only 4 of 12 comparisons (33.3%) support a positive correlation between voter need for orientation and the agenda-setting effect of television for October, a far weaker relationship than was true for the newspaper comparisons.

TABLE 4
Need for Orientation and Newspaper Agenda-Setting
(October 1972)

Need for Orientation			Uncertainty Scales
Hi	I .68*	I .16	
Mod	II .59	II .24	(X)
Lo	III .29	III .33	
	I .58	I .51	
	II .52	II .19	(Y)
	III .29	III .33	
Relevance Scales	(C)	(E)	

*Indicates that the agenda of national issues consiered most important by Group I respondents (those with a high need for orientation) was correlated .68 (Kendall's tau) with the "official agenda" of the *Observer* in October 1972; that the agenda of Group II respondents (those with a moderate need for orientation) was correlated .59 with the *Observer* agenda; and that the agenda of Group III respondents (those with a low need for orientation) was correlated .29 with the *Observer* agenda.

Note. Two measures are needed to define an individual's level of need for orientation: a measure of relevance and a measure of uncertainty. To sgrengthen the analysis in this table a number of different measures are used to operationalize the two concepts defining need for orientation.

See Table 1 for the list of specific indicators.

Implications for Voting

How does this affect voting behavior and the outcome of elections? For voters with a strong party or candidate preference – those with low or moderate need for orientation – it probably means what already has been found in research on politics and the press: issue and candidate information most often reinforces our intentions to vote in line with our preferred party and candidate.

Reinforcement is the opposite of change and some have pointed to this alleged ability of the press to cement our views in place and concluded that the press has little effect in changing our views.[10]

Yet this view ignores voters who are highly interested in politics and undecided about how to vote. In short they as yet have no views to cement in place. The close 1960 presidential election furthermore showed us that it does not take many of these people to determine the direction of a national election.

Voters and Issues

DeVries and Tarrance argue there is a growing number of persons who split party tickets in voting and that these ticket-splitters are a younger, educated

TABLE 5
Need for Orientation and Television Agenda-Setting
(October 1972)

Need for Orientation			Uncertainty Scales
Hi	I .59*	I .27	
Mod	II .49	II .24	(X)
Lo	III .49	III .52	
	I .37	I .28	
	II .52	II .29	(Y)
	III .49	III .52	
Relevance Scales	(C)	(E)	

*Indicates that the agenda of national issues consiered most important by Group I respondents (those with a high need for orientation) was correlated .59 (Kendall's tau) with the "official agenda" of issues from ABC, CBS, and NBC nightly news television broadcasts in October 1972; that the agenda of Group II respondents (those with a moderate need for orientation) was correlated .49 with the combined TV agenda; and that the agenda of Group III respondents (those with a low need for orientation) was correlated .49 with the combined TV agenda.

Note. Two measures are needed to define an individual's level of need for orientation: a measure of relevance and a measure of uncertainty. To sgrengthen the analysis in this table a number of different measures are used to operationalize the two concepts defining need for orientation.

See Table 1 for the list of specific indicators.

group who use media more than most other people.[11] If so, these may be the very voters who can tip an election one way or another; at the same time these voters potentially are most susceptible to an agenda-setting influence of mass media.

This appears to mean that for voters with a high need for orientation about politics, mass media do more than merely reinforce. In fact, mass media may teach these voters the issues and topics to use in evaluating certain candidates and parties, not just during political campaigns, but also in the longer periods between campaigns.

One timely example of this teaching function can be seen in the heavy coverage given the Watergate scandal during the period between the 1972 presidential election and the 1974 gubernatorial and senatorial elections. By keeping this issue at the top of the news agenda for so many months, news media in effect told many voters it was an important criterion for judging political parties and candidates, even after President Nixon resigned in August 1974, three months before the fall elections. The dramatic Democratic wins in these elections at least in part may be interpreted as a testament to the agenda-setting power of the press and relative impotency of short-term editorial endorsements and political campaigns.

If voters highly interested and highly uncertain about which party or candidate to support are most susceptible to media news emphasis, this places a great responsibility on reporters not just to report certain politically-related events and issues as fairly as possible, but also to choose which events and issues to cover with just as much fairness.

NOTES

1. Maxwell E. McCombs and David H. Weaver, "Voters' Need for Orientation and Use of Mass Communication." Unpublished report prepared for presentation to International Communication Association, Montreal, Canada, 1973.

2. Edward C. Tolman, *Purposive Behavior in Animals and Men* (New York: Appleton-Century. 1932).

3. Bruce H. Westley and Lee Barrow, "An Investigation of News Seeking Behavior." *Journalism Quarterly*. 36:431–38 (Fall 1959).

4. Maxwell E. McCombs, "Editorial Endorsements: A Study of Influence." *Journalism Quarterly*. 44:545–48 (Autumn 1967).

5. John E. Mueller, "Choosing Among 133 Candidates." *Public Opinion Quarterly*. 34:395–402 (Fall 1970).

6. Actual questions are in the Appendix. The political interest index was constructed from two variables: interest in the presidential campaign in June and concern over the outcome of the presidential campaign in June. These variables were summed because they loaded highly on one factor (.66 and .67 respectively) and negligibly on all other factors when factor analyzed with other variables, using a principal components method with varimax rotation.

7. The political discussion index was formed by summing two June variables: frequency of discussion of specific political issues and frequency of discussion of politics in general. These variables loaded .74 and .84 on one factor and negligibly on the others, using principal components factor analysis with varimax rotation.

8. Frequency of mass media use for political information was measured in all instances by a Guttman quasi-scale composed of three variables: frequency of newspaper use for news about political candidates and issues, frequency of television viewing of news about political candidates and issues, and whether or not the respondent subscribed to a news magazine. Coefficient of reproducibility for the scale was .88 and coefficient of scalability was .65.

9. The June 1972 agendas of ABC, CBS, and NBC nightly news broadcasts were combined into one TV agenda because of their high rank-order correlation (.96 between ABC and CBS, .57 between ABC and NBC, and .61 between CBS and NBC, all measured by Spearman's Rho).

10. The October 1972 agendas of ABC, CBS, and NBC nightly news broadcasts were combined into one TV agenda because of their high rank-order correlation (.89 between ABC and CBS, .64 between ABC and NBC, and .75 between CBS and NBC, all measured by Spearman's Rho. See Chapter 3).

11. Maxwell E. McCombs, "Mass Communication in Political Campaigns: Information, Gratification, and Persuasion." In F. Gerald Kline and Philip J. Tichenor (eds.). *Current Perspectives in Mass Communication Research* (Beverly Hills: Sage Publications, 1972), pp. 169–94.

12. Walter DeVries and V. Lance Tarrance, Jr., *The Ticket-Splitter: A New Force in American Politics* (Grand Rapids: William B. Eerdmans Publishing Company, 1972).

15 Viewer Characteristics and Agenda-Setting by Television News*

David B. Hill

During the recent past a fragile consensus has emerged among researchers which holds that television news programs can influence the relative salience of political issues in the minds of the American public—that is, that they are capable of setting the public agenda. Generally, however, there have been few efforts to redress a problem noted by Iyengar (1979: 398), that "most previous agenda-setting studies . . . document the congruence between media content and issue salience without attempting to identify variables which strengthen or weaken the relationship. . . ." The research reported in this article responds directly to this criticism by examining the impact of viewer characteristics and modes of news exposure on the agenda-setting effects of television news.

The data analyzed here were gathered as part of a larger study of the public's use of television. The methodology of that study is described in substantial detail by the co-principal investigators in their own report of their findings (Frank and Greenberg, 1980). Study participants were interviewed between late 1977 and early 1978 and asked to complete an extended recall diary of all television viewing, on a program-by-program basis, for the fortnight prior to the interview. Thus the data consist of self-reports of the number of times, if any, that respondents watched national news programs during a two-week period. Furthermore, for each program watched during that period, respondents were asked to report on several traits of their viewing (e.g., attentiveness), again on a program-by-program basis. Finally, separate from the

*Reprinted from *Public Opinion Quarterly* (1985, Vol. 49, pp. 340–350) by permission of The University of Chicago Press.

viewing diary portion of the study, respondents were asked more general questions about their attitudes toward television and other matters, including a series of items assessing interest in various news and public affairs issues.

Data reported here are based on interviews with 1204 adult research subjects whose viewing diaries indicated that they had watched a national news program on at least one occasion during the two-week reporting period.

ANALYSIS OF AGENDA SETTING

The methodology used here to measure and evaluate agenda setting is similar to that reported in other cross-sectional studies of the phenomenon. The content of news programming prior to the interviews was content analyzed, and news topics were rank-ordered to establish the media agenda. This media agenda was then compared with the rank-ordered personal issue agendas of news watchers. Unlike many other studies that have measured personal agendas only in the aggregate, the survey data utilized here make it possible to compare media agendas with individual-level as well as aggregate personal agendas.

The measurement of the media's agenda was constrained to some extent by the individual issue salience questions. The latter were fixed choice items that asked respondents to rank (on a four-point scale from "extremely interested" to "not interested at all") their interest in 59 political and social issue topics. The Vanderbilt Abstracts of the three national network news programs (ABC, CBS, and NBC) were consulted to determine the number of news stories that made mention of each issue topic during the two weeks prior to the first interview day and throughout the remainder of the interviewing time frame. Only 20 of the 59 issue topics received substantial and consistent coverage during the time period investigated.[1] These 20 issues, shown in Table 1 with the number of news stories in which each topic was mentioned, were then rank-ordered from highest to lowest on the media agenda.

Aggregate personal agendas were determined by calculating the percentage of the sample that reported the highest level of interest ("extremely interested") in each social and political issue.[2] The issues were then rank-ordered according

---

[1]The issue content of the national news programs was analyzed within every two-week period between September 15, 1977 and January 7, 1978. Issues that received heavy coverage during some blocks of time, but little or no coverage during other times, were excluded from the analysis. This technique has the advantage of tapping longer-term issue agendas of the media.

[2]Personal agendas are often measured by items that assess the perceived importance of various issues rather than the interest generated by these issues. While in many instances we would expect respondents to attach importance to interesting issues and vice versa, these two dimensions of issue salience (perceived importance and interest) are not likely to coincide for all issues. Because this

TABLE 1
National News Program and Aggregate Personal Agendas

	Number of Stories	Aggregate Personal Agenda Ranking
Conflict in Middle East	729	(15)
National economy	696	(7)
National unemployment	330	(8)
Sources and uses of energy	309	(5)
The stock market	235	(18)
Air transportation (planes, jets, ect.)	202	(17)
Agriculture and arming	140	(13)
Froeign policy	127	(19)
Labor unions in the U.S.	125	(12)
Medical sciences (anatomy, physiology, etc.)	124	(10)
Education and schools	113	(1)
Arms race	101	(14)
Space travel	101	(16)
Balance of trade	65	(20)
Managing money (finances, taxes, etc.)	56	(2)
Women's rights/roles	49	(9)
Prolems of drug abuse	42	(4)
Health and nutrition	29	(6)
Causes and prevention of crime	20	(3)
Rights of minority groups	7	(11)

to those percentages to create the aggregate personal agenda. These rank orders are presented in Table 1. A comparison of the media agenda and personal agendas reveals only a weak relationship between the two. Of the 10 issues given most attention by the media, only three rank in the top half of the public's agenda.

A similar pattern of weak correlation was observed in the individual-level analysis. *Individual-level personal agendas* and their rankings were established using the four-point scale of interest in each social and political issue. The use of a four-point scale necessarily created numerous tied rankings of issue salience, a somewhat undesirable artifact of the fixed-choice question format as a means of assessing relative issue salience.[3] For example, if a respondent rated 2 of the 20 issues as ones in which he or she is "extremely interested," then those two issues would be assigned a tied ranking of 1.5 out of 20. Other ties were assigned numerical rank values by standard rank-ordering proce-

---

study focuses on the interest dimension alone, the results reported may not generalize to the importance dimension of issue salience.

[3]Clearly, the many tied ranks of issue salience do not reflect respondents' real attitudes. For example, most respondents would be able to differentiate their levels of interest in each of the issue topics in which they were forced to report being "extremely interested." By assigning all such issues the same ranking, a substantial amount of measurement precision is lost.

dures. The media agenda for the 20 issues was then correlated with each individual-level personal agenda (and with the aggregate personal agenda where appropriate). The coefficients (values of Kendall's tau) resulting from these individual-level correlations will be referred to as the *agenda-setting score* for each respondent. The mean agenda-setting score for all news viewers was $-.10$, indicating a weakly negative relationship between the media and individual agendas. Thus, *among news viewers as a whole,* agenda setting is not confirmed by either the aggregate or individual analyses. It is possible, however, that agenda setting is more evident among news viewers with the characteristics and viewing habits described by the hypotheses stated previously.

First-order correlations between the individual level agenda-setting scores and viewer characteristics also produced values that are generally very small. The coefficients range from a null value (for watching alone) to .19 (for persons who are exposed to print news). The small magnitude of these correlations, along with the poor fit observed in the aggregate and individual level data, could be taken as evidence that agenda setting is not occurring, no matter what the nature of viewers' exposure to news programs. Such a conclusion would be unnecessarily pessimistic, however. In part, the small size of these correlations can probably be explained by research design constraints. A review of previous research suggests that cross-sectional studies such as this one reveal weaker effects than longitudinal studies. And by focusing on a set of 20 issues, rather than on a single issue (or two or three), the odds of achieving a mirror image relationship between media and personal agendas is significantly reduced. Furthermore, the measure of individual-level agendas is based on very elementary survey data which are likely to introduce a fair amount of "noise" into the analysis. Therefore, we proceed with the analysis assuming that the actual extent of agenda setting is underestimated here. And because the *fundamental purpose of this research is to identify contingent conditions that affect agenda setting the most,* not to measure the precise dimensions of the phenomenon, the actual magnitude of agenda setting discovered here is relatively unimportant.

A comparison of the bivariate correlations between the agenda-setting scores and the independent variables indicates that the most important viewer characteristics are prior exposure to news topics, i.e., print media exposure ($r = .19$), some college education (.16), the presence of a color television in the household (.12), giving undivided attention to news programs (.12), choosing unilaterally to watch the news (.11), and planning in advance to watch the news (.10). Two other factors proved to be of slightly less importance: viewers' belief that television is informative (.07), and the fact that viewers frequently watched television with the intent of relaxing or escaping from everyday cares ($-.07$). The latter variable, as hypothesized, was negatively related to agenda setting. Watching news programs alone was unrelated ($-.00$) to agenda setting.

The relative importance of educational attainment and print media exposure suggests strongly that general news awareness influences the agenda-setting process. News awareness doubtless stimulates an attentiveness and a sensitivity to news items that does not occur among the less informed. In short, the news-rich become richer while the news-poor lag behind. News awareness also facilitates superior comprehension and understanding of the news which, in turn, may affect the process of agenda setting.

Because the bivariate analyses show that no single characteristic of news-viewing can unilaterally explain substantial variation in agenda setting, it is desirable to develop a multivariate model which combines the effects of several viewer characteristics in order to evaluate their collective impact on agenda setting.

The most important result of the multivariate analysis has to do with quantity of news exposure. The regression exercise suggests that the frequency of exposure by news viewers is much less important than the characteristics of viewers and their viewing habits. All nine viewer characteristic variables outrank quantity of exposure as a predictor of agenda setting. In order to evaluate this finding further, the six "best model" viewer characteristic variables and frequency of exposure were regressed together on the absolute level of interest in each of the 20 issues ranked highest on the agenda of television news, i.e., 20 separate regression analyses with 7 independent

TABLE 2
Results of Multiple Regression on Individual Agenda
Setting Scores

	Best 6 Variable Model		Full 10 Variable Model	
	b	Beta	b	Beta
Intercept	$-.14$		$-.18$	
Print media exposure	.07*	.15	.06*	.14
Full attention given to news programs	.06*	.14	.04*	.11
College education	.04*	.10	.03*	.09
Color TV in household	.02*	.08	.02*	.07
TV judged informative	.01*	.08	.01*	.08
Relaxation/escape motivation for viewing TV	$-.01*$	$-.07$	$-.01*$	$-.07$
R chose news programs			.03*	.08
Plans viewing of news programs			.02	.08
Watches news programs alone			$-.02$	$-.04$
Frequency of news viewing			.01	.03
	$R^2 = .08$		$R^2 = .08$	

*F significant at .01.

variables in each. *In every single instance, frequency of exposure to national news programs failed to be a significant positive predictor of interest in the news topic.* In 10 of the resulting equations, frequency of exposure was negatively related to interest in the topic. These were not significant, however. Results of 2 of the 20 regression analyses are presented in Table 3 for illustrative purposes. The standardized regression coefficients presented in the table indicate that print media exposure, college education, and paying full attention to news programs are the strongest and only significant predictors of interest in these news topics. While frequency of viewing is not the weakest predictor in both equations (it is, in fact, the fourth strongest predictor of interest in the Middle East), it is not a significant variable in any of these equations. Across the 20 equations, frequency of exposure was the weakest or next to the weakest independent variable in a majority of cases. Thus, after news viewers achieve a minimum threshold of quantitative exposure, their personal characteristics and viewing habits, particularly their news knowledge and attentiveness to news programs, are more important in establishing agendas than mere time spent in front of the TV set.

DISCUSSION

This study has substantiated some of the conclusions and speculations of previous studies of agenda setting. For example, the rather weak indications of agenda setting reported herein are consistent with the notion that it is more difficult to demonstrate the phenomenon in cross-sectional surveys, particularly when considering attitudes toward as many different issues as were considered here. Longitudinal experiments and quasi-experiments designed to probe the impact of television news on the salience of one particular issue or

TABLE 3
Results of Regression on Interest in the Middle East and the
National Economy

	Middle East — Beta	National Economy — Beta
Print media exposure	.18*	.18*
College education	.16*	.13*
Full attention given to news programs	.10*	.09*
Frequency of news viewing	.04	.00
Color TV in household	.03	.01
Relaxation/escape motivation for viewing TV	− .02	− .05
TV judged informative	− .01	− .05

*F significant at .05.

class of issues (e.g., foreign policy matters) probably reveal more robust effects.

This study has also confirmed the apparent importance of "news awareness" (indirectly indicated by print media exposure and educational attainment) in conditioning the effects of exposure to television news. While previously only MacKuen (1981) had formally scrutinized the effect of educational attainment on agenda setting, the role of news awareness as a contingent condition of news recall and comprehension has been fairly well established. In this context, perhaps the most significant aspect of this study has been to argue that education and other variables which affect news recall and comprehension may similarly affect agenda setting. In order for the two literatures to be properly reconciled, however, future research should directly ascertain the effects of news recall and comprehension on the process of agenda setting.

Another important finding of this study concerns the *relative* impotency of quantity of television news exposure as a factor in agenda setting. This result has implications not only for the study of agenda setting, but also for the study of other media effects. As studies by Levy (1978) and Hill (1983) seem to indicate, quantity and quality of news viewing are two independent concepts. And whereas prior research into almost all media effects has focused on the quantity of exposure alone, it may be that researchers need to focus now on some of the relevent characteristics of viewers and their viewing traits other than frequency of exposure.

REFERENCES

Frank, R., and M. Greenberg, 1980 The Public's Use of Television. Beverly Hills: Sage Publications

Hill, D., 1983 "Qualitative dimensions of exposure to political television." Social Science Quarterly 64:614–623

Iyengar, S., 1979 "Television news and issue salience." American Politics Quarterly 7: 395–416

Levy, M., 1978 "The audience experience with television news." Journalism Monographs 55.

MacKuen, M., 1981, 1981 "Social communication and the mass policy agenda." In M. MacKuen and S. Coombs (eds.), More than News, Beverly Hills: Sage Publications.

IV Shaping Public Policy Agendas

Media matter. As the readings in the previous sections show, media may influence significantly the agenda priorities as well as the views of the general public. These influences sometimes occur in subtle and complex ways. The impact of news may be greater or lesser, depending on the amount of media attention, the timing of the coverage, the nature of the issues covered, and the medium itself, among other things. But no one questions that the phenomenon of media agenda-setting — once an hypothesis — now is a demonstrated empirical reality.

Nowhere is the agenda-setting influence of media more clearly or consistently shown than in the research on political campaigns. Studies indicate that news coverage of elections often influences what the public and the candidates themselves come to view as the important issues of the campaign. As political scientist Thomas E. Patterson (1980) stated in the opening lines of *The Mass Media Election:*

> Today's presidential campaign is essentially a mass media campaign. It is not that the mass media entirely determine what happens in the campaign, for that is far from true. But it is no exaggeration to say that, for the

149

large majority of voters, the campaign has little reality apart from its media version. Without the benefit of direct campaign contact, citizens must rely on the media for nearly all their election information. Moreover, the media are now without question the basis for the candidates' organizations. (p. 3)

What is far less clear, however, is the influence that media have *after* the campaign is over. Are the *political* agendas that were set during election campaigns transformed into the *public policy* agendas of the winning candidates? Does ongoing media coverage of government set the policymaking priorities of citizens and elected officials? Do media have an effect on massive governmental bureaucracies staffed by *non*elected officials? Can media exposure of governmental wrongdoing or coverage of societal ills *change* the public's and policymakers' agendas?

Conventional democratic theory answers these questions in the affirmative. It holds that media impart information about policy matters to citizens, who in turn pressure officials to act on their concerns and priorities. Whether the policymaking process actually reflects this linear interplay of media, citizens and policymakers is the subject of lively debate. Some media critics have suggested that the press plays this role all-too-well; that it has become too powerful of an agenda-setting force for the democratic process to work as it should. The selection by William L. Rivers, for example, calls the media a "shadow government" that became "firmly in control" after Watergate.

In *Making An Issue of Child Abuse,* Barbara Nelson examines how the media's discovery and sustained coverage of a social problem ultimately led to its rise on both the public's and policymaker's agendas. Using content analysis of child abuse coverage, she finds that "The (news) articles can be considered the point at which an invisible problem became a public concern, and soon a major policy issue." Nelson's conclusions typify the conventional democratic view of the media's agenda-building role.

A rather different conclusion about this role is reached by Northwestern University researchers who studied the impact of investigative reporting on public opinion and government policymaking. The article by David L. Protess and his colleagues finds that policymakers' responses to investigative stories often occur independently of any change in the public's agenda priorities. In fact, changes in policy priorities sometimes are orchestrated by journalists and policymakers acting in concert, with the public playing a bystander role. The conclusions are based on four case studies of media influence. As with Nelson's findings, the reader should be cautioned against making firm generalizations from a limited number of cases.

Agenda-setting research is concerned mainly with how issues become salient in the first place. But what forces *maintain* an issue's agenda status, or cause it ultimately to *decline* in salience? Fay Lomax Cook and Wesley G. Skogan address these questions by examining the rise and fall from the Congressional agenda of criminal victimization of the elderly. They find that just as news scrutiny of this problem helped to bring it to policymakers' attention in the early 1970s, so declining media coverage led to its legislative denouement by the end of the decade. The relative priority of *other* issues on the Congressional agenda during this period needs to be studied further to test the authors' theory of "convergent" and "divergent voices."

Clearly, the debate over the media's policymaking role centers on differing views of the relationship between journalists and their official sources. Some have described this relationship as symbiotic. Others have emphasized a theme of mutual antagonism. Metaphors abound to describe the journalist–policymaker relationship, ranging from dance partners to professional wrestlers.

It is our view that each of these characterizations has some basis in reality. Under some conditions, the media may play a traditional democratic role of neutrally supplying information to the public, which in turn influences policy priorities. Under other conditions, the media may actually influence the agendas of both citizens and policymakers. Under still different circumstances, the media themselves may react to the agendas of others.

The issue of media "influence" over public policy thus is an empirical question. Under what conditions and in what ways do media matter? The readings that follow provide some interesting answers.

While each of these readings sheds light on the media's role in shaping governmental agendas, none should be viewed as definitive. Of all the subjects in this anthology, the one most in need of additional research is the connection between media and policy. Certainly, none is more important for understanding the workings of American governing institutions.

16 The Media as Shadow Government*

William L. Rivers

Official Washington is majestic and orderly, erratic and tasteless. Its architecture represents the impossible simplicity and systematic character of the U.S. Constitution. It also reflects the labyrinthine complications and overelaboration that were the inevitable products of the Industrial Revolution, of Manifest Destiny, of one civil and two world wars, of bread-and-circus electioneering—the inevitable products, in other words, of two centuries of human foible.

But there is another side to Washington—another government. The Other Government—the Washington news corps—has come to consciousness of its power and is gradually moving into larger, more official, less eccentric structures. . . . they have acquired the authority and sometimes even the power of a shadow government.

The Washington press corps has certainly acquired the trappings of power. Privileged as no other citizens are, the correspondents are listed in the *Congressional Directory;* they receive advance copies of governmental speeches and announcements; they are frequently shown documents forbidden even to high officials; and they meet and work in special quarters set aside for them in all major government buildings, including the White House. Fantastic quantities of government time and money are devoted to their needs, their desires, and their whims. Some White House correspondents talk with the president more often than his own party leaders in the House and in the

*Reprinted from *The Quill* (March 1982) by permission of the author and publishers.

Senate, and there are Capitol correspondents who see more of the congressional leaders than do most other congressmen.

No wonder, then, that Washington correspondents feel what one presidential assistant has termed an "acute sense of involvement in the churning process that is government in America." A close view of this involvement so impressed Patrick O'Donovan, a former Washington correspondent for the London *Observer,* that he said, "The American press fulfills almost a constitutional function."

Indeed, in Washington today, correspondents who report for the news media possess a power beyond even their own dreams and fears. They are only beginning to become aware that their work now shapes and colors the beliefs of nearly everyone, not only in the United States but throughout most of the world.

For the American public, full acceptance of the media's new authority and responsibility came at the end of the Watergate crisis, when the president of the United States posed his word against that of the press and lost. But Watergate was less coup d'état than it was climax. It was the end of a long evolution that was first observed by a newsman nearly fifty years ago, during the trial of the Lindbergh baby's kidnapper and killer. At that time, Walter Lippmann commented that in our democracy "there are two processes of justice, the one official, the other popular. They are carried on side by side, the one in the courts of law, the other in the press, over the radio, on the screen, at public meetings."

Lippmann's observation remains true today, yet those who would end this discussion on the question of the court verdict versus the popular verdict are missing a much greater issue. For the basic question is not just whether we have two parallel systems of justice in this country, but whether we have two governments. Do we have a second, adversarial government that acts as a check on the first and controls public access to it? Indeed we do—and this Other Government is made up primarily of the more than two thousand news correspondents stationed in Washington.

In our daily lives, we trace a path from home to work and back. Without the news media, we would know almost nothing beyond our own sphere of activity. The public's knowledge of national government depends not on direct experience and observation, but on the news media; and it is the media that set the agenda for public discussion and decision.

To a large degree, the employees of the government—including the president himself—must also depend on the reports of the news media for information about some of their most important concerns. In government, as elsewhere, each worker is circumscribed, and his sphere is small. A congressional assistant may spend much or all of one day absorbing details about the religious leaders of Iran and learning much more than is published or broadcast about the imminence of all-out war in the Middle East. But he hasn't the time to inform all of his colleagues about his new knowledge, and he is likely to know less about House debate that day than any tired tourist from North Carolina who wandered into the public gallery to give his feet a rest. Both the tired tourist and the congressional assistant must depend on the newspapers to find out what happened that day in the Senate.

In an article for a journal of political science, former Senator H. Alexander Smith of New Jersey made it clear that members of Congress are not Olympians who learn what they know in closed-door hearings and secret communiqués. They, too, must depend on the media. Senator Smith listed thirteen different sources of information for congressmen; but the news media, he wrote, "are basic and form the general groundwork upon which the congressman builds his knowledge of current events. The other sources . . . are all supplements to these media."

Even presidents, with their vast and powerful apparatus of information, often end up relying as much on the press as on their own informational systems. John Kennedy admitted that he acquired new information from *The New York Times* about his own secret sponsorship of the Bay of Pigs invasion. Eleven days before the invasion that the CIA had been shepherding so carefully, the editors of the *Times* informed Kennedy that their correspondent, Tad Szulc, had discovered the secret and that a detailed news report was imminent. Kennedy persuaded the publisher to postpone publication until after the landing in Cuba. But, during the discussions with the *Times* editors, the president picked up new information about the mounting of the invasion.

Afterward, in regret at the fiasco, Kennedy said to Turner Catledge, the executive editor of the *Times,* "If you had printed more about the operation, you would have saved us from a colossal mistake."

Even the strongest and most capable president requires such reporting; for he is *always* insulated from the realities of his administration by the fears and ambitions of his subordinates. He cannot possibly sort and absorb all of the vital information that is produced by governmental agencies and activities. Many believe that the fall of Richard Nixon was foreordained by his hatred of and isolation from the media.

The influence of the Washington press corps is also recognized in the third branch of the federal government. Justice Potter Stewart said in 1975, with something like wonder: "Only in the two short years that culminated last summer in the resignation of the president did we fully realize the enormous power that an investigative and adversary press can exert."

The courts have long been suspicious of that power, and over the years, they have waged a largely silent battle with trial reporters over the reporters' access to and publication of courtroom proceedings. Moving ponderously, the courts have attempted to close off much of the access of the news media. Moving quickly and sometimes deviously, the media have anticipated and occasionally foreclosed these efforts, very often using one judge against another.

The Other Government wins some, loses some. During the fifty years since Walter Lippmann's observation about public and private trials, legal maneuvers between the federal government and its courts and the national news media have resembled a very intricate and symmetrical minuet. The courts move to gag orders and to secret trials. The media, stalemated, take the issues to higher courts and begin to employ attorneys as reporters.

But the dance does not always include willing partners, and the Other Government is usually less effective than official Washington at some of the more subtle steps. Often the official government will make the news media an unwitting participant in the never-ceasing warfare among its various branches and agencies.

In 1978, philosopher-novelist Aleksandr Solzhenitsyn — an outsider, a Russian — observed, with considerable disapproval, that "The press has become the greatest power within Western countries, more powerful than the legislature, the executive, and the judiciary." How could he believe that? What of the overwhelming power of an attractive and canny president? What of the sheer size of the bureaucracy and its countless daily actions and decisions, which can vitally affect the course of society? Is it possible, despite the odds, that Solzhenitsyn is on to something?

We must remind ourselves periodically that the American republic's founders granted to the press, alone among private business institutions, the task of protecting the U.S. Constitution. Contemporary Washington correspondents are well aware of this responsibility and are proud of their independence from the official government and from the biases of their editors, publishers and station owners back home.

This independence marks the sharpest difference between Washington correspondents and their local brethren and between the Washington press corps today and that of previous generations. In 1936, Leo Rosten made this statement to a group of newspaper correspondents and asked whether it was true in their experience: "My orders are to be objective, but I *know* how my paper wants stories played." Slightly more than sixty percent of the correspondents replied yes, that they felt at least subtle pressure from their editors and publishers. In 1960, the mark came down dramatically; only 9.5 percent replied yes to the same question.

That difference is so dramatic that one may think there was a misunderstanding or a mistake. Another statement, which also tested freedom from home-office pressure, drew a similar response, however. Rosten asked the correspondents in 1936 whether this could be said of their work: "In my experience I've had stories played down, cut or killed for 'policy' reasons." Slightly more than fifty-five percent of the correspondents answered yes. In 1960, only 7.3 percent affirmed the same statement. During the twenty years since 1960, that downward trend has continued.

Yet, as my own experiences with President Kennedy and Congressman Rooney indicate, the independence of the contemporary Washington correspondents may be something of a mirage. In any event, what counts is not so much the independence of the reporters as it is their service of the public interest. How well do the news media serve our interests? How much do they show us of official Washington?

Learning about the national government from the news media is like watching a tightly-directed play. The director features the president at some length, the leading congressmen as secondary players, and the cabinet and justices of the Supreme Court as cameos and walk-ons. There are seldom any other entries in the dramatis personae, although there are *three million* employees of the national government. Any effort to move beyond the stage to see the undirected reality is useless. We must understand this: that the *reality* of government is often quite different from that reported by the two thousand news correspondents who help to create that image.

The public and the government are awash in a torrent of media reports. Yet, inquiring into how the news media actually serve the public yields a different perspective. Radio and television are mainly useful in signaling news events, providing the immediate — and sketchy — reports that announce happenings. More and more, we depend on television, despite the fact that our understanding is distorted by the brevity of the news reports. Broadcast journalists skim the top of the news, working with headlines, leads, and the bulletins that alert the public. Only occasionally does a documentary flesh out the news. Av Westin, a news executive of the American Broadcasting Company, has said: "I think television news is an illustrated service that can function best when it is regarded as an important yet fast adjunct to the newspapers. I know what we have to leave out; and if people do not read newspapers, news magazines, and books, they are desperately misinformed."

Newspapers cannot compete with radio and television for rapid transmission, and they cannot compete with television for the sheer impact of seeing and hearing news in the making. But a newspaper is available at any time, and it can provide a vast range of information on many subjects. The importance of the newspaper has been described best by a man who was interviewed during a newspaper strike: "I don't have the details now; I just have the result. It's almost like reading the headlines of the newspaper without following up the story. I miss the detail and the explanation of events leading up to the news."

Most magazines can treat their subject in greater depth than newspapers, but they generally cannot cover as many *different* subjects. Even the news magazines, which attempt to cover a wide range of subjects in some depth, do not publish as much information in their weekly issues as can be found in a single issue of a large daily newspaper. Like people who write books, those who write for magazines can seek out the unreported, flesh out the information that has been presented only in silhouette in broadcasts and newspapers, and report matters that the faster media have missed in the rush to meet deadlines.

It would seem that such a division of labor would help us to learn about *everything* that goes on in the government: radio and television rapidly reporting the action; newspapers putting most of the stories into context; and the magazine writers and book authors reporting the major stories more fully, and with more grace and flavor. But this range of public-affairs reports, however carefully some may be fashioned, often seems the reflection of a faulty mirror. The mirror is first held this way, then that way, but how narrowly it is focused! The presidency, the congressional leaders, the State Department, and the Department of Defense are in view. Only occasionally is mention made of such bureaus as the Departments of Energy, of Transportation, or Agriculture, or of such agencies as the Federal Communications Commission, the Food and Drug Administration, the Interstate Commerce Commission, and the many other agencies that figure so importantly in our everyday lives. Only a few such agencies ever make it to the front page, to the television screen, to the radio interview.

Protesting the narrow focus of the Washington press corps, Derick Daniels, former executive editor of one of the Knight-Ridder newspapers, argued that journalists must recognize the reader's needs and desires:

> Yes, yes, we understand that the poor slob in the kitchen is interested in the price of soap when she *ought* to be interested in Congress. But I mean recognizing squarely, as a matter of intellectual honesty, that the kitchen is really, *in fact,* just as important. . . . the amount of knowledge and information collected, and the studies available through the U.S. government, are nearly limitless. A single document—the yearbook of the Department of Agriculture—contains more useful information in its pages than most newspapers report in a year.

The media are thus confronted with a dilemma. It is impossible for any news organization, no matter how large, to cover fully the entire federal government every day. And even if it were possible, no one would want to sift through such reports. So the real question is not whether the media are at fault for not covering the entire government all the time, or for printing only a small portion of what is knowable about the government. The more appropriate questions are: How good is the judgment of the Washington press corps as to what parts of the government to watch and which of its actions to record or investigate? And how good is the judgment of the Washington news bureaus and their outlets in deciding what information to print and to broadcast every day?

These are two important questions—as important as any questions we can ask about our official government in Washington; for, in a sense, the two governments — the official government and the national news media — increasingly form part of a single, symbiotic unit. The major difference between the real government and the media government begins with the conscious and deliberate action by most officials to insert the image they desire into the media process. The government nearly always attempts to create an image of itself. Whether this will be successful depends on the reporter. In some cases, the image of the officials vies with the reporter's own concept of those officials. In other cases, the images are a match.

Ben Bagdikian, one of the most powerful media critics in the United States, commented on the interrelationships between government image-making and press image-making when he made a study of newspaper columnists. He talked to many federal assistant secretaries for public affairs about how they briefed their bosses and how they preferred to break government news. Bagdikian found the secretaries were heavily influenced by what they saw in the news media, that they accepted this as what the media would respond to, and that, as a result, they fashioned their output to serve what they perceived to be the media interest. Thus, the work of the Washington columnists, Bagdikian speculated, "includes guessing what the government is doing." This produces a double-mirror effect, in which each side responds to what the other is doing, while at the same time adjusting itself to the other side's anticipated needs.

Thinking about the mirrors of politics, John Kenneth Galbraith commented wryly: "Nearly all of our political comment originates in Washington. Washington politicians, after talking things over with each other, relay misinformation to Washington journalists who, after further intramural discussion, print it where it is thoughtfully read by the same politicians. It is the only completely successful closed system for the recycling of garbage that has yet been devised."

Viewed in the rawness of this circus of political reporting, government news seems very complicated — and dangerous. It is true that since the Vietnam War and the Watergate crisis, Washington correspondents are much more suspicious of the announcements of government officials. More and more correspondents every year are asking sharp questions of officials.

The questions are important because there have been times in the past fifteen years when *no one* in the official government knew what was true. Phil Goulding, assistant secretary of defense for public affairs in the second Nixon administration, once said: "In our office, the secretary's office, or the White House, we never knew how much we did not know." Again, in reference to the Nixon years and the Watergate scandal, Senator Charles Mathias has said: "The more a president sits surrounded by his own views and those of his personal advisers, the more he lives in a house of mirrors in which all the views and ideas tend to reflect and reinforce his own."

When it became evident in 1973 that Nixon had been living in a world of mirrors — that he saw only the image that he had manipulated — Dr. Edward

Teller, who had developed the hydrogen bomb in strict secrecy twenty years earlier, wrote ruefully, "Secrecy, once accepted, becomes an addiction." He might also have noted that secrecy, once the routine practice and defense of the official government, had, by 1973, finally given way to the angry probings of the Other Government.

By the time the Watergate case had brought an end to the presidency of Richard Nixon, the Other Government was firmly in control. One wonders if this is what the founding fathers had in mind.

17 Making an Issue of Child Abuse*

Barbara Nelson

Agenda-setting is the course by which issues are adopted for Governmental consideration and perhaps remedy. Although agenda-setting can be approached from an economic or issue-oriented perspective, the focus of this work is on decision making in organizations. The objective was to find out how officials learn about new problems, decide to give them their personal attention, and mobilize their organizations to respond to them. To answer these questions we examined four situations where child abuse achieved important agendas: the U.S. Children's Bureau, the mass and professional media, state legislatures, and Congress. In the process we discovered how child abuse, originally a private-sector charity concern, became additionally a public-sector social welfare issue.

The social problem we call abuse is about a century old, even though evidence of maltreatment exists all through human records. This apparent paradox is resolved by understanding that a social problem is a social construct. A social problem depends not only on the existence of conditions unacceptable to some people, but also on organization to redress those conditions and a modicum of social support for such efforts. The invention of child abuse as a social problem rested in part on the increasingly popular ideal of a "protected" childhood in the home, an ideal which took hold in American culture in the decades after the Civil War. In 1874, New York City was rocked by the reports that Mary Ellen Wilson was regularly beaten by her stepmother.

*Reprinted from *Making an Issue of Child Abuse,* University of Chicago Press (1984) by permission of the author and publisher.

161

Outraged charity workers and their supporters formed the New York Society for the Prevention of Cruelty to Children. Interest in the problem declined as Progressivism superseded the Scientific Charity movement. It was not until the 1950s and 1960s, when new research was undertaken, that the problem again came to the fore.

By examining how child abuse achieved these agendas we expected to understand better how new categorical social service policies are initiated. It was immediately evident, however, that child abuse was emblematic of another group of policy issues dealing with violence in intimate situations. Governmental response to child abuse made it easier for issue partisans to promote more sensitive governmental response to rape, as well as recognition of such "new" problems as spouse abuse, child sexual abuse, child pornography, and abuse of the elderly. In this sense, child abuse was an agenda-leading issue.

The valence, i.e., noncontroversial, character of child abuse allowed its rapid adoption on each agenda. Initially the problem was constructed as parenting gone crazy, the awful violence that individual adults inflicted on individual children. This construction gave the issue support from conservatives as well as liberals. Indeed, when abuse first achieved governmental agendas, all but the most orthodox conservatives felt that the government's fiduciary role toward children included protecting them from physical violence. Policymakers were very wary, though, of associating abuse with physical discipline. They did not want to appear to be undermining the "natural authority" of parents over their children and were careful not to construct the problem as one of unequal power within the family. Such a construction (redressing unequal power within the family) defeated the second Domestic Violence bill in Congress.

Contemporary governmental interest in abuse and neglect was part of a larger social current pushing issues of equity to the fore. In the period when abuse was rediscovered, the civil rights, welfare rights, and feminist movements captured the imagination of many people. Although the underlying problems raised by these movements — racism, poverty, and patriarchy — were not adequately addressed by minority scholarships, school lunches, or "equal pay for equal work" legislation, a spirit of optimism and good will prevailed. In part this generous spirit was a result of the greatest economic boom in American history — real GNP more than doubled between 1950 and 1970. Consequently, governmental support of child protection did not invoke a zero-sum argument.[1] Funding for child abuse programs, never large in any event, was only marginally in competition with the war in Vietnam, Food Stamps, or subsidized airport construction.

Over a period of twenty years, child abuse was *recognized, adopted, priorities* about its importance set, and interest *maintained* in three public institutions and the mass and professional media. First, the U.S. Children's Bureau became interested in child protective services and then physical abuse.

Its model child abuse reporting law (aided by escalating media coverage) spurred states to adopt similar legislation. The demands of influential lobbyists for child protective services, good service models, and adequate funds prompted Congress to pass legislation providing research and demonstration support and, to a lesser degree, social service monies. The history of agenda setting for this issue shows clearly how one public institution helps to set the agendas of others.

The Children's Bureau

The Children's Bureau provides a perfect example of "unplanned" agenda-setting. The Bureau was, first and foremost, an "issue-sensing" organization. After identifying an emerging child welfare or health problem, the Bureau's staff, aided by outside experts, undertook research to develop practical responses. In 1955, the Bureau learned of the American Humane Association's research on child protective services and immediately included the findings in its communication stream. The priority of the problem increased when the Bureau also became interested in the research by Dr. C. Henry Kempe on the battered-child syndrome. To encourage reporting, the Children's Bureau drafted (in 1962) and circulated (in 1963) a model child abuse reporting law.

The Bureau committed funds out of its small yearly research budget to pay for the development of the model statute. Immediately thereafter, however, the Bureau's research budget grew astronomically. Congress bankrolled a new era of research by the Children's Bureau when it passed the 1960 Maternal and Child Welfare amendments to the Social Security Act. (The money was not available until fiscal year 1962.) The issue of child abuse benefited from being in the right place at the right time. Projects on child abuse received a large share of the newly available research funds. Between 1962 and 1968, the Bureau spent an estimated one million dollars on child abuse and family law research.

These funds changed the nature of the Children's Bureau, however. Very rapidly, the Bureau went from being an issue-sensing and internal research agency to a grant-managing agency. Consequently, when the Nixon administration wanted to reorganize HEW on a functional rather than population basis, it practically destroyed the Bureau by assigning the Maternal and Child Health programs, which funded most of the Bureau's research, to the Health Services and Mental Health Administration. The agency had no more money for outside research and went into rapid decline.

Only the national child abuse legislation, which created the National Center for Child Abuse and Neglect (NCCAN) and placed it within the Bureau, saved the Bureau from total obscurity. But the remission was short. President Reagan's budget cuts pared research on abuse and neglect from $17 million in fiscal year 1980 to $2 million in fiscal year 1982.[2] In October, 1981, the

Administration on Children, Youth, and Families, where the Bureau now resides, began the layoffs and job changes which were designed to eliminate 443 jobs by fiscal year 1983, including thirty-three Washington positions in the Bureau and twenty-five in the regions. Such budget and staffing cuts signal an extremely limited presence for the Bureau and NCCAN in the early Reagan administration. Even the increased appropriations expected in the 1983 Reconciliation Act cannot easily replace the expertise lost through staffing cuts.

Media Attention to Abuse

The role of the media was not important when child abuse first achieved the agenda of the Children's Bureau. But initial consideration in state legislatures and Congress benefited from sustained coverage in professional journals, popular magazines, and newspapers. Between 1950 and 1980, professional journals carried 1,756 articles on abuse and neglect, popular magazines published another 124 articles, and the *New York Times* printed 652 stories on the subject. Virtually all of them were published after Dr. C. Henry Kempe's famous article "The Battered-Child Syndrome" appeared in the July 7, 1962 edition of the *Journal of the American Medical Association*. Indeed, Kempe's article so focused attention on the problem of child abuse that it is customarily used to date the "rediscovery" of the issue in this century. . . .

With the publication of this article, a tiny trickle of information grew into a swollen river, flooding mass-circulation newspapers and magazines and professional journals alike. In the decade prior to the article's appearance doctors, lawyers, social workers, educators and other researchers and practitioners combined published only nine articles specifically focusing on cruelty to children. In the decade after its publication, the professions produced 260 articles. Similarly, mass-circulation magazines carried twenty-eight articles in the decade after Kempe's article, compared to only three in the decade before, two of which recounted instances of bizarre brutalization.[14]

Even television displayed an interest in the problem. Although it is harder to document this medium fully, it seems that child abuse was virtually absent from early television scripts, whereas after "The Battered-Child Syndrome" appeared, soap operas and prime-time series alike created dramas based on the problem. The plight of Mary Ellen's fictional brothers and sisters was first beamed into millions of households in episodes of *Dr. Kildare, Ben Casey, M.D.,* and *Dragnet.*[15]

These figures on the emergence of child abuse in the media suggest that Downs's formulation of the issue-attention cycle needs to be amended. Contrary to Downs's hypothesis, media attention to child abuse grew steadily rather than declined, and the public has sustained a loyal interest in what might on the surface be thought of as a small, even unimportant, issue. Admittedly,

Downs does not speculate on how long the issue-attention cycle takes to run its course. Nonetheless, findings so strikingly at variance with the tenor of Downs's formulation deserve closer attention.

Four factors contribute to the continuing coverage of child abuse and suggest that media attention to a host of issues can be more long-lived than previously assumed. These factors include topic differentiation, issue aggregation, the link between the professional and the mass media, and the growing appeal of human interest stories (especially ones with a medical deviance twist).

First and foremost, coverage of abuse increased because stories about *specific types* of abuse were added to the earlier, more general reports. In other words, coverage increased because the general problem of abuse was differentiated into more narrowly defined topics such as the relationship between illegitimacy and abuse, or abuse within military families.[16] Second, child abuse coverage increased because the issue was also linked with larger, more overarching concerns, such as intrafamilial violence, which now includes abuse of a spouse, parent, or even grandparent.[17] The scope of the problem is thus simultaneously decreasing and increasing.

Topic differentiation and issue aggregation are themselves explained by a third factor which encourages sustained media attention to child abuse. To a large extent the mass media carefully and consistently monitor professional and scientific journals in search of new stories. This symbiotic relationship is perhaps the most neglected factor contributing to ongoing media coverage of issues. Despite the lack of attention paid to it, the relationship between the mass media and professional outlets is well institutionalized, and serves both parties admirably, providing fresh stories for journalists and (for the most part) welcome publicity for scholars. Moreover, this relationship provides a regular source of "soft (i.e., interesting) news" about child abuse. Indeed, the fourth factor contributing to the durability of child abuse coverage is the fact that "soft news" — human interest stories — has been added to "hard news" stories, which have traditionally focused on child abuse cases as crime news. This last factor should not be confused with the first two. Soft news stories extend the range of story *types,* whereas differentiation and aggregation extend the range of story *topics.*

By investigating each of these factors we can show how media coverage both created the demand for, and was a product of, governmental action. The first three factors — differentiation, aggregation, and the relationship between the professional and mass media — can be considered together. These three factors are linked through the recognition that child abuse was initially a research issue, and that research on a problem has a life cycle of its own. This life cycle can greatly affect the prominence of an issue in the media.

As chapter 3 has shown, physical abuse was a research problem long before it was a public policy issue in the conventional sense. During the decade between 1946 and 1957 radiologists reluctantly pieced together evidence revealing that a fair number of children had bruises and broken bones, the cause of which could only be parental violence. This research, however, never crossed the bridge from scientific publications to the mass media. Indeed, not until 1960 did the Children's Bureau even mention these medical studies in its *Annual Report.*[18]

Much has been made of the fact that the radiological research failed to create a stir outside roentgenological circles. The cause is often attributed to the low status of radiology within medicine, and, in fact, only one of the early articles was published in the prestigious AMA *Journal.* But importantly, this article—by P. V. Woolley and W. A. Evans, Jr.—stopped short of crediting injuries to willful parental violence.[19] Instead the authors suggested that the injuries were due to "indifference, immaturity and irresponsibility of parents."[20] Thus it was more than the low status of radiologists which kept the social origins of physical abuse from being determined; it was also a pronounced distaste for acknowledging parental behavior so at odds with the ideal.

In 1962 the situation changed, however. Dr. C. Henry Kempe and his colleagues published "The Battered-Child Syndrome" in the AMA *Journal.* The article and its companion editorial caused a storm in medical circles and in the mass media as well. Indeed, the article and editorial are routinely used to date the rediscovery of abuse. In this instance, medical research and opinion did cross the bridge to the mass media, primarily through the vehicle of the AMA press release "Parental Abuse Looms in Childhood Deaths."[22] The message of the article and editorial was clear: Kempe and his co-workers had "discovered" an alarming and deadly "disease" which menaced the nation's children. The article was measured in tone and eminently professional, although its findings were later sensationalized through less careful retelling. But the editorial presented problems from the beginning.

The most important characteristic of the article is that it provided a powerful, unifying label in the phrase "the battered-child syndrome." Kempe purposefully chose the term to emphasize the medical, and downplay the criminal, aspects of the problem. The year before, as a hardworking member of the American Pediatric Association's convention program committee, he had the opportunity to organize a panel on any topic he chose. Naturally he chose the topic of his current research, the physical abuse of children. Colleagues warned him, however, that a panel using that title might scare away just the audience he sought to inform. Kempe agreed and changed the title to "The Battered-Child Syndrome." As it turned out, his choice of label was inspired. Like others who promoted the issue, Kempe saw the need to diffuse anxiety and promote consensus through the choice of a nonthreatening label. For the same kinds of reasons, legislators frequently employed the term "child abuse," which conjured up severe maltreatment yet avoided any taint of association with "discipline."

The editorial was equally powerful but more problematic. Based on what would now be considered very dubious epidemiological evidence, the editors of the AMA *Journal* proclaimed: "It is likely that [the battered-child syndrome] will be found to be a more frequent cause of death than such well recognized and thoroughly studied diseases as leukemia, cystic fibrosis and muscular dystrophy and may well rank with automobile accidents."[23] Then as now, the difficulties in determining accurate figures about child abuse, even mortality figures, were enormous. The death rate may have been as high as the editors presumed, perhaps even higher, but they could not have known that with certainty using existing data. However, supported by data or not, the editors annointed the problem with the most durable of unctions: they established the significance of the problem by asserting its frequency.

The AMA's news release repeated Kempe's findings and the *Journal's* opinion to a wider audience. Like many professional associations, the AMA routinely issues press releases about important findings reported in its journal. This practice constitutes the first link in a chain which keeps mass media personnel abreast of medical, scientific, and technical developments. At the other end of the chain are the beat reporters who cultivate the sources behind the news releases. The chain, little studied in the policymaking literature but well institutionalized, transmitted Kempe's findings to journalists responsible for medical news.

Within a week of the news release, *Time* magazine summarized the article as the second feature in its "Medicine" section. (The lead medical article, garnered from the *Medical Letter,* and the AMA *Journal,* touted the fact that oral contraceptives "have proved to be 'virtually 100% effective.' ") *Newsweek,* however, beat *Time* to the punch. In the April 16, 1962 edition of *Newsweek,* the findings of "The Battered-Child Syndrome" were reported. This article coincided with the fiftieth anniversary of the Children's Bureau. Although the exact origins of this article are no longer known, its genesis appears to have been a celebratory news release by the Children's Bureau. Together, *Time* and *Newsweek* informed millions of readers that a new "disease" imperiled the nation's children.[24]

If these two magazines informed a somewhat selective and small audience, the *Saturday Evening Post* and *Life* had more popular appeal. The *Post* published an article entitled "Parents Who Beat Children: A Tragic Increase in Cases of Child Abuse Is Prompting a Hunt for Ways to Select Sick Adults Who Commit Such Crimes" on October 6, 1962.[25]

Like the news magazine articles, the author of the *Post's* article interviewed the medical experts: Kempe, and other physicians such as Dr. Vincent Fontana, Chief of Pediatrics at New York's St. Vincent's Hospital, Dr.

Frederic N. Silverman, chief radiologist at Cincinnati Children's Hospital (and one of the coauthors of "The Battered-Child Syndrome") and Dr. John L. Gwenn, radiologist at Los Angeles Children's Hospital. The Chief of the Children's Bureau, Mrs. Katherine Oettinger, and her deputy, Dr. Katherine Bain, were also interviewed. But in the *Post* article, these interviews were juxtaposed with a recitation of the gory details of child abuse.

Charles Flato wrote the *Post* article, in which he leaned heavily on the *Newsweek* piece written but not signed by current "Medicine" editor Matthew Clark. No highbrow restraint fettered Flato in the *Post* article. On the first page of this article in a respected family magazine, Flato unleashed his journalistic talents to describe abuse:

> In the United States generally, at least two children a day are savagely assaulted by their own parents. The most common form of parental abuse is beating. The second is burning — with matches, cigarettes or electric irons, or by holding the child's hands, arms or feet over an open flame. Many are deliberately scalded with whatever happens to be bubbling on the stove.
>
> Others are strangled, thrown, dropped, shot, stabbed, shaken, drowned, suffocated, sexually violated, held under running water, tied upright for long periods of time, stepped on, bitten, given electric shocks, forced to swallow pepper or buried alive. The reports of the injuries read like a case book of a concentration-camp doctor: bruises, contusions, welts, skull fractures, broken bones, brain injuries, burns, concussions, cuts, gashes, gunshot and knife wounds, ruptured vital organs, bites, dislocated necks, asphyxiations, eyes gouged out.[26]

The list of types of abuse, its length, detail, and thesaurus-like completeness, could only inflame readers — so too, the reference to a concentration camp, a reference with uncanny and probably unknown significance. Charles Flato was probably unaware that C. Henry Kempe had fled Nazi Germany. The article goes beyond the inflammatory, however. Flato also describes the difficulty encountered in the treatment of child abuse cases, which was then believed to stem from the absence of laws requiring the reporting of child abuse. The article concludes with an upbeat note that the Children's Bureau "has drafted a model [reporting] law for submission to state legislatures" to remedy the problem.[27]

In a double-barreled shot, photojournals and news magazines introduced child abuse to the American public. The articles can be considered the point at which an invisible problem became a public concern, and soon a major public policy issue. The popular agenda was set and the problem was defined as one of medical deviance — the broader concerns went unmentioned. . . .

Once child abuse was rediscovered as a social problem, newspapers began to cover cases more frequently and intensively. But not all the growth in the coverage of child abuse was a result of papers' interest in bizarre brutalization. As legislative response to child abuse grew, so did that type of newspaper coverage. Every state passed a child abuse reporting law between 1963 and 1967, and all amended and reamended their law several times, with each legislative action renewing newspaper interest in the problem. In addition, newspapers also began to run human interest stories on child abuse, in part aided by the now defunct Women's News Service, which provided feature stories on child abuse for the home, style, and fashion pages of subscribing newspapers. Local human interest stories focused on nearby programs to prevent or treat abuse, and special training sessions for county and state workers.

In deciding to investigate or publish a particular story, journalists quickly learn that "hard" and "soft" news are not accorded the same value. "Hard news," according to Gaye Tuchman, "concerns important matters and soft news, interesting matters."[50] Soft news does not have the "quickening urgency" which Helen MacGill Hughes asserts is the lifeblood of newspapers.[51] In other words, soft news is timeless and durable — although many would say insignificant — which means it appears at the back of a newspaper.

The special titillation of violent deviance accounts for the durability of child abuse as soft news. Newspapers usually feature such news in the portions of the papers devoted to women's interests. These stories often dwell on the fact that most reported abusers are women, even while mentioning that this finding is not surprising since women traditionally bear the burden for most child care. The abuser is characterized as an "unnatural" woman, one who does not adequately love and protect children, and who finds child care less than totally rewarding. Human interest stories are frequently described as instances where a "man bites dog," not the reverse. What better fits the "man-bites-dog" category than the case of a mother who beats her child? The deviant aspect of child abuse cases lets the coverage glide easily into the category of soft-news coverage.

The role of human interest stories in sustaining newspaper coverage of child abuse can be seen by examining the *New York Times* stories in 1964 and again in 1979. The sixteen stories on child abuse published in 1964 split evenly between cases and legislative reports. Fifty child abuse stories made the *Times* in 1979. In that year the activities of various charitable groups and the results of numerous scientific research projects constituted *one-half* of the coverage. Cases, legislation, even criminal proceedings took a back seat to soft-news articles.

The pattern of newspaper coverage of abuse and neglect over the last thirty years is quite illuminating. Once again relying on the *New York Times Index,* we find that during the early 1950s child abuse stories were quite common, thinning to just a few stories a year until the late 1960s when coverage took a dramatic jump. The sheer volume of coverage is remarkable. Between 1950 and 1980 the *Times* published 652 articles pertaining to abuse, certainly enough to keep the issue in the public's eye.

Of course, the media can lead the public to water, so to speak, but cannot always make it drink. The information was available to anyone who wanted it, but how many people read which articles (or watched which television programs) cannot be ascertained. And the information grew year by year, to an unprecedented volume, providing a climate of public awareness which initially encouraged elected officials to recognize the problem and ultimately caused them to maintain an interest in it.

In sum, we can say that child abuse achieved the public's agenda because the interest of a few pioneering researchers crossed the bridge to mass-circulation news outlets. Public interest was sustained and grew, however, because the media have both many *sources* of news and many *types* of audiences to whom they present the news. Through topic differentiation, issue aggregation, professional and mass-circulation linkages, and the growth in human interest newspaper reporting, child abuse remains a lively topic of media coverage. The public's interest in this newly recognized social problem prompted state legislatures into action. And act they did, out of humanitarian interest to be sure, but also from the recognition that child abuse was the premier example of no-cost rectitude. . . .

18

The Impact of Investigative Reporting on Public Opinion and Policymaking: Targeting Toxic Waste*

David L. Protess
Fay Lomax Cook
Thomas R. Curtin
Margaret T. Gordon
Donna R. Leff
Maxwell E. McCombs
Peter Miller

This article reports the fourth in a series of field experiments that test the agenda-setting hypothesis (McCombs and Shaw, 1972) for news media investigative reports. Our goal is to treat these field experiments as case studies from which we can develop empirically grounded theory that specifies the conditions under which investigative reports influence public agendas and policymaking priorities. Unique to studies of agenda-setting is our use of pretest-posttest research designs, made possible by journalists' disclosure of forthcoming investigative stories to the research team with adequate time for pre- and postpublication survey interviewing. A further distinctive feature is our concern with detailed tracing of the life course of a media report from an examination of the initial investigation by journalists, to the publication of the report, the effects on the general public and policymakers, and eventual policy outcomes.

The first of these studies (Cook et al., 1983) found that a nationally televised investigative news report on fraud and abuse in the federally funded home health care program had significant effects on the agendas of both the public and policymakers. The study found that home health care-related issues (and not unrelated issues) became significantly more important to citizens and policymakers exposed to the televised report than to nonviewers. Yet, actual policy changes after the report's publication resulted more from direct pressure

---

*Reprinted from *Public Opinion Quarterly* (1987, Vol. 51, pp. 166–185) by permission of The University of Chicago Press.

for change by the journalists themselves than from demands by the general public or political constituencies.

The second study (Protess et al., 1985) measured the impact of a Chicago *Sun-Times* investigative series disclosing government improprieties in the reporting and handling of rape against Chicago area women. The effects of the newspaper series were considerably more limited than in the first study, in part because the pretest disclosed an already high level of awareness and concern about the problem. The most striking result was a sharp increase in the number, length, and prominence of stories about rape in the *Sun-Times* — that is, the largest measurable effect was on the medium itself rather than on its audience. However, as in the home health care study, policymaking effects included legislative hearings and related "symbolic" political actions (Edelman, 1964).[1]

The effects of the third investigative report, a five-part local television series about repeatedly brutal Chicago police officers, provided an "in-between" case (Leff, Protess, and Brooks, 1986). The series had significant effects on viewer attitudes about police brutality but not on their assessment of the priority or salience of the problem in comparison with other social concerns. Nonetheless, the series resulted in major policy changes within the Chicago Police Department, in part because its publication coincided with a hotly contested Chicago mayoral election in which mayoral challenger Harold Washington used the series to help make the Department an issue.

Why is it that some investigative reports "catch on" and affect the views of members of the public and policy elites, while others do not? Why is it that all three investigative reports had some form of policy impact, despite the fact that they did not all have effects on the public and policymakers? In answer to the first question, several explanations have tentatively been suggested in our earlier work: the nature of the medium of presentation (print versus television); the style of presentation (unambiguous, with clear villains and heroes, versus ambiguous, where fault is not clear and where solutions seem difficult to find); the "age" of the issue on the media's agenda (a new issue that has infrequently been presented in the past and about which the public has little knowledge versus an old issue that has recurred over time on the media's agenda and about which the public is aware).

None of these explanations provides a possible answer to the second

---

[1]Symbolic acts have been described as "dramatic in outline and empty of realistic detail" (Edelman, 1964:9). Here we use the term to describe policy "changes" that are largely rhetorical. Thus, when a public official responds to a media exposé by making speeches about the problem, by convening governmental hearings, or by announcing as news previously approved legislation, we call these acts symbolic. Conversely, "substantive" reforms are tangible regulatory, legislative, or administrative changes that occur after an investigative story is published. In making this distinction, we do not mean to suggest that substantive reforms are necessarily more likely than symbolic reforms to lead in the long run to the *correction* of the problem disclosed by the media.

question concerning the investigative reports' impact on policy. Regardless of the above factors, some form of policy impact occurred in all the cases we have examined to date. In the home health care and rape cases, the impact was symbolic with legislative hearings and proposals for policy changes. In the police brutality case, the impact was substantive with actual, major policy changes occurring. Clearly, more case studies are needed before we can develop an empirically grounded theory that specifies under what conditions and with what kinds of issues media investigations influence public agendas and policymaking processes.

The current study examines the public opinion and policymaking impact of a local television investigative series concerning the toxic waste disposal practices of a major Chicago university. In this case, the publication format was virtually identical to the earlier police brutality study: a multipart television report, aired during a "ratings sweeps" period, by the same correspondent on the same local television station. Further, one of the primary "targets" of the series was also a city regulatory agency, the Chicago Fire Department, which was accused of failing to enforce its environmental safety regulations. However, here we examine a different kind of issue—i.e., toxic waste disposal—at a different point in the city's political history—i.e., a year into Mayor Harold Washington's first term, when he was locked in a struggle with the City Council over control of Chicago's city government.

This article first will discuss the attitudinal impact of the toxic waste series on the general public and policy elites. Next, we trace the effects of the series on public policymaking in Chicago, focusing on the Fire Department's response to disclosures about its shortcomings. Finally, we analyze the findings of the four studies and try to identify and explain emerging patterns.

RESEARCH DESIGN

The pretest, posttest experimental design is highly appropriate, but not traditionally utilized, in research involving nonlaboratory studies of media effects (Cook and Campbell, 1979). More typical in such research endeavors is the use of cross-sectional (McCombs and Shaw, 1972; McLeod, Becker, and Byrnes, 1974; Erbring, Goldenberg, and Miller, 1980) or panel study designs (Tipton, Haney, and Baseheart, 1975; Shaw and McCombs, 1977; MacKuen, 1981). In this study, however, two factors made field experimentation practicable: the reporters' cooperation with researchers and the lengthy preparation time of the report, which made advance planning by the researchers possible. Thus, researchers were able to obtain prepublication measurements of public and policymaker attitudes about the precise subject matter of the forthcoming television series. Survey questions about unrelated matters were used to obtain control data.

The resulting television series, "Wasted Time," was broadcast on three successive nights beginning 13 May 1984 on WMAQ-TV, Channel 5, a Chicago-based station owned and operated by the National Broadcasting Company (NBC). The reporter was Peter Karl, a well-known local investigative journalist who also served as correspondent on the police brutality series that was the subject of our third study. The series was promoted heavily by the television station, since it was broadcast in the middle of a highly important ratings period.

The series disclosed that the University of Chicago was storing potentially hazardous toxic chemical and radioactive wastes beneath several of its buildings, including some classrooms. Stories alleged that the storage violated Chicago Fire Department regulations, as well as the environmental standards of several state and federal agencies, including the U.S. Environmental Protection Agency (EPA), the U.S. Occupational Safety and Health Administration (OSHA), and the U.S. Department of Energy. Each night, the broadcast described an assortment of delays by the University in constructing relatively inexpensive facilities to ameliorate the waste disposal problem, thus giving the investigative report its title "Wasted Time." At no time did the series state that anyone at the University was in immediate danger, but the use of pictures of chemical explosions and fires that had occurred on the campus a decade earlier suggested the potential harm involved. One implication of the series was that the violations would not have persisted over time if certain federal, state, and local agencies were doing their jobs properly (i.e., the EPA, OSHA, the U.S. Department of Energy, and the Chicago Fire Department).

General Public

Through random-digit dialing techniques, 395 respondents from the Chicago Metropolitan area were contacted two weeks before the television series aired. Telephone numbers were generated from listings in area directories. The last digit of each chosen number was replaced with a random digit to ensure that unlisted telephone numbers were included in the sample. Those who refused to be interviewed were found to be similar to respondents in gender, age, education, and the area of residence.

The telephone sample was then stratified by the respondents' self-reported television viewing habits into regular watchers of Channel 5 news (N = 208), and watchers of other evening newscasts or non-watchers of any television news (N = 186). We expected that Channel 5 newswatchers were likely to be exposed to the investigative series, while others would constitute a quasi-experimental comparison group. One week after the broadcast of the series, researchers recontacted the entire sample. As indicated in Table 1, 235 persons agreed to be reinterviewed, comprising the general public sample in this study. The respondents in this sample, though proportionately more female than the

TABLE 1
Quasi-Experimental Design Distribution of Respondents

Respondent Groupings	Pretest	Posttest
TV 5 Watchers/Nonwatchers		
Treatment (watchers)	208 (52.7%)	131 (55.7%)
Comparison (nonwatchers)	186 (47.0%)	103 (43.9%)
Unclassified	1 (0.3%)	1 (0.4%)
Total	395 (100.0%)	235 (100.0%)
Series Aware/Nonaware		
Treatment (series-aware)	NA	83 (35.3%)
Comparison (series-unaware)	NA	146 (26.2%)
Unclassified	NA	6 (2.5%)
Total	NA	235 (100.0%)

pretest respondents, did not differ significantly in educational level, age, or ethnic or racial background from the individuals who refused to be reinterviewed or who could not be recontacted after the pretest.[2]

Since general viewing habits are not perfect predictors of the public's actual *exposure* to a specific television series, respondents were asked at the conclusion of the posttest interview whether they had "seen, read, or heard anything about recent news media investigative stories about toxic waste disposal problems at the University of Chicago." Follow-up questions were then asked about the source and extent of the exposure. Those responding "yes" to the question were considered "series-aware" group members, while those responding "no" were defined as a comparison group. Respondents in these two groups did not differ significantly in gender, educational level, age, or ethnic or racial background. Table 1 shows the distribution of respondents in this analysis. It is important to emphasize that respondents in both analyses are from the same overall sample. It is only the definition of "treatment" and "control" that changes.

To avoid sensitizing respondents to the subject of the investigative series, researchers embedded questions related to toxic waste disposal and other environmental problems among questions about crime, unemployment, police

---

[2]Of respondents interviewed for the pretest, 59% were female, while 64.7% of the posttest respondents were female. The change in gender corresponds to a chi-square value of 7.2035 with one degree of freedom ($p < .01$) after completing the Yates correction for the continuity of the data. No other demographic changes between pre- and posttest were statistically significant. Moreover, no significant demographic differences were found between the Channel 5 viewers and nonviewers (identified in Table 2). The percentage of respondents who agreed to be reinterviewed (60%) was slightly higher than in two of our previous three studies. Nonetheless, the attrition rate was still fairly substantial, due in large measure to the problem of keeping respondents in panels in which they are given no inducements to participate.

brutality, child abuse, and governmental corruption. Of the forty separate items in the questionnaire, twelve were related to general environmental issues and six to chemical or radioactive waste disposal problems. We hypothesized that change would occur among the Channel 5 viewers on questions about the environment and toxic waste, while responses to other questions would remain constant from pre- to posttest. We expected the comparison groups' responses to remain constant on all questions.

The questions can be divided into three categories: (1) attitudes and agendas, (2) affective responses, and (3) changes in behavior. We asked respondents to rate the importance of environmental issues compared to other problems; to evaluate the performance of federal, state, and local governmental agencies, including some related and others unrelated to the environment; to describe their level of anxiety about various environmental problems and their personal reactions to news stories about them; and to discuss what they have done to avoid environmental hazards. We hypothesized that in posttest interviews, the treatment groups would consider toxic waste and related environmental problems to be more important and would change their attitudes, feelings, and actions about them.

Policymakers and Policymaking

A purposive sample of forty policy elites was selected for their interest and potential influence on environmental policymaking. Those surveyed included public administrators from Illinois and federal environmental protection agencies, state legislators, members of the Chicago City Council, University officials, and lobbyists from public interest groups and private waste disposal companies. Persons who were considered likely to know about the investigative series prior to pretest interviewing were excluded from the sample. Interviews were conducted by telephone; 31 of the 40 respondents were reinterviewed after the television broadcast.

As in our previous studies, we made no attempt to establish a group of nonexposed elite respondents. We expected that persons with significant interest in the subject of an investigative report would almost certainly hear about it, even if they failed to view the particular stories. Indeed, 23 of the 31 respondents indicated in posttest interviews that they "saw, read, or heard" something about the series. Statistical analyses were performed on the self-defined "exposed" and "unexposed" groups.

The policymakers were asked a series of questions that were identical to those in the survey of the general public. The questions included items both related and unrelated to the subject of the investigative series. In addition, the elite respondents were asked about their past, present, and anticipated future policymaking activities related to toxic waste disposal problems.

After the series, researchers tracked policy developments that might be attributable to the Channel 5 investigation by interviewing an expanded sample of policymakers and conducting analyses of related budgets, legislation, and regulatory and administrative initiatives. Content analyses of local media coverage of environmental issues were also performed both as an additional indicator of the level of governmental response to the series and as a measure of its impact on the news media's agendas.

IMPACT OF THE INVESTIGATIVE REPORT ON THE GENERAL PUBLIC

In examining public attitudes before and after the broadcast of the Channel 5 investigation, we wanted to determine whether changes occurred on questionnaire items related to the subject of the series. To test whether the changes between the pretest and posttest were different for the exposed group from the nonexposed group, we used analysis of covariance (ANCOVA), employing the pretest score as the covariate. Table 2 shows the mean responses and significance levels for Channel 5 viewers and nonviewers as well as for the series-aware and unaware groups.

The data show no effects of the series, as measured by the ANCOVA analysis. Some items bordered on significant change, however, giving slight indications of change in perception due to the series. In particular, compared to those unaware of the series, those exposed to the reports were slightly more likely to say that environmental news stories cause confusion. Both series-aware and unaware respondents reported worrying somewhat less about improper storage and disposal of chemical waste at the posttest. Both groups of respondents tended to decrease their evaluation of the Chicago Fire Department, which suggests that other stimuli produced a small judgmental change. Evaluation of environmental agencies other than the Fire Department remained constant, as did measures of respondents' behavior concerning environmental problems.

In short, the agenda-setting hypothesis was not supported by the findings. Responses to questions about the importance of toxic waste disposal in relation to other issues did not change significantly. In comparison with other problems, toxic chemical and radioactive waste disposal was consistently at or near the bottom of their reported agendas.

IMPACT OF THE INVESTIGATIVE REPORT ON POLICYMAKERS AND POLICYMAKING

Table 3 reports the mean responses of policymakers to the surveys before and after the investigative report. The small size of the nonexposed group and the

TABLE 2
Mean Responses for General Public[a]

	Channel 5 Viewers (N = 131)		Channel 5 Nonviewers (N = 103)			Series-Aware (N = 83)			Not Aware (N = 146)		
	Pre	Post	Pre	Post	Sig.[b]	Pre	Post	Sig.[b]	Pre	Post	Sig.[b]
Cognitive Items											
Importance of toxic wase disposal	3.48	3.43	3.53	3.41	ns	3.51	2.42	ns	3.50	3.42	ns
Fire Dept. does its job	3.67	3.52	3.67	3.53	ns	3.69	3.50	ns	3.68	3.55	ns
U.S. Dept. of Energy does its job	2.66	2.72	2.40	2.53	ns	2.48	2.58	ns	2.57	2.64	ns
U.S. EPA does its job	2.61	2.57	2.41	2.56	ns	2.45	2.39	ns	2.55	2.65	ns
OSHA does its job	2.63	2.76	2.52	2.75	ns	2.48	2.65	ns	2.63	2.80	ns
NRC does its job	2.56	2.61	2.22	2.37	ns	2.35	2.37	ns	2.46	2.59	ns
Fed. officials adequately enforce toxic waste disposal regulations	2.50	2.48	2.41	2.42	ns	2.49	2.43	ns	2.44	2.43	ns
Fire officials regularly inspect buildings for hazards	2.44	2.55	2.48	2.63	ns	2.43	2.57	ns	2.47	2.59	ns
Local universities have influence in the city	2.47	2.55	2.58	2.64	ns	2.39	2.44	ns	2.62	2.68	ns
Affective Items											
Worry of improper storage and disposal of chemical waste	3.36	3.23	3.27	3.13	ns	3.44	3.21	ns	3.27	3.17	ns
Worry of danger from radioactive accidents	3.13	3.03	3.12	2.96	ns	3.12	3.04	ns	3.15	3.00	ns
News stories frustrate me	1.77	1.73	1.73	1.72	ns	1.74	1.76	ns	1.76	1.69	ns
News stories confuse me	1.54	1.60	1.58	1.59	ns	1.57	1.69	ns	1.56	1.56	ns
News stories make me feel helpless	1.61	1.70	1.63	1.68	ns	1.67	1.78	ns	1.59	1.65	ns
News stories anger me	1.74	1.73	1.75	1.75	ns	1.78	1.77	ns	1.73	1.74	ns
News stories make me feel indifferent	1.29	1.32	1.31	1.40	ns	1.28	1.35	ns	1.32	1.36	ns
Shrug off or don't remember stories	1.52	1.18	1.26	1.25	ns	1.12	1.16	ns	1.25	1.23	ns
Behavioral Items											
Have you acted to solve problems on the report?	1.38	1.36	1.29	1.29	ns	1.39	1.35	ns	1.30	1.31	ns
Have you acted to avoid risks?	1.54	1.56	1.55	1.55	ns	1.55	1.62	ns	1.55	1.52	ns

[a]Higher numbers indicate more psoitive responses (4 equals "very important," "agree strongly," and "very adequate").
[b]Significance levels are based on distributions of f ratios from Analyses of Covariance (ANCOVA) adjusting for initial between-group differences (Reichardt, 1979).

TABLE 3
Mean Responses for Policy Elites[a]

	Exposed (N = 23)		Unexposed (N = 8)		Sig.[b]
	Pre	Post	Pre	Post	
Agency Evaluations					
Chicago Fire Department	3.42	2.79	2.71	2.71	ns
U.S. Department of Energy	2.50	2.05	2.71	3.00	*
U.S. Environmental Protection Agency	2.91	2.27	3.13	3.13	*
Occupational Safety and Health Administration	2.33	2.00	3.13	3.25	*
Department of Streets and Sanitation	2.83	2.72	3.00	3.00	ns
Bureau of Inspectional Services	2.20	2.07	2.75	2.75	ns
Police Department	2.84	2.84	3.57	3.57	ns
Park District	2.60	2.55	3.20	3.20	ns
U.S. Social Security Commission	2.56	2.50	3.00	3.50	*
U.S. Department of Immigration	2.29	2.21	3.00	3.17	ns
U.S. Department of Health & Human Services	2.45	2.40	3.17	3.17	ns
Agenda-Setting					
Importance of toxic waste disposal	3.52	3.61	2.63	2.63	ns
Importance of environmental pollutants	3.09	3.27	2.63	2.25	*
Importance of violent crime	3.48	3.39	3.38	3.50	ns
Importance of unemployment	3.74	3.61	3.75	3.75	ns
Importance of police brutality	2.76	2.67	2.00	2.00	ns
Importance of child abuse	3.32	3.18	3.50	3.17	ns
Behavioral					
Past time spent on toxic waste problems	2.39	2.57	2.38	2.38	ns
Ideal time spent on tixoc waste problems	2.64	2.73	2.50	2.63	ns
Expected future time spent on toxic waste problems	2.50	3.05	2.50	2.25	*

[a]Higher numbers indicate more psoitive responses (4 = "very important" or does job "very well").
[b]Significance levels are based on distributions of f ratios from Analyses of Covariance adjusting for initial between-group differences (Reichardt, 1979).

nonprobability sampling procedure make generalization from these data tentative. Recognizing the limitations of inference from these data, we believe that the findings in Table 3 indicate stronger support for the hypotheses than do the survey results for the general public.

Policy elites were asked to evaluate the performance of eleven government agencies. We expected that the investigative report would result in policy elites' lowering their assessments of the jobs done by four agencies – the Chicago Fire Department, the U.S. Department of Energy, the EPA, and OSHA. The changes were statistically significant ($p < .05$) for the performance evaluations of three of the four government agencies targeted by Channel 5 as bearing responsibility for the problems disclosed. Change in the evaluation of the fourth agency, the Chicago Fire Department, was in the expected downward direction ($p < .10$). Change was also significant for one of the seven unrelated agencies added as controls – the U.S. Social Security Commission – but this appears to be a chance change by the unexposed policy elites whose evaluations increased to more positive ones while the series-exposed elites' evaluations did not change.

Marked changes also occurred on one of the questions designed to measure the behavior of policymakers. When asked, "In the coming months, how much of your time do you think *will* be spent on toxic waste disposal problems?" the group exposed to the series changed significantly in the direction of "more" time. This finding is consistent with our analysis of the actual policymaking consequences of the investigative series. Since the series aired, each of the governmental agencies named by Channel 5 initiated actions to monitor the University's compliance with toxic waste disposal regulations.

Perhaps the most dramatic of these enforcement efforts was made by the Chicago Fire Department. On the morning after the first broadcast, a team of high-ranking Department officials inspected the buildings where chemical wastes were stored, and cited the University for failing to comply with 20 of the City's safety regulations. The Department gave the University 30 days to comply with its standards and threatened publicly to initiate criminal proceedings if it failed to do so.

Media coverage of the Fire Department's initiative was swift. A Chicago *Tribune* headline in the newspaper's next edition read: "City Faults U of C on Fire Safety," and the *Sun-Times* reported that the "U of C Is Cited as Fire Violator." The *Hyde Park Herald,* a weekly newspaper serving the community surrounding the University, headlined: "UC Responds to Hazard Charge" and called editorially for a study of the problem. All three newspapers credited the Channel 5 investigation as the catalyst for the governmental actions.

Channel 5 itself reported the "Fire Department crackdown" on its evening newscast later the same day. (The station's television competitors ignored the story, however.) Pictures of the Department's inspections were shown, and the story was repeated in the remaining two segments of the investigative series. The television station claimed that the action was taken "in response to our series on hazardous waste disposal problems at the University." In fact, however, Channel 5 correspondent Peter Karl had discussed the possibility of an inspection in several telephone conversations with Fire Department officials two days *before* the first part of the series was aired. The officials had agreed both that the inspection would occur and that it would not take place until the morning *after* the airing of the initial broadcast. Channel 5, in turn, covered the inspection as if it occurred at the initiative of the Fire Department, i.e., without direct prodding by its investigative reporter.

This form of journalist-policymaker collaboration has been described in our earlier studies (Cook et al., 1983; Molotch, Protess, and Gordon, 1987). What is significant here is that general public and policymaker respondents were exposed to news media stories about governmental "reforms" before the allegations in Channel 5's three-part series had been completely aired. Thus, the public's perceptions of the series may have been colored somewhat by media reports that included the presentation of both a problem and its "solution."

Interviews by researchers with Fire Department officials at the end of the 30-day compliance period indicated that the University had, in fact, corrected the fire hazard aspect of its waste disposal problem. The University also was implementing plans for the much-delayed facility to provide a more permanent solution to its environmental difficulties. However, content analyses of Channel 5 and other media revealed that the media did not cover these *post*series developments. Unlike our study of the *Sun-Times* rape series, the issues of toxic waste disposal at the University of Chicago or elsewhere did not rise on the news media's agenda of concerns. Content analysis of the Chicago *Tribune* for 3-month periods both before and after the publication of the Channel 5 series showed a slight *decline* in column inches of news stories and editorials on toxic waste disposal problems. A review of the assignment log at Channel 5 for the same periods showed only a minor increase in the frequency of such stories.

Similarly, Table 3 shows that policymakers' assessments of the *importance* of toxic waste disposal as an issue did not change significantly after the broadcast of the series. Perhaps this was because by the end of the series and the time of the posttest interview, the problems were being eliminated. There is no indication that the series produced any substantive initiatives (i.e., legislative, regulative, or budgetary) to deal with larger questions of toxic waste disposal, either on college campuses or elsewhere in the U.S. society. Thus, we call its policy impact "individualistic" because it was specific only to the particular problem documented at the University of Chicago.

DISCUSSION OF FINDINGS

With the completion of this fourth study, we are somewhat better able to compare the varying impacts of the different investigative reports. Table 4

TABLE 4

Summary of Four Case Study Findings of the Impact of Investigative Reports on the Public, Policy Elites, and Policy

Subject of Case Study	Medium	Format	Journalists' Involvement with Policymakers	General Public Impact	Elite Impact	Policymaking Impact
1. Home health care fraud and abuse ("The Home Health Hustle")	Network television	Single report	Extensive	Yes	Yes	Yes (Symbolic)
2. Assaults against women ("Rape: Every Women's Nightmare")	Local newspaper	5-part series	Minimal	No	No	Yes (Symbolic)
3. Policy brutality ("Beating Justice")	Local television	5-part series	Minimal	Yes	No	Yes (Substantive)
4. Toxic waste disposal ("Wasted Time")	Local television	3-part series	Extensive	No	Yes	Yes (Individualistic)

summarizes the results of the four case studies. Both the home health care broadcast and the police brutality television series were found to have greater *public* impact than either the toxic waste or the rape series. Nonetheless, like the police brutality series, the toxic waste investigation resulted in significant changes in the attitudes and actions of *policymakers*. The policymaking impact of the current case is the most focused. It appears to be attributable more to journalistic lobbying with Fire Department officials than to the published investigative reports themselves. This is similar to the developments that occurred in the home health care investigation, where we found that it was not the members of the public who were so aroused by the report that they pressured their representatives to act. Rather, it was the active collaboration between journalists and policymakers during the prepublication phase of investigation that generated the policy outcome. In the two other cases that we studied, no such collaboration occurred, but policy changes nonetheless resulted.

What factors account for these similarities and differences? This question probably has a different answer depending on the target of impact that one wishes to understand — on the public, on elites, or on policy itself. For public attitudes to change, two factors seem to be important — the nature of the media portrayal and the frequency of attention by the media to the issue in the past. When the media portray an issue in an unambiguous way with dramatic, convincing, and clear evidence, public attitudes are more likely to change (see also Tyler and Cook, 1984:706). For example, the police brutality series documented the seriousness of the problem thoroughly, including a statistical analysis of brutality cases against the police and a 5-year review of all lawsuits filed against police in federal courts in Chicago. Its interviews with brutalized victims and action shots of identified "villains" made for powerful drama. In all these respects, the series was most similar to the home health care television report. Both investigations had significant impacts on the public.

On the other hand, like the *Sun-Times* rape series, Channel 5's "Wasted Time" investigation was stylistically ambiguous. Villains and victims were not well-defined. Rather, the television station attributed the problem to "bureaucratic delays," not venal conduct. The harm alleged was more *potential* than actual, and the presentation of the findings contained frequent exceptions and caveats. For example, the second part of the series began with the statement by correspondent Karl that "this is not a scare story of radioactive contamination on the campus of the University of Chicago."[3]

---

[3]The script for the series "Wasted Time" is replete with statements that may have limited its impact. It refers repeatedly to the *"potential* for problems," rather than actual problems; it states that "no questions have been raised about the reported levels of radiation in various classrooms . . ."; it defines the source of the problem as "bureaucratic and academic red tape" and "a possible conflict of interest"; and admits that "plans for the structure [that would wipe out the danger] will finally be submitted to the EPA for approval" (Transcribed Manuscript, "Wasted Time,"

Moreover, the edge of the toxic waste series' potential impact may have been dulled by the simultaneous presentation of problems and their solution, which created the impression that the danger was under control. The repeated mention that a permanent solution would result from the University's construction of an inexpensive facility (which had already been planned) further circumscribed the scope of the problem.

The equivocal nature of the presentation may help to explain why there was a tendency for posttest anxiety about the problem to be reduced. It may also help to explain why respondents in the exposed groups were somewhat more likely to be " 'confused' [about] news stories about environmental problems, like chemical or toxic wastes. . . ." In sum, the actual importance or seriousness of a problem may be less significant for influencing public attitudes than its "mediated reality" (Nimmo and Combs, 1983).

The second factor that seems important for influencing general public attitudes is the nature of the issue that the media are addressing. Certain issues receive fairly consistent treatment by journalists. Their place on the news media's agenda of interests may be higher or lower at different times, but they regularly tend to be the object of reportorial scrutiny. Examples include news about crime, governmental waste and corruption, and corporate windfall profit making. Borrowing from terminology used in a somewhat different context, we call these topics "recurring issues" in the news (Walker, 1977). Investigative stories about recurring issues have lower impact potential. Media effects are limited by the routine discussion of such issues in news stories, creating an information blur that may obscure the transmission of even unique disclosures. Further, as information is accumulated about a particular issue over time, the effect of subsequent communication tends to diminish (Saltiel and Woelfel, 1975; Downs, 1972). Thus, the impact of investigative reports about rape, toxic waste, and police brutality in Chicago may have been circumscribed by their appearance in the midst of a recurring stream of news events on these subjects.

On the other hand, issues that become the subject of breakthrough news reports have a greater opportunity to produce effects. The home health care report provides an example of a "nonrecurring issue" in the news, one that has received infrequent or no prior attention from journalists. Investigative news stories about such issues have higher impact potential because they reveal matters that may be relatively unknown before their publication. The public's lack of accumulated information on these issues may increase its susceptibility to investigative media messages (Cook et al., 1983), although the effects may

---

WMAQ-TV, 13–15 May 1984). When interviewed about the reason for the wording of the script, correspondent Karl stated that "we could only say what we had. I wish we could have made it stronger, but the findings didn't allow it" (Interview by David L. Protess with Peter Karl, 4 June 1984).

Media Portrayal of Issues

		Unambiguous	Ambiguous
Frequency of Past Media Attention	Recurring Non-recurring	STRONG EFFECTS (e.g., "Home Health Hustle")	MODERATE EFFECTS (e.g., early Watergate coverage)
		MODERATE EFFECTS (e.g., "Beating Justice")	WEAK EFFECTS (e.g., "Rape . . ." & "Wasted Time")

FIGURE 1. A Typology of the Effects of Investigative Reports on Public Attitudes.

not be long-lasting (Watt and van den Berg, 1981; Saltiel and Woelfel, 1975; Downs, 1972).

We would suggest that news media investigative reports with the maximum ability to produce attitude change are those that involve unambiguous presentations of nonrecurring issues. This may explain why the home health care investigation, which spotlighted an "undiscovered" problem by showing greedy agency directors victimizing the elderly and handicapped, had the strongest public impact of the four case studies. Conversely, ambiguously presented reports on recurring issues, like the rape series and toxic waste investigation, have the least opportunity to change public attitudes.

Other types of investigative reports tend to produce in-between cases. The effects of the unambiguous police brutality series may have been delimited by the recurring nature of its subject, at least in Chicago. These kinds of investigative stories may result in significant *attitude* changes on particular items, while falling short of producing a change in the public's *agenda* priorities. We would hypothesize similar "in-between" effects for ambiguously presented, nonrecurring issues. As shown in Figure 1, it is the combination of an issue's "newness" on the media's agenda and its portrayal that may determine the impact of investigative reporting on public attitudes.[4]

Explanations for the effects of news media investigations on policy elites and on policy are more complex and less well understood. Two of the four cases showed effects on elites, and in all four cases, policymaking effects occurred. A review of the four case studies suggests that many factors may

---

[4]We recognize that other factors, including audience receptiveness to particular media messages, have been found to explain the differential effects of news stories (Graber, 1984). However, our findings here and in the previous case studies do not show statistically significant differences between respondents with varying degrees of attentiveness to the investigative reports or with differing demographic characteristics. The effects of these and other factors will be examined further in future field experiments.

influence the nature and extent of governmental responses to investigative reporting. These factors include the timing of the publication in relation to political exigencies, the extent of journalistic collaboration with policymakers, the level of general public and interest group pressures, and the availability of cost-effective solutions to the problems disclosed.

In the toxic waste series, the proximate cause of the initial governmental response was the involvement in the policymaking process of the Channel 5 correspondent. The level of involvement was sufficient to prompt an immediate effort to correct the specific problem at the University of Chicago. Likewise in the home health care case, the policy impact (legislation hearings and proposals for change) resulted from the active collaboration between journalists and policymakers (i.e., high-level staff members of the Senate Permanent Investigations Subcommittee).

In the other two cases, journalists did not orchestrate the policy impacts. In the rape study, we found that the series provided a platform for those already pushing for reform of rape legislation. Policymakers who already had proposals and programs ready to recommend before the series made their announcements soon after publication of the series, using the investigative report as a backdrop for their announcements.

In the police brutality study, the series also provided a platform but in a different way from that described above. The investigative report's results were used by Chicago mayoral challenger Harold Washington as ammunition against incumbent Mayor Jane Byrne, who had appointed the police superintendent. When elected, Washington was responsible for many of the policy changes in the police department.

Do investigative reports always result in some form of policy response? Investigative reports uncover problems in the social fabric of society. Officials directly responsible for the particular domain in which a problem is uncovered may feel obligated to take some action to show they are "responsive" and "responsible." Since our cases are small in number and are not necessarily representative of all investigative reports, we cannot generalize. However, the results to date suggest that investigative reports may have more influence than previously thought. The evidence that such reports present about social conditions serves to put policymakers on the defensive. They must either attempt to justify the problem or act to solve it. Actions—symbolic, individualistic, or substantive—are the responses seen in the cases analyzed here.

The web of influences that affect the policymaking process is intricate and variable, as are the conditions for public attitude formation. Additional case studies are necessary to identify other influential factors, and to build and refine additional models of influence. As we continue to examine investigative reporting, we will try to understand further the link between media messages, the nature of the problems that are revealed, and the opinion and policy responses to them.

REFERENCES

Anderson, D. (1976) Investigative Reporting. Bloomington: Indiana University Press.

Cook, F. L., T. R. Tyler, E. G. Goetz, M. T. Gordon, D. Leff, and H. L. Molotch (1983) "Media and agenda-setting: Effects on the public, interest group leaders, policy makers, and policy." Public Opinion Quarterly 47:16–35.

Cook, T. D., and D. T. Campbell (1979) Quasi-Experimentation: Design and Analysis Issues for Field Settings. Chicago: Rand McNally.

Downs, A. (1972) "Up and down with ecology: The 'issue attention cycle.' " Public Interest 28:38–50.

Edelman, M. (1964) The Symbolic Uses of Politics. Urbana: University of Illinois Press.

Erbring, L., E. Goldenberg, and A. Miller (1980) "Front-page news and real-world cues: A new look at agenda-setting by the media." American Journal of Political Science 24:16–49.

Graber, D. (1984) Processing the News. New York: Longman.

Hallett, J. (1984) "Issues management letter." August 1, p. 6.

Lang, G., and K. Lang (1983) The Battle for Public Opinion. New York: Columbia University Press.

Leff, D., D. Protess, and S. Brooks (1986) "Changing public attitudes and policymaking agendas." Public Opinion Quarterly 50:300–314.

MacKuen, M. B. (1981) "Social communication and the mass policy agenda." In M. B. MacKuen and S. L. Coombs, More Than News: Media Power in Public Affairs. Beverly Hills: Sage.

McCombs, M., and D. L. Shaw (1972) "The agenda-setting functions of the mass media." Public Opinion Quarterly 36:176–187.

McLeod, J. M., L. B. Becker, and J. E. Byrnes (1974) "Another look at the agenda-setting function of the press." Communication Research 1:131–166.

Mollenhoff, C. (1981) Investigative Reporting. New York: MacMillan.

Molotch, H., D. Protess, and M. T. Gordon (1987) "The media-policy connection: Ecologies of news." In D. Paletz (ed.), Political Communication: Theories, Cases, and Assessments. New Jersey: Ablex.

Nimmo, D., and J. Combs (1983) Mediated Political Realities. New York: Longman.

Protess, D. L., D. R. Leff, S. C. Brooks, and M. T. Gordon (1985) "Uncovering Rape: The watchdog press and the limits of agenda-setting." Public Opinion Quarterly 49:19–37.

Reichardt, C. S. (1979) "The statistical analysis of data from nonequivalent group designs." In T. D. Cook and D. T. Campbell, Quasi-Experimentation: Design and Analysis Issues for Field Settings. Chicago: Rand McNally.

Salisbury, H. E. (1980) Without Fear or Favor. New York: Times Books.

Saltiel, J., and J. Woelfel (1975) "Inertia in cognitive processes: The role of accumulated information in attitude change." Human Communication Research 1:333–344.

Shaw, D. L., and M. E. McCombs (eds.) (1977) The Emergence of American Political Issues: The Agenda-Setting Function of the Press. St. Paul: West Publishing Company.

Tipton, L., R. Haney, and J. Baseheart (1975) "Media agenda-setting in city and state election campaigns." Journalism Quarterly 52:15–22.

Tyler, T. R., and F. L. Cook (1984) "The mass media and judgments of risk: Distinguishing impact on personal and societal level judgments." Journal of Personality and Social Psychology 47:693–708.

Walker, J. L. (1977) "Setting the agenda in the U.S. Senate: A theory of problem selection." British Journal of Political Science 7:423–445.

Watt, J. H., Jr., and S. van den Berg (1981) "How time dependency influences media effects in a community controversy." Journalism Quarterly 58:43–50.

19 Convergent and Divergent Voice Models of the Rise and Fall of Policy Issues*

Fay Lomax Cook
Wesley G. Skogan

A growing literature in the policy sciences and in mass communications focuses on agenda-setting (i.e., how issues come to receive serious attention by authoritative decision makers). Far less attention has been given to understanding the life course of policy issues, especially the question of why issues move off policy agendas.

The number of potential policy issues far exceeds the capabilities of Congress to process them. Thus, issues must compete for a place on the policy agenda. In the competition, some issues achieve visibility and others do not. Between 1970 and 1978, the issue of crime against the elderly made it onto the Congressional agenda, also receiving attention from the news media, the federal bureaucracy, elderly interest groups, and some academic and professional publications.

Figure 1 depicts the life course of the crime against the elderly issue within (a) the news media (as exemplified by a content analysis of *The New York Times*); (b) the bureaucracy (as exemplified by the number of grants on the topic funded by Law Enforcement Assistance Administration); and (c) the relevant academic and professional communities, as indexed by publications. First to peak were accounts of crimes against the elderly in *The New York Times*. These increased from 1 in 1970 to 33 in 1973 and to 95 in 1974. The number of accounts dealing with the issue remained at about this level from

---

*This is a revised version of an article appearing in the November 1990 issue of *Government and Politics*. Reprinted by permission of the authors.

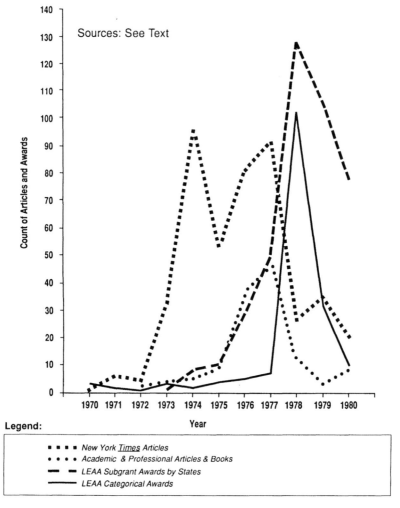

FIGURE 1. Attention to crime and the elderly by the media, the bureaucracy, and academic/professional publications.

1975 to 1977, but began to drop in 1978, although not quite to the level of 1970–1972.

The numbers of Law Enforcement Assistance Administration (LEAA) categorical awards on crime and the elderly remained low between 1970 and 1977, as did subgrant awards to states. However, in 1978, there was a tremendous spurt to 102 categorical and 128 subgrant awards related to crime and the elderly. By 1980, the number of awards granted had substantially decreased.

Figure 1 also shows the rise and fall in the number of articles in academic and professional publications. They ranged between 0 and 9 from 1970 to 1975. Then there was a sharp increase to 35 in 1976 and 47 in 1977. In 1978, the number tapered off to 13; in 1979, 3; in 1980, 8.

Figure 2 illustrates the course of the crime and the elderly issue in the U.S. Congress during the 1970s. The number of hearings ranged between 0 and 5 from 1970 to 1975. In 1976, they increased to 7; in 1977, there were 6; in 1978, 5; in 1979, 5; in 1980, only 1. The solid line in Figure 2 shows the number of times in Congress that a legislator mentioned the topic of criminal victimization of the elderly in a speech or in introducing legislation. Ranging between 0 and 3 for the years 1970–1974, Congressional mentions increased to 15 in

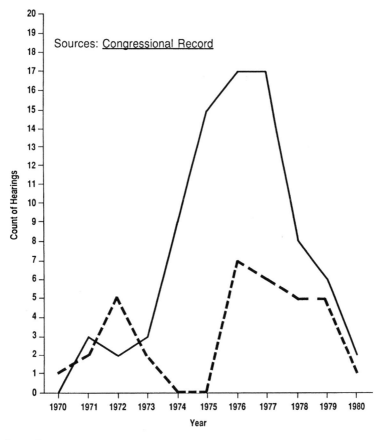

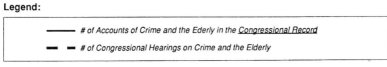

FIGURE 2.   Congressional attention to crime and the elderly.

1975, 17 in 1976, and 17 in 1977. They then began to drop somewhat: 8 in 1978, 6 in 1979, and 2 in 1980.

Thus, within one decade, the salience of the crime and the elderly issue rose and fell on the formal policy agenda of Congress, and the same is true for some agency, media, and scholarly agendas. The decline was not due to public resistance to the issue, for opinion data suggest that there was a favorable "climate" for the issue throughout this period. Indeed, a national survey conducted in 1974 for the National Council on the Aging found that 50% of all Americans thought that "fear of crime" constituted a "very serious problem" for the elderly (National Council on the Aging, 1975), whereas the same question asked in 1981 showed that 74% of the public thought fear of crime was a major concern for the elderly (National Council on the Aging, 1981). Nor was the decline due to the decrease in crimes against the elderly. Indeed, Census Bureau indicators suggest that the real level of victimization did not change for the elderly at all in the 1970s. During the period described by Figures 1 and 2, rates of criminal victimization of the elderly remained virtually unchanged (Cook & Skogan, 1984). There is no evidence that concern in Washington over this issue waned because of decreasing public concern, nor that it was driven by shifts in the actual level of the problem at hand. Rather, the dramatic ups and downs in attention and activity depicted in Figures 1 and 2 appear to be due to agenda-setting processes that are little understood.

COMING ON THE AGENDA:
A CONVERGENT VOICE MODEL

Cook (1981) developed the convergent voice model to depict how this particular policy issue arose. The model describes the rise of issues that are independently and similarly articulated by several different groups or notables both within and outside of government at about the same time. First, the model requires a "ripe" issue climate for the issue to gain salience. It is not difficult to see that criminal victimization of the elderly emerged in a ripe issue climate. The issue is fundamentally composed of three subthemes: crime, victims, and the elderly. By the early 1970s, each of these separately commanded attention. There was concern about increasing crime rates, about an undue emphasis on the rights of criminals rather than their victims, and about the health and welfare of the ever-growing number of elderly persons in America. Crime against the elderly neatly encompassed all these concerns in a single issue. Moreover, in Nelson's (1984) terms, the issue seemed to be a "valence" issue, one that elicits a "single, fairly uniform emotional response" (p. 27) from all audiences and allows only one position to be taken.

The second stage in the convergent voice model requires that multiple sources voice concern about the issue. In the case of criminal victimization of the elderly, this process of articulation occurred during 1971 and 1972. In 1971, the White House Conference on Aging recommended that "police protection of the elderly should become a top priority" (Toward a National Policy on Aging, p. 74). At about the same time—and independently of the White House Conference—a Special Committee of the U.S. Senate held hearings on housing needs of older Americans. In 1971, and extending into 1972, these hearings became re-focused on problems of crime against senior citizens, first in public housing, then in public and private housing, and finally on crimes in general against elderly people. The consensus of those who testified and those senators who participated in the hearings was expressed in Senator Williams' rhetorical questions: "Do we need any more proof that a crisis in crime exists? Do we need any more reason to act on an emergency basis?" (U.S. Congress, 1972b, p. 481). The news media helped push the issue onto the policy agenda in a series of stories appearing in the *Boston Herald,* the *Boston Globe,* and the *Hartford Courant,* which focused on crimes against elderly persons in federally funded housing. These stories were one of the impetuses to White House Conference planners to add a Special Concerns Session on "Legal Aid and the Urban Aged" and were widely quoted in the Congressional hearings.

The third stage in the convergent voice model of agenda-setting requires the legitimization of the issue. This occurred during the 1972–1975 period. First, the news media covered the issue of criminal victimization of the elderly extensively. Our content analysis of *The New York Times* coverage of crime against the elderly stories shows a dramatic increase, from 1 story in 1970 to 95 stories in 1974 about criminal victimization of the elderly. Attention to the issue by the media anticipated that by the other sectors described by Figures 1 and 2. Second, several key officials within the legislative and executive branches of government helped legitimize the issue by speaking out publicly about the elderly's problem of criminal victimization. These key officials included the President, senators, representatives, and the directors of the FBI, LEAA, and the Administration on Aging (AoA). Third, organizations of elderly persons spoke publicly about the problem and began to think about how best to attack it. Fourth, the legitimacy of the issue was enhanced by documentaiton of the problem. The AoA funded a study that examined crimes against elderly persons in Kansas City. Despite the fact that only older victims were studied, the report's conclusions made comparative statements such as, "of all persons who become targets of a criminal act, the elderly suffer most" (Cunningham, 1975, p. 6). These findings were used to back the claim that crimes against the elderly were a "crisis." This claim appeared in print (e.g., *Chicago Sun Times,* June 6, 1975, p. 1; Goldsmith & Tomas, 1974) and was widely cited at the 1975 National Conference on Crimes Against the Elderly.

The fourth stage in the model requires policy specification and program development. Beginning in 1975 (and continuing through 1978), policies and programs were proposed to deal with the problem. For example, the Crime Control Act of 1976 required that states receiving LEAA discretionary grant funds include plans for projects assisting the elderly in their state's comprehensive law enforcement plan—unless a state found the requirement inappropriate. The Victims of Crime Act of 1978 (defeated but repeatedly reintroduced) included special entitlements for elderly victims, and several bills were introduced (but not passed) calling for stiffer sentences for criminals who victimized older persons. In addition, a National Bicentennial Conference on Justice and Older Americans brought together researchers, advocates, and practitioners in 1976. The national FBI Academy added a course on the topic to its curriculum. The International Association of Chiefs of Police used LEAA funds to develop model projects to fight crime against the elderly. AoA and LEAA contributed $200,000 to demonstration projects in six cities, and both agencies sponsored pamphlets on elderly crime prevention and victim assistance. The only other positive federal action was the creation of a direct bank deposit program for Social Security and Supplemental Security Income recipients.

Clearly, the issue of criminal victimization of the elderly reached formal agenda status on the Congressional policy agenda as it moved through the stages of agenda-setting from 1970 to 1978. It emerged as an issue at a time when the elderly, crime, and victims were all "hot" topics and brought them together in one neat issue "package." It was articulated as an issue by delegates to the White House Conference on Aging, by commentators who testified at hearings before the Senate Select Committee on Aging, and by the senators at those hearings. The final spark that put the issue on the Congressional agenda was the legitimization of the issue's importance by multiple actors whose voices converged in agreeing on crimes against the elderly as an important issue about which the federal government should be concerned and act. These actors included the media, officials in federal agencies, influential Congressmembers, the President, and scholars.

After 1977, the issue declined in salience almost to the level it had prior to reaching formal agenda status. The question is why?"

GOING OFF THE AGENDA

An important feature of the decline of elderly victimizaton on the Congressional agenda was the breakdown of an early consensus about the nature of the problem. In the early 1970s, no reliable evidence was available to identify the relative magnitude and nature of the problem of crime against the elderly, thus creating opportunities for advocates to define the terms of the debate. Whatever knowledge there was came from media reports, testimonials by victims, and studies of samples of elderly victims. All left the impression that rates of victimization against the elderly were high when compared to other age groups.

The first systematic empirical evidence on the issue came from the National Crime Surveys (NCS), conducted by the Census Bureau to measure the yearly level of crime victimization in the United States. Although begun in 1973, it was not until November 1974, that an advance report on its findings for the first 6 months of 1973 was released and not until 1976 that the first full report on all of 1973 was released to the public. These data revealed that the elderly were not the most likely age group to be victimized. In fact, the opposite seemed true, for in nearly all crime categories they were the least likely age group to be victimized.

These survey-based conclusions about crime rates could not be readily ignored. It could not be claimed, for example, that the victimizations only appeared to be lower for the elderly because older persons were less likely to report crimes to the police, for the data in question did not come from police reports but from many thousands of in-person interviews conducted by Census Bureau interviewers with a random sample of Americans. As one highly placed staff member for the Select Committee on Aging said of the NCS in one of our interviews, "We didn't want to believe the data about rates. . . . We talked to several very respected criminologists and social scientists to be sure we could trust the data. They didn't tell us what we wanted to hear [i.e., that the data couldn't be trusted]. . . . They said it was good data." Thus, the highly credible and increasingly visible social science evidence undercut all the individual case studies of elderly crime victims, leaving the impression that the elderly were uniquely spared from crime rather than uniquely exposed to it. Given the robustness of the data and their ability to withstand critical scrutiny, it was difficult for advocates to argue that criminal victimization of the elderly was a significant national problem.

An early stage in Downs' (1972) "issue-attention cycle" is one of alarmed discovery and euphoric enthusiasm. At this stage, the public becomes aware of a particular problem and alarmed about it. This alarm is accompanied by an enthusiasm to solve the problem. Downs did not speculate about what might happen if, during the "alarmed discovery" stage, the public and other participants in the policymaking process are informed that the problem is not quite what they thought it was and should be redefined. Yet, this is what happened with criminal victimization of the elderly.

To examine how the issue of crime against the elderly was defined in Congress between 1970 and 1981, we used the *Congressional Record*. We coded how the problem was defined in (a) each speech that a member of Congress gave and (b) each news article or editorial that was inserted into the *Record*. At least two researchers coded each *Record* entry and revealed high levels of intercoder agreement (90%). Figure 3 shows what percentages of all discussions of crime and the elderly were about (a) rates of crime, (b) the

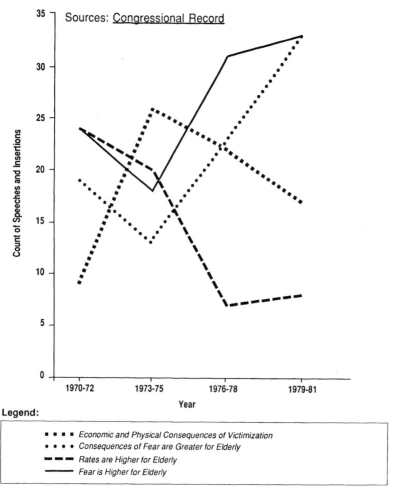

FIGURE 3.   Problem formulation and reformulation about crimes against the elderly.

economic and physical consequences of crime, (c) fear of crime, and (d) the behavioral consequences of such fear. Thus, the figure depicts the way the problem of criminal victimization of the elderly was formulated and reformulated in Congress.

In the early years, 1970–1972, the preponderance of the claims were about rates (the elderly are more likely to be victimized than other age groups) and fear (these high rates of crime make the elderly more fearful of crime than other age groups). In the period 1973–1975, early findings from the NCS began to circulate in research and policy circles, making it difficult to claim that the rates of crimes were higher against the elderly. Instead, the economic consequences of victimization experiences came to be stressed.

Steiner (1980) has noted how conflicting claims about the magnitude of a problem can make it difficult to solidify support for policy and can enable its detractors to chip away at its support. One can see that process at work in this case, as policy entrepreneurs sought to redefine the nature of the problem they were seeking to solve. The terms of the policy debate shifted. Congressman Morgan Murphy's address on the floor of Congress in 1977 illustrates a frank acknowledgment that the problem was not one of high crime rates for older Americans, but rather — as he argued — fear of crime and the possibility that crimes against the elderly have more severe physical and economic consequences:

Crime against the elderly is a problem of growing concern to senior citizens, policy officials, and legislators. *The reason is not that older persons are victimized more than other age groups or that crime against the elderly is dramatically increasing.* Rather, as a recent house study noted, it is the recognition that older Americans are financially, physically and emotionally the least able to cope with the effects of crime. Perhaps the most devastating impact of crime against the elderly is that fear that it creates (*Congressional Record,* August 2, 1977, p. E5066; italics added)

However, those who accepted the "consequences" rationale were soon on the defensive as well. Although doubts about the differential severity of consequences of victimization for the elderly had been raised earlier (Cook & Cook, 1976), it was not until 1978 that they began gaining visibility. At the hearings held by the U.S. House of Representatives Subcommittee on Aging in January of that year, research results were presented that further questioned the conventional wisdom. It was revealed that the elderly do not suffer more severe physical and economic consequences than other age groups.

As figure 3 indicated, by the 1976-1978 period, the problem most often mentioned in connection with crime against the elderly was not the problem of rates or consequences. Rather it was that the elderly were believed to be the group most fearful of crime. In testimony before the House Select Committee on Aging in 1978, the Associate Administrator of LEAA noted this, and its effects on the policy debate:

While statistics indicate that the elderly are victimized less frequently than other age groups, such statistics do not convey the effect of crime on older persons — their despair, depression, worry, and fear. In fact, the statistics tend to dilute emphasis and urgency for affirmative action in this area. (U.S. Congress, June 3, 1978, pp. 103)

The fear rationale was on a firmer footing than others, for many surveys available in 1975 showed higher fear levels among the elderly. The major difficulty with the fear formulation was that it was not intuitively as important as rationales for action based either on uniquely high victimization rates or on a disproportionate degree of financial and physical harm. Indeed, the lower rates of victimization among the elderly made the fear rationale vulnerable to the charge that the fear in question was "irrational." Although the fear rationale has remained salient to this day and little disconfirming evidence has been widely circulated, it is a rationale without obvious effective remedy. Short of accomplishing the seemingly impossible task of significantly reducing the crime rate, how does one reduce the elderly's fear of crime?

We have seen that over the decade of the 1970s, the problem of crime and the elderly was given at least three different formulations, each emphasized at a different time. One major impetus for these reformulations was descriptive research results coming from a government-financed national data collection system (the NCS) that provided the capacity to test claims being made to justify attention to the problem. NCS data suggested that important elements in the "common consensus" about crime were wrong, indicating that the problem for the elderly was neither one of rates nor of physical or economic consequences. Thus, the sands of the debate shifted, with the shifts serving to make the problem of crime and the elderly seem less important.

Bureaucratic Involvement Declined

An often overlooked factor in the Congressional agenda-setting literature is executive agency involvement in an issue (for an exception see Nelson, 1978, 1984). For an issue to remain salient on the legislative agenda, it can be important that one or more agencies give it special attention (e.g., by funding research or demonstration projects, preparing information for distribution to the public or Congress, and providing testimony in Congressional hearings). This is a form of "recurring maintenance" described by Nelson (1984) that helps sustain interest in an emerging problem.

The two relevant agencies for crime against the elderly were the Administration on Aging (AoA) and the Law Enforcement Assistance Administration (LEAA). They were each interested enough in the crime and the elderly issue that in 1976 they collaborated in funding demonstration projects in six cities in an attempt to reduce the impact of crime against the elderly. Each agency also independently funded research studies and demonstration programs related to the crime and elderly issue as well as major national conferences on crime and the elderly.

Nonetheless, their initial involvement in the issue did not persist. LEAA was the federal agency with the most resources for dealing with crimes against the elderly. But LEAA was also the agency with the most intimate knowledge of the findings of the NCS. As early as 1975, LEAA and FBI officials were saying in public that crime rates against the elderly were lower than against other groups. Knowledge of the negative relationship between age and the likelihood of victimization served to slow the momentum toward action. So, too, did widespread belief within the agency that targeting the elderly might not have much impact on crime and, moreover, that the business of the federal government was to prevent crime and improve the criminal justice system for all Americans, not just for the elderly. Figure 1 documented how sharply LEAA state-level and federal categorical grants dropped off after their peak in 1978.

Bureaucratic involvement in the issue of crimes against the elderly declined because countervailing agency priorities emerged in each of the agencies reducing the motivation to fight for this issue. Arthur Fleming, the Commissioner of Aging from the early 1970s to 1976, was extremely interested in the problem of crime against older people. But in 1977 a new commissioner on aging, Robert Benedict, was appointed by recently elected President Carter. Like Secretary of HEW Joseph Califano, Benedict's primary concern was reducing health-care costs, and the priority issue on his mind was home health care. One former official reminded us laughingly in an interview, "Remember, also, that the crime issue was an NIH issue for the new commissioner [NIH means Not Invented Here], and incoming administrators want to deal with new issues." Resources were not "slack" in either AoA or LEAA (Nelson, 1978; Walker, 1977). Alone, these facts may not have caused AoA to relegate criminal victimization of the elderly to a lower priority, for civil servants there continued to be interested in the issue. However, combined with the NCS data showing that the elderly did not have a special problem in regard to crime, these events made it easier to give higher priority to other issues.

Countervailing priorities also existed within LEAA. By the mid-1970s, efforts were afoot to shift the focus of the agency in the direction of emphasizing efficiency and fairness in the processing of criminal defendents, rather than continuing to try to get the national crime rate down. One result of this re-focus would be that the police, prosecutors, and judges would become the principal "targets" of the agency's money (then approaching $1 billion a year); with this new direction, agency officials believed they would be more able to demonstrate measurable accomplishments than they did while pursuing their previous goal of reducing crime.

A Cohesive Policy Community Failed to Develop

Active policy communities are important in maintaining an issue on the agenda. The last two decades in the United States have witnessed the formation of communities of experts around problems such as vocational education, water pollution control, or judicial administration (Heclo, 1978).

Policy communities are made up of persons involved in the politics and policymaking of a restricted policy area (Walker, 1977). It is among such networks that policy issues tend to be defined, the relevant evidence debated, and alternative options worked out.

The loose policy grouping around the crime and the elderly issue never developed into a cohesive community. This was not due to lack of available opportunities. The 1975 National Conference on Crimes Against the Elderly brought together agency officials from the Law Enforcement Assistance Administration and the Administration on Aging, members of the U. S. Congress, practitioners in the aging and law enforcement areas, and social scientists. So did the 1976 Conference on Justice and Older Americans. Yet these different persons and relevant groups never joined forces in any meaningful way. Why was this?

There seemed to be two major and related reasons. First, there was little agreement about a solution to the problem; the shifting issue of crime and the elderly never got hooked up in a realistic way to a limited set of plausible federal policy alternatives on which all could reach consensus. It was not clear where the federal government could target the problem — at the street level, by increasing the number of policemen on the beat in areas with a higher percentage of elderly persons? In courtrooms, by having elderly "court watchers" monitor each case of a person accused of victimizing an elderly person? At the sentencing and prison levels, by enacting mandatory stiff sentences for criminals who victimized an elderly person? Or should the federal government push crime prevention education programs for the elderly? Or is the proper focus to work on target-hardening strategies (i.e., installing locks and bars on elderly persons' homes)? Or should there be legislation to compensate financially the elderly victim of crime? All of these proposals were made by members of what could be called the policy community. However, advocates for the elderly could never join in supporting one or two specific and seemingly substantial programs. Thus, a dizzying number of alternative actions was proposed, around which no consensus emerged.

The second, and related, roadblock to the development of a policy community was the widely perceived intractability of the problem of crime against the elderly to any practical solution. We do not have ways of combating crime that are simple, demonstrably effective, and congruent with democratic values. It could not be documented that any of the proposed programs for the elderly actually would work, although that might not have been fatal had any of the proposed programs seemed plausible enough to make a significant dent in any of the shifting definitions of the issue. In this respect, criminal victimization of the elderly was quite different from other "technically solvable" problems in the aging policy arena, problems such as home health care for which solutions apparently are clear and the divisive issues are money and personnel. A truly cohesive policy community for the crime and the elderly issue never emerged to coordinate activities, to press for one policy alternative, or to advocate continued study of the problem.

Media Attention Declined

As was shown in Figure 1, media attention to the problem of crimes against older adults declined markedly beginning in 1978. Why did this occur? Crime news is "easy news" (Gordon & Heath, 1981). It is cheap to obtain, and can be turned up predictably whenever an exciting "filler" story is needed. Information about individual crimes is readily available; the basic facts are contained in records conveniently available to reporters from the police; and police officers are accepted by reporters' editors as credible, reliable sources. Crime news sells newspapers because it is dramatic and exciting. As one intern was told, "bad news, good story; good news, bad story" (Tuck, cited in Gordon & Heath, 1981, p. 232).

Crime against the elderly has, therefore, the potential to generate press coverage of dramatic individual incidents of crime that can become interesting brief stories or dramatic features, even if crime against the elderly is not on the increase. All that is required are dramatic criminal events with elderly victims. However, as it became more widely known that the Census Bureau found low rates of victimization and no distinctive consequences of crime for the elderly, stories about crime and the elderly became less clear and easy to tell. There were still dramatic individual stories, but when reporters called participants in the policy community for material (e.g., to help them document a "national trend"), they often got mixed signals. Both the current authors (and other researchers they know) can personally attest to the confusion of reporters and television editors who called us for background information and for help in identifying "what the story is." Journalists' confusion about the large facts surely contributed to some of them devoting less attention to criminal victimization of the elderly and made the issue harder to depict in responsible media outlets.

The Legislative Fate of the Issue

By the early 1980s, proponents of a legislative attack on the problem of crime against the elderly realized that it was difficult to make a valid case that elderly adults were "special" victims. Advocates for older adults believed that fear of crime was a special problem but realized the difficulty of devising credible policies and programs directed toward fear. As a result, representatives of aging interest groups (National Council of Senior Citizens and the National Retired Teachers Association/American Association of Retired Persons) began to work with the staff of the Senate Special Committee on Aging to develop age-neutral legislation that focused on all victims, regardless of their age – the Victim's Protection (S. 2420) and the Victim's Compensation Bill (S. 704). The idea was that victim protection and compensation programs aimed at all victims would "trickle down" to help elderly adults in need. Some observers also thought that focusing on all victims would mobilize broader based support for action.

The Victim's Compensation Bill did not pass, but the Victim's Protection Bill became the Omnibus Victim's Protection Act of 1982 (PL 97-291). It amends Rule 32 of the Federal Rules of Criminal Procedure to (a) require that pre-sentence reports contain information assessing the impact on and cost to any person who was a victim of a federal offense and (b) authorize federal courts to order the defendant to make restitution for any offense. Further, it directs the Attorney General to develop federal guidelines for the fair treatment of crime victims and witnesses, including ensuring that victims receive prompt social and medical services. In contrast to the rhetoric associated with the crime and the elderly issue, and in comparison to the programs that were suggested along the way, this was – to say the least – a minor legislative response.

GOING OFF THE AGENDA:
A DIVERGENT VOICE MODEL

Based on this analysis of the decreasing salience of the crime against the elderly issue, we propose a general model of issue decline on the Congressional policy agenda. Figure 4 summarizes the divergent voice model of issue decline.

First, a strong and credible counter voice emerges that challenges the accepted formulation of the issue. For an issue that is already on an institutional agenda, seems universally supported, and offers obvious symbolic political advantages to then decline in salience, something must happen that convincingly redefines the issue, undermines the consensus, and makes problematic its apparent political advantage. There are a variety of potential "voices" in the policy process. Interest group theory would have us look for the reactive mobilization of elites and organizations whose interests are threatened by the progress of an issue or who want to capture for their own purposes those resources that are targeted at some other issue. Americans' recent affection for "investigative journalism" suggests that prominant negative attention by the media may serve as an effective "divergent voice," although some research on how the journalistic enterprise really works in this regard suggests that such "investigations" are not necessarily independent of government interests (Cook et al., 1983). In the present case study, the divergent voice was provided by the circulation of research findings. The data were collected by the U. S. Census Bureau for a research arm of the Justice Department. The results of these surveys were widely available in technical reports, were cited

A Model of Issue Decline on Policy Agendas[1]

FIGURE 4.   A Model of Issue Decline on Policy Agendas.

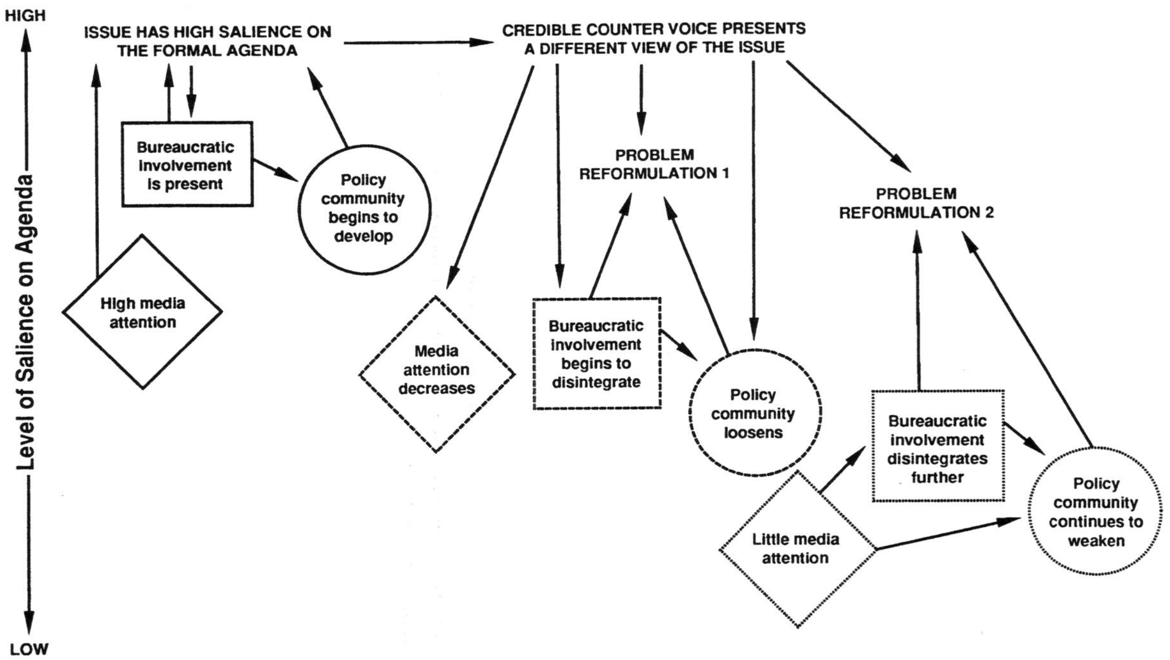

[1] The model attempts to show that issues can decline in salience on policy agendas due to the interaction of five factors, with the first factor being the precipitating factor: (1) a strong and credible counter voice (such as social science data or a well organized, articulate opposition group) emerges showing the problem to be less severe than commonly believed; (2) the problem as originally defined undergoes reformulation again and again; (3) bureaucratic involvement of federal agencies does not continue at a high level; (4) a cohesive policy community interested in ameliorating the problem fails to develop; and (5) attention from the mass media decreases

203

heavily by researchers, and came to the attention of the media. What they revealed did not square with the succession of definitions of "the problem."

The critical issue is what happens next. The key actors are the executive branch agencies, participants in the policy community, and the media. If the involvement of the relevant bureaucratic agencies begins to disintegrate in the face of the attack on the problem; if policy community interest in ameliorating the problem loses its cohesiveness or does not develop; and if media attention declines, thus not continuing to fuel public and political interest in the issue, it will begin to die. One response of those who want action taken on the issue usually will be to reformulate the problem. This will work only if that new formulation closes the fatal wound opened by the counter voice. Most issues go through some redefinition as they are tested in the heat of the policy debate, but they survive only if they can retain or rekindle bureaucratic agency, policy community, and media interest.

Bureaucratic involvement in nascent issues is important to an issue's life but is sometimes fickle. Agency officials want to be seen as working on important problems, and typically many issues are jockeying for a finite amount of attention. Consequently, their attention has to be selective. Some problems are never treated in serious fashion, or the initial interest in them wanes as other issues come to command attention due to (a) media pressures, (b) the responsiveness of the bureaucracy to the legislative agenda, or (c) the need new senior bureaucrats often feel to impose their own agendas and to neglect the agendas of their predecessors. If, in the face of a divergent voice, the relevant agencies treat the problem in less serious fashion, lose some of their interest in it, and reduce their level of involvment in the issue, this declining bureaucratic attention will contribute to a decline of an issue's prominence on the legislative agenda as well.

A credible counter voice may be a necessary condition for an issue to decline on agency "must" lists, but it is not sufficient. For example, in the early 1970s much concern existed about teenage drinking, and spokespersons of the National Institute on Alcohol Abuse and Alcoholism (NIAAA) claimed that drinking of alcohol among teenagers was increasing at a faster rate than ever before and that it constituted a severe problem. Even when credible social science data emerged showing that the prevalence of alcohol use among teenagers had remained stable over the past 10 years, NIAAA maintained its rhetoric about the severity of the problem because the "problem" was important to the mission of the agency (Chauncy, 1980). On the other hand, agency reorganization and political considerations quite unrelated to the substance of its mission can divert bureaucratic attention from an issue and undermine its agenda status for reasons having nothing to do with the problem at hand (Nelson, 1984). But for an issue to remain high on the national policy agenda, the federal agencies must be interested and concerned about the issue.

Next, policy communities also are important in maintaining issues on the agenda. It is among the networks of group representatives, interested legislative and agency staff, editors of journals and magazines, hardware vendors, potential contract recipients, consultants employed by research and development firms, and academic specialists that form around issues that the relevant evidence is distributed and debated and policy alternatives are worked out. They play an important role in defining the credibility of the emergent counter voice, and when it undermines their interest in a particular issue, its days on the policy agenda are numbered.

The interest of federal agencies can have an independent effect on the development of policy communities, as well as vice versa. For example, agencies can fuel issues by funding research carried out by academics and by funding demonstration programs overseen by interest groups. In fact, in a survey of 564 interest groups, Walker (1983) found that government agencies are important patrons of many interest groups — including groups of interested academics whose welfare depends on a particular problem — and that after 1945 the proportion of groups in the not-for-profit sector started up with government grants more than tripled. He noted that "patrons are not likely to support groups for any purposes that do not share their general approach to public policy" (p. 401). If bureaucratic support decreases, actors within the policy community often begin to lose interest in a particular policy issue, especially if they have other issues to which they can turn their attention.

Finally, the role of the mass media is important to the extended life course of policy issues. During the last decade, interest has developed among mass communication researchers in the influence of the print and electronic media on policy agendas (Cook at al., 1983; Lang & Lang, 1981; McCombs & Shaw, 1972; Protess et al., 1987; Shaw & McCombs, 1977; also see review of literature in Roberts & Bachen, 1981). There appear to be important linkages — of debatable magnitude, to be sure — between the mass media and the development of the legislative agenda. However, less attention has been paid by communication researchers to the linkage between media attention and issue decline.

The mass media always are on the alert for dramatic, personalized stories that will command public attention. There is an ample supply of potential stories of this nature nestled in almost any social problem, ranging from malnutrition to emergency-room malfeasance; as a result, portraits of individual miseries provide them with "easy news." The frequency with which these human interest stories appear is affected by such factors as organizational needs (to fill empty space), the cost of gathering them (which is lower when they appear in the wire services), and fashion (what are the "quality papers" carrying?). Studies of the varying frequency with which newspaper and television crime stories appear over time or across jurisdictions document that crime coverage has little to do with the frequency or nature of local crime *problems* at all (Antunes & Hurley, 1977; Cohen & Young, 1973; Dolminick, 1973; Fishman, 1978; Jones, 1976).

However, to link together individual instances of a problem in order to document a major trend, or to peg them to incipient policy responses, the media need to reach out to "experts" and politicians in policy communities. It is at this point that the existence of a credible divergent voice can matter. It makes it more difficult for reporters to cite "authorities," cast broad generalizations, and draw conclusions with the simple clarity that their audience requires. If competing topics do seem to admit to clear conclusions and apparent policy consensus, those stories will be easier to tell. The divergent voice model of issue decline posits that, just as the media can play a role in increasing the salience of issues on the policy agenda, so it can have a role in the declining salience of issues.

V THE MEDIA AGENDA

Most discussions of agenda-setting are about the influence of the news media on the agenda of the public. Usually, it is the agenda of issues facing the country, but sometimes it is an agenda consisting of political candidates or the attributes of these candidates. Nevertheless, McCombs and Shaw never intended that this concept about the transfer of salience should be limited to a single aspect of the mass communication process. Because of the strong interest in mass media effects that prevailed in 1968, the media/audience interface was simply a compelling starting point to explore this new perspective. In recent years, some scholars have shifted their attention to earlier points in the mass communication process.

The keystone of this new work is the news media agenda. Several aspects of this expanded work on agenda-setting are previewed here. "Who sets the media's agenda?," asks Judy VanSlyke Turk. She examines how much influence the public information offices of six state government agencies have on the news content of the eight major daily newspapers in Louisiana. There is strong support for agenda-setting in the results. News content does reflect the agenda of the news releases. Turk's findings set the stage for discussion of two important topics in journalism: the effectiveness of public relations and the dependency of the news media on their sources.

A major source of national news, of course, is the president of the United States. Numerous books about the Washington press corps assert that the president is the nation's number one newsmaker. If this is so, then is the president a major agenda-setter for national issues? Sheldon Gilberg and his colleagues examine one of the president's major television appearances, the annual State of the Union address, which is delivered before a joint session of Congress with members of the Cabinet, Supreme Court, and diplomatic corps present. Not only is it a major presidential speech, it is really the only occasion that the president presents a systematic agenda of national priorities. Contrary to the original hypothesis, the Gilberg et al. study finds that the press set President Carter's agenda. Was this unique to the Carter presidency?

Another version of the question, "Who sets the media's agenda?", has revived interest in the flow of stories and story ideas among the news media. News sources, such as the president and state government agencies, are important in setting the tone of the daily news. But these sources have direct contact with only a few journalists. The news agenda of the local newspaper or the local television station is more likely to be influenced by the play of stories in elite newspapers, such as *The New York Times,* and by the daily diet of news offered to local news outlets by the wire services.

This revival of gatekeeping research is extended by Charles Whitney and Lee Becker's study of 52 Ohio newspaper and television journalists whose duties regularly include selecting wire service stories. This experimental study, based on two versions of a typical day's file of stories available on the wire, yields strong evidence for agenda-setting. These new studies significantly shift the focus in gatekeeping research. Previous research looked for characteristics of wire editors, such as attitudes and opinions, that shape their decisions on which stories to select. The agenda-setting paradigm shifts attention to environmental influences that affect the selection of stories from the wire.

Other major news organizations, such as *The New York Times* and *Washington Post,* also influence the play of topics on the news agenda. Stephen Reese and Lucig Danielian examine the leadership role of five major newspapers, the three TV networks, *Time* and *Newsweek* in the 1986 news coverage of the cocaine problem, a topic that also occupied a prominent position on the public agenda and the Congressional agenda that year. Taking the lead in placing the cocaine story on the press agenda was *The New York Times.* Although the frequent agenda-setting role of the *Times* is part of contemporary journalism mythology, Reese and Danielian are among the first scholars to document this role with precise, quantitative evidence.

In preparing the daily agenda, editors do considerably more than make decisions about what topics will be covered and presented. They also make critical decisions about how these topics will be presented. In other words, editors determine the frame of reference for a story. As Wenmouth Williams,

Mitchell Shapiro, and Craig Cutbirth note, how a story is framed has significant effect on its agenda-setting impact. For example, when network news stories about major public issues are explicitly framed as presidential campaign issues there is significant agenda-setting. In the absence of an explicit campaign frame, there is no evidence of agenda-setting. Merely reporting an issue is not enough. It must be explicitly identified as relevant to the public agenda of campaign issues.

Fields of research evolve over time. The agenda of the news media recently has become a principal focus of attention in the agenda-setting process. Concern with the effects of mass communication is far less dominant now than it was in the late 1960s when McCombs and Shaw designed the original agenda-setting study in Chapel Hill. Increasingly, scholars and students are concerned with the messages of the mass media. One is tempted to say that the field has come full circle because content analysis of newspaper stories is one of the oldest lines of research in journalism and mass communication, dating back to Malcolm Willey's *The Country Newspaper* published in 1926. But a more apt expression would be "come full spiral." Those early content analyses were descriptions based largely on common sensical categories. Contemporary studies of the media agenda have greater depth and take an analytical view of mass media messages. These studies inform a theoretically based criticism of journalism and advance our understanding of the agenda-setting process and public opinion.

20 Public Relations' Influence on the News*

Judy VanSlyke Turk

The world the public sees through the mass media's eyes is not a mirror image of reality, nor a true picture of events, people, places and issues. The media's news window on the world is, instead, a reflection of the media's own construction of reality.[1]

The media provide their own account of reality, a pseudo-environment of "a background and setting in which a few objects and selected attributes are highlighted."[2] Therefore, the information presented in the media, and the importance the media attach to this information, can be interpreted as the media's agenda of what is important.

But how does this construction of reality come into being? Who and what helps to set the media agenda?

Individuals working for media organizations do decide what gets on the agenda of important "news" presented to the public in media content. Even more of an influence on the media news agenda are the values shared by those engaged in the craft of journalism.[3] And there is no denying the power of the deadline or of the size of the "news hole" in influencing what is included in media content.

Even though journalists and the conventions of the media for which they work play a role in shaping the media agenda, the sources of the raw material of information upon which journalists rely may ultimately have as much to do

*Reprinted from the *Newspaper Research Journal* (1986, Vol. 7, No. 4, pp. 15-27) by permission of the author.

with the media's agenda as the selection processes of the journalists themselves.

As Gandy notes, the interaction between journalist and source is what "makes" news:

> Whereas the journalist selects from an array of sources and events on the basis of perceived utility in producing news that will meet organizational requirements, sources select from an even wider array of information and techniques for conveying that information on the basis of perceived effectiveness in being covered, reported and transmitted in the right form, at the right time, and in the right channel . . .[4]

Sources from all walks of organizational life provide information on which journalists rely for their news coverage of the days' events. But journalists perhaps depend most heavily for information on one particular group of sources — government information officials — because the complexity of government makes it difficult for reporters to adequately "cover" government themselves:

> So vast and complicated is the operation of government today . . . the press would find it virtually impossible to perform even its basic function without the assistance of the growing army of government information officers.[5]

This study, conducted in 1984 and 1985, examined the assistance one group of government information officers — the public information officers (PIOs) for six state agencies in Louisiana — provided to eight Louisiana daily newspapers in covering state government news. The study measured the influence these PIOs had on the agenda of news reported about their agencies.

RESEARCH QUESTIONS AND ASSUMPTIONS

The purpose of the study was to examine how much influence state government PIOs had on daily newspaper content through the handouts of information they provided journalists.

Several assumptions about the relationship between journalists and public information officers were tested:

Assumption 1: When provided with information in news releases or other public relations "handouts" from government public information officers, daily newspaper gatekeepers are more likely to use than to discard that information.

Although Jeffers suggests reporters and public information officers are at philosophical odds, with reporters viewing publicists as "obstructionists" to obtaining full "truth,"[6] it's clear that journalists nevertheless *do* use the information contained in news releases and other public information "handouts."

Fishman, for instance, noted that journalists, in an attempt to make their information-gathering more efficient, view society as bureaucratically structured, and rely on "official" points of view for what they include in their news reports.[7] Gandy noted bureaucratic, official sources of information are frequently used by journalists because those sources are viewed as reliable.[8]

And several researchers have concluded that news releases substantially influence news media stories even though not all news releases are published. Cutlip[9] found 35% of newspaper content came from public relations handouts, while Martin and Singletary[10] reported 59% of one organization's news releases generated at least one newspaper article.

Assumption 2: The most important factor in a daily newspaper's decision to accept or reject a news release or other "handout" it receives from a public information officer is whether the information conforms to craft newsworthiness norms of oddity/conflict, prominence, significance and timeliness.

There is considerable support for the notion that newsworthiness is the most frequently-used "test" of whether raw information should be turned into a news story. Harris, for instance, found editors discarded publicity releases because the releases contained too few facts, did not deal with timely information or did not contain "new" information.[11]

Gans, while noting available space or staff and deadline pressures also influenced media gatekeepers' selection decisions, concluded newsworthiness was the primary test of whether information was usable.[12]

Assumption 3: The agenda of activities and issues presented in PIO handouts turns up as the subsequent agenda of activities and issues covered by the media.

While Newsom found that a group's agenda of issues, as reflected in its internally generated media (newsletters and annual reports), was different from the agenda of issues presented by the media,[13] there is considerable support for the notion that the agendas of news sources and the media are congruent.

Erbring, Goldenberg and Miller noted a nation's political agenda typically includes the same issues that receive substantial attention in the news media,[14] and McCombs, Gilbert and Eyal found that to be the case when comparing presidential agendas in State of the Union addresses and subsequent media coverage.[15]

Weaver and Elliott, in a comparison of city council agendas and media coverage, found the news coverage generally reflected the council's agenda.[16]

And Hale, comparing press releases and newspaper coverage of court decisions, found newspapers emphasized the same types of decisions as the court's own news releases.[17]

Assumption 4: Public information officers with state agencies who view their role as providers of persuasive "propaganda" serving the interests of their agencies are less successful in getting their news releases and other "handouts" into print than are PIOs who view themselves merely as providers of "straight," "objective" information.

Journalists, who often carp that government public information officers are "flacks" who try to control the press and who try to disguise propaganda as fact,[18] might be expected to place greater trust in information from PIOs who don't seem to be trying to selfishly persuade either media or public.

RESEARCH METHODS

Both quantitative and qualitative methods were used to examine the hypothesized relationships between the media's agenda and the agenda of state government agencies.

The media agenda examined was the editorial content of the newspapers. Agency agendas were the information PIOs provided newspapers. Both were measured through content analysis. How and why PIOs disseminated information and why the media did or didn't use that information also were studied through interviews and observation.

A period of eight weeks, from Sept. 16 through Nov. 10, 1984, was the time frame for content analysis of both newspaper stories and the information provided by agency PIOs to the media.

Six of 17 cabinet-level departments of the State of Louisiana were selected to represent government agencies: agriculture, commerce and industry, justice, public safety, revenue and taxation, and the secretary of state's office. These six agencies provided a cross-section of public relations "styles" or philosophies.

Eight daily newspapers in three Louisiana cities were selected to represent the media: morning, afternoon and Sunday papers in Baton Rouge; an all-day and a Sunday newspaper in New Orleans; and morning, afternoon and Sunday papers in Shreveport. These cities (New Orleans with more than one million, Baton Rouge with almost 500,000 and Shreveport with almost 400,000) account for almost half of the state's population.

These cities also presented another advantage of residents having access to newspapers both in the morning and in the evening. All three cities also have Sunday newspapers.

The newspapers studied also have the largest circulations among daily newspapers in Louisiana, and all have full-time correspondents at the Louisiana State Capitol in Baton Rouge whose primary, if not sole, responsibility is providing news on the activities of state government.

ANALYSIS OF AGENCY INFORMATION PROVIDED

The six Louisiana state agencies disseminated a total of 444 information handouts to the eight Louisiana daily newspapers during the eight-week study period. The Department of Justice public information officer was the most active, providing 121 news releases and other handouts, and the Department of Revenue and Taxation's PIO was least active, disseminating only seven during the period.

Reporters working for Baton Rouge newspapers—the *Morning Advocate* and the *State-Times*—received more public relations handouts, 106 and 107 respectively, than their colleagues at either New Orleans or Shreveport papers. The three Sunday newspapers received the least public relations information— only five of the total 444 subsidies.

Public information officers and journalists offered similar plausible explanations for this distribution. Because Baton Rouge is the state capitol, almost all state government is *local* news, and therefore fits readily into the Baton Rouge newspapers' view of news as local, close-to-home occurrences.

For New Orleans and Shreveport papers, the local angle was much less automatic. Public information officers said they rarely sent information to Shreveport or New Orleans journalists unless the information either had obvious statewide impact or a specific local appeal to Shreveport or New Orleans newspaper audiences.

The majority of informational handouts (78%) originated with the public information officers—that is, the PIOs volunteered the information without a specific request from the journalists. Included in those PIO-initiated subsidies were 215 written news releases, 8 news conferences, 5 face-to-face conversations with journalists, 27 copies of agency documents and 20 telephone calls to reporters.

Information provided at the request of journalists resulted from 143 telephone queries from reporters and 26 requests from journalists, made either by telephone or in person, for specific agency records or documents.

Almost half of all public relations information was provided in written news release form. And for some agencies the percentage was even higher: almost 80% for the Departments of Commerce and Industry and Agriculture. Agency PIOs said they prefer written handouts over other methods because the written releases can be prepared and disseminated efficiently, and serve as a permanent, written record of just what information was given to journalists.

The PIOs acknowledge some journalists probably would rather receive a quick phone call than a written release, and agree that press conferences, with the opportunity for journalists to ask questions, might permit more give-and-take between source and media.

The largest number of releases and other handouts (94 or 21%) dealt with election campaigns and politics, while the issue focus of the smallest number (13, or 4%) was recreation, culture and tourism, as shown in Table 1.

When the information was initiated by a PIO, it was most likely to deal with public safety or criminal matters, probably because so many releases were issued by the Department of Public Safety which by its very policy mandate concentrates its activities in this issue area. When information was provided in response to a reporter's request, the subject addressed was most likely to be election campaigns and politics.

The data indicate despite the PIOs' claims they try to disseminate only information with local impact and interest — because they know that's what journalists define as newsworthy — there was little attempt to localize the information provided to these newspapers.

The same news release, for instance, was generaly made available to *all* newspapers, whether there was a specific local angle or not. The same news releases or telephone calls went to journalists at *each* of the newspapers in more than 6 of 10 instances.

Information viewed as appropriate and newsworthy for one of the newspapers — *any* one of the newspapers — was viewed equally appropriate for all in most cases, although the Department of Public Safety and the Secretary of State's Office were more likely than the other agencies to localize their information.

The PIOs did better at living up to their claims of using timeliness — present-day impact — as a news criterion. More than 70% of the handouts dealt with events that occurred within the 24 hours prior to release, although a glaring exception was a news release issued by the Secretary of State's Office

TABLE 1
Issue Categories Addressed by Subsidies

Issue Category	# of Subsidies (A = 444)	% of Subsidies*
Election Campaigns and Politics	94	21%
Economics and Finance	80	18
Environment and natural resources	37	8
Public health	70	16
Public Safety and Criminal Matters	89	20
Recreational, Culture and Tourism	13	3
Ceremonial Events and Celebrations	19	4
Administrative and Personnel Actions	42	9

*Does not add to 100% because of rounding.

about a groundbreaking for a new state archives building that was released to newspapers three days after the event had taken place.

In disseminating information to newspaper journalists, the PIOs hoped to influence newspaper content — the media's agenda. They acted on the assumption their information would be used by journalists in stories because it was free and so easily available.

Was their assumption warranted? That question can be at least partially answered by examining newspaper use of PIO-provided information.

USE OF PIO INFORMATION

Analysis of stories published in the eight Louisiana newspapers, supplemented by "memory-recall" interviews with state capitol correspondents for each of the newspapers, showed the newspapers used information from 225, or 51%, of the 444 information contacts they had with an agency PIO.

The PIOs therefore were successful slightly more than half the time in gaining newspaper publication of the information they provided in news releases and other public relations handouts.

Use of these 225 handouts resulted in the publication of 183 separate news stories, or 48% of all 383 stories the newspapers published about the six agencies during the eight-week period.

Discrepancy between the number of *subsidies* used and number of *stories* that used PIO information can be explained at least in part by the fact that several published stories included information from more than one news release or telephone call.

For example, a news release on proposed amendments to the Louisiana constitution was combined into just one story with two other election/political issue news releases, one on projected voter turnout for the amendment election and the other on first-time use of computerized vote tallying in that election.

This practice of using information from multiple releases in one story was not uncommon among the journalists studied. All indicated that "use" of information frequently meant the information would be combined with other available information to create one story.

The published stories about state agencies which could not be traced back to a PIO handout — 200 of them — were based on information provided by someone other than an agency PIO.

Other sources *outside* the six agencies, such as a legislative or judicial source within government or a source with a private-sector organization, provided the information used in 151 of those stories that did not use public relations information. The rest were based on information the journalists obtained from an agency official other than the PIO. . . .

REASONS FOR USE OR REJECTION

Inquiry into the reasons PIO-provided information was used or rejected by newspapers in this study indicates newsworthiness was the most important consideration 82% of the time. The to-use or not-to-use decision on 365 of the 444 information handouts received was based on whether journalists judged the information to be timely, important to the public and readers, a report of unusual as opposed to routine happenings or a report involving prominent individuals or organizations.

Organizational considerations of space, available resources (staff), "management" policy as to how someone or something should be treated and deadline pressures were a factor in only 18% of their information-selection decisions, journalists said.

Newsworthiness' importance was even more clear when the information used was examined separately from that which was rejected. Journalists said newsworthiness was the deciding factor for virtually every bit of public relations information they used. Fewer than 1% of the subsidies used were accepted because of other types of considerations.

The specific criterion of newsworthiness journalists cited most often as justification for accepting or rejecting information from PIOs was presence or absence of a local angle. If there *was* a local angle, or some local impact, the information got used, according to journalists. But if there wasn't, the subsidy was discarded as non-news.

Some information was rejected primarily because it wasn't timely—the information was "old" or "stale," according to journalists.

Journalists seemed to apply the same to-use, not-to-use selection criteria to both agency-initiated subsidies and to those subsidies resulting from a reporter's specific request for information. While newsworthiness might seem almost a "given" in reporter-requested information (information volunteered without a journalist's cue might get tougher scrutiny), that was not the case. Newsworthiness criteria were applied in decisions affecting 93% of the agency-initiated information and 92% of the reporter-requested information.

PIO INFLUENCE ON THE MEDIA'S AGENDA

As the data show, about half the information provided by these PIOs to daily newspapers was used in subsequently-published news stories. Half of their news releases and other information handouts were "used" by the newspapers to which they provided information. Almost half the news stories written about these state agencies included information provided to journalists by the PIOs.

But how well did the PIOs do in making newspaper content different from what it might have been without the information they provided? Several tendencies emerge from closer examination of the data.

At first glance, there seems to be a positive relationship between the volume of information provided by a PIO and how much of that information was used in newspaper coverage of his agency. After all, the Department of Justice, which provided the largest number of information handouts, was the subject of the largest number of subsidized stories.

But it is important to remember a public relations practitioner's information, even though it might be used, is not necessarily the *only* information used in writing news stories about the organization he represents. Even though the PIO may be successful in "placing" his information in newspaper stories, a newspaper may publish additional stories which the PIO did not influence.

Therefore, a more important relationship than number of handouts to number of stories using PIO information is the proportion of *all* stories published about his agency over which a PIO had some influence.

It appears that the Department of Agriculture, not the Department of Justice, actually had proportionately more influence on newspaper content. Information from the Department of Agriculture's PIO was used in 84% of all stories written about his agency even though he disseminated only 69 handouts of information.

The Department of Justice by comparison provided 121 handouts to journalists, the largest number of any agency, but only 55% of all stories written about the department used the Justice PIO's information.

By this same standard, the Department of Revenue and Taxation was the least successful in influencing media content — its subsidies were used in only 18% of all stories written about it, as shown in Table 4.

A second tendency the data reveal is that persuasive public relations tactics aren't as effective with journalists as providing information intended to inform without necessarily persuading.

Other variables, such as the perceived newsworthiness of the information

TABLE 4
Subsidy Influence on Newspaper Stories

Agencies	Subsidies (n = 444)		Stories		
			Subsidized	Total	% Subsidized
	Number	Percent	(n = 444)	(n = 444)	(n = 444)
Agriculture	69	16%	43	51	84%
Commerce/Industry	38	9	8	18	44
Justice	121	27	56	102	55
Public Safety	96	22	41	145	28
Revenue/Taxation	7	2	2	11	18
Secretary of State	113	25	33	56	59

provided, undoubtedly also influenced whether a PIO's news release or handout was used in a published news story. But as Grunig's four models of public relations behavior suggest,[19] persuasive intent might influence a communication's use by journalists.

Comparison of those agencies that practiced persuasive versus non-persuasive models of public relations indicates those whose public relations behavior is straightforward are more successful in getting their information into published news stories than those who attempt to be persuasive.

The Department of Agriculture, an agency that describes itself as a disseminator of straightforward information, was most successful of all six agencies in actually influencing newspaper content. The agency that was least successful — the Department of Revenue and Taxation — was one whose public relations behavior was described by its PIO as predominantly persuasive.

SUPPORT FOR ASSUMPTIONS

Do the data support this study's assumptions? Generally, yes.

The first assumption — daily newspapers are more likely to use public relations information in published stories than to discard it — was supported by the data. But published stories about government are not more likely to be based on "official" handouts of information than on information obtained from other sources.

Although 51% of the news releases and other handouts were accepted, they resulted in only 183 news stories, 48% of the total stories published about these six state agencies during the eight-week period. Therefore, even though more than half of the PIO-generated information was accepted, public relations handouts influenced less than half of the total news coverage given these agencies.

Another assumption — newsworthiness is the most important factor in a newspaper's decision to accept or reject agency information from a PIO — also was supported by the data. In fact, support for this hypothesis is quite strong, since newsworthiness of a subsidy was the reason journalists gave for acceptance or rejection 81% of the time.

A third assumption — the agenda of agency activities presented in newspaper stories using information from PIOs mirrors the activity agendas of the agency information handouts — also was supported. Rank-order correlation of issues in agency handouts and in newspaper stories that used PIO information was strong and statistically significant, as shown in Table 5.

The implications of this positive correlation are important for agencies and their public information officers, and perhaps for journalists as well. Stories that incorporate information provided to journalists by PIOs more accurately reflect the issues agencies consider salient than does the broader group of *all*

TABLE 5
Issue Rank-Order Correlation: Subsidies, Subsidized Stories and
All Agency Stories

Issue	Subsidies (n = 444)	Subsidized Stories (n = 183)	All Stories (n = 383)
Election Campaigns and Politics	1 (*n* = 444)	2 (*n* = 44)	3 (*n* = 59)
Public Safety and Criminal Matters	2 (*n* = 89)	1 (*n* = 46)	1 (*n* = 136)
Economics and Finance	3 (*n* = 80)	3.5 (*n* = 32)	2 (*n* = 82)
Public Health and Consumer Protection	4 (*n* = 70)	3.5 (*n* = 32)	4 (*n* = 50)
Administrative and Personnel Actions	5 (*n* = 42)	6 (*n* = 4)	8 (*n* = 6)
Environment and Natural Resources	6 (*n* = 37)	5 (*n* = 22)	5 (*n* = 28)
Ceremonial Events and Celebrations	7 (*n* = 19)	7 (*n* = 2)	7 (*n* = 9)
Recreational, Culture and Tourism	8 (*n* = 13)	8 (*n* = 1)	6 (*n* = 13)

Kendall's tau-b correlation coefficients: agency subsidies with subsidized stories .84 $p < .01$; agency subsidies with all stories .57 $p < .05$; subsidized stories with all stories .69 $p < .02$.

stories written about the agencies. Agency information sources (the PIOs in this case) transmit importance of information as well as raw facts to journalists.

The last assumption examined — agencies practicing persuasive public relations behavior are less successful in getting their information published than those using non-persuasive tactics — also was supported by the data.

Although not enough agencies were represented in this sample to permit broad generalization, there is at least a strong suggestion that straightforward presentation of information, with no organizational "spin" on it, may be better received by the media than information intended to "sell" an organization's point of view.

NOTES

1. Gaye Tuchman *Making News: A Study in the Construction of Reality* (New York: The Free Press, 1978), pp. 210-211.

2. Max McCombs and Sheldon Gilbert, "News Influence on Our Pictures of the World," in *Perspectives on Media Effects,* ed. Jennings Bryant and Dolf Zillman (Lawrence Erlbaum Associates, forthcoming), p. 4.

3. Joseph Bensman and Robert Lilienfeld, *Craft and Consciousness: Occupational Techniques and the Development of World Images* (New York: John Wiley, 1973), p. 1.

4. Oscar H. Gandy Jr., *Beyond Agenda-Setting: Information Subsidies and Public Policy* (Norwood, N.J.: Ablex Publishing Co., 1982), p. 14.

5. Wilbur J. Cohen, "Communication in a Democratic Society," in Ray Eldon Hiebert and Carlton E. Spitzer, ed., *The Voice of Government* (New York: John Wiley & Sons, 1968), pp. 13-14.

6. Dennis W. Jeffers, "Performance Expectations as a Measure of Relative Status of News and PR People," *Journalism Quarterly* 54: 299–306 (1977).

7. Mark Fishman, *Manufacturing the News* (Austin, TX: University of Texas Press, 1980), p. 50.

8. Gandy, *Beyond Agenda-Setting,* pp. 11–12.

9. Scott M. Cutlip, "Third of Newspapers' Content PR-Inspired," *Editor and Publisher* May 26, 1962, p. 68.

10. William P. Martin and Michael W. Singletary, "Newspaper Treatment of State Government Releases," *Journalism Quarterly* 58: 93–96 (1981).

11. David H. Harris, "Publicity Releases: Why They End Up in the Wastebasket," *Industrial Marketing* 46: 98–100 (1961).

12. Herbert J. Gans, *Deciding What's News: A Study of CBS Evening News, NBC Nightly News, Newsweek and Time* (New York: Pantheon Books, 1979), pp. 147–175.

13. Douglas Ann Johnson Newsom, "Creating Concepts of Reality: Media Reflections of the Consumer Movement," Ph.D. dissertation, University of Texas, 1978.

14. Lutz Erbring, Edie N. Goldenberg and Arthur H. Miller, "Front-Page News and Real-World Cues: A New Look at Agenda-Setting by the Media," *American Journal of Political Science* 24:1 (February 1980), pp. 16–49.

15. Maxwell McCombs, Sheldon Gilbert and Chaim Eyal, "The State of the Union Address and the Press Agenda: A Replication," unpublished paper, Syracuse University, 1983.

16. David Weaver and Swanzy Nimley Elliott, "Who Sets the Agenda for the Media? A Study of Local Agenda-Building," paper presented to the Association for Education in Journalism and Mass Communication, Gainesville, Fla., August 1984.

17. F. Dennis Hale, "Press Releases v. Newspaper Coverage of California Supreme Court Decisions," *Journalism Quarterly* 55: 696–702 (1978).

18. Stephen Hess, *The Government/Press Connection: Press Officers and Their Offices* (Washington: The Brookings Institution, 1984), p. 3.

19. James A. Grunig and Todd Hunt, *Managing Public Relations* (New York: Holt, Rinehart and Winston, 1984) chapter 2.

21 The State of the Union Address and the Press Agenda*

Sheldon Gilberg
Chaim Eyal
Maxwell McCombs
David Nicholas

For national news, one of the major sources of this daily flow of news is the president, the nation's number one newsmaker. Being a major source of news places the president in a strategic position to influence the agenda of the news media and the agenda of the public. Every U.S. president prior to the Civil War sought to make sure that he had a sympathetic newspaper to which he could feed information. Abraham Lincoln broke this tradition by relying not upon a particular newspaper, but instead relying heavily upon the new Associated Press. His perspective was national.

In more recent decades U.S. presidents have been able to attempt to influence the national agenda directly through televised press conferences and, most importantly, through direct televised addresses to the nation.[1] Another setting which offers the president great potential for agenda-setting is the annual State of the Union address. The immediate audience is the Congress of the United States, but the effective audience for the marshalling of public opinion is the general public since the State of the Union address now is routinely televised during prime time.

Since the State of the Union address is a multi-faceted report typically touching on a wide variety of national issues, it also has the potential for extensive subsequent coverage in the press. While the immediate coverage might simply reflect the president's address, it may also provide a set of cues

---

*Reprinted from *Journalism Quarterly* (1980, Vol. 57, pp. 584–588) by permission of the editor.
[1]D.S. Rutkus, "Presidential Television," *Journal of Communication,* 26:73–8 (1976).

for media coverage and initiative going well beyond the next-day follow-up news story.

The State of the Union address is an explicit attempt by the president to influence the perceived salience of selected issues in the public mind and among members of Congress. To the extent that the press is swayed by this presentation or sees the address as the source of cues about the important topics of the day, the press agenda in subsequent days should reflect the priorities of the State of the Union address. In short, this study hypothesizes that *the agenda of issues presented by the president in his State of the Union address will influence the subsequent agenda of the national press.*

METHODOLOGY

To test this hypothesis about the president's role as news-maker and agenda-setter, President Carter's second State of the Union address, delivered on January 18, 1978, was content analyzed to determine the major issues and themes that the president and his staff chose to speak about. This analysis resulted in the identification of eight issue categories: 1) Jobs, 2) Energy, 3) Defense, 4) Peace, 5) Human Rights, 6) Middle East, 7) Panama Canal and 8) Taxes. The issues were rank-ordered on the basis of the number of column inches accorded each topic. This describes the emphasis and priority given each issue in the president's address.[2] The list of issues above represents the actual rank-order.

Next, all news stories on these eight issues were identified and counted in the Washington *Post,* New York *Times* and evening news broadcasts of ABC, CBS and NBC for a two-month period surrounding the president's State of the Union address. All the news stories on these topics were located and marked initially by Gilberg and subsequently verified by Nicholas. The abstracts prepared by the Vanderbilt University Library Television Archive were used for the network broadcasts. Because of the high inter-correlations among the three networks, an aggregate measure of the television agenda is presented here.

This set of 4,026 stories summarized in Table 1 was content analyzed to determine the number of stories for each of the eight issues[3] during three time periods:

- 28 days of coverage on these eight issues *prior* to the State of the Union address;

---

[2] *Vital Speeches of the Day.* 44:226–30 (1978).

[3] A story was assigned to an issue category on the basis of its dominant theme. A reliability check by Nicholas on this coding and the recording of such routine data as the date and medium revealed coder disagreement on less than three percent of the items coded.

TABLE 1
Number of News Stories on the State of the Union Issues

	Washington Post	New York Times	TV Networks	Total
Pre-Speech	579	801	506	1,886
Synchronous	108	121	84	313
Post-Speech	706	757	364	1,827
	1,393	1,679	954	4,026

- three days of *synchronous* coverage — the day prior to the address, the day of the President's appearance before the Congress and the day immediately following;
- 28 days of coverage on these eight issues *subsequent* to the address.

The key period for the testing of the hypothesis is the four weeks of coverage subsequent to the State of the Union address. Since most press coverage of issues, such as those discussed by President Carter, is episodic and event-oriented, this is an ample span of time in which to observe press response to the set of priorities set forth by the president.[4] The hypothesis predicts that this coverage will reflect the president's emphases in the State of the Union address.

The four-week period prior to the State of the Union address was added as a *control* to sharpen our view of the correlations between the president's agenda and the subsequent press agenda. Even though these latter correlations might be substantial, the pattern of press coverage could simply be a continuation of trends which were in motion before the State of the Union address. Content analyzing the four weeks prior to the address provides better evidence on the nature of the shifts in the press coverage following the State of the Union address.

Since it was expected that the coverage immediately before and immediately after the State of the Union address would largely be factual accounts of the contents of the address, either anticipated or as actually delivered, this three-day period was separated from the other data.

To test the hypothesis, the eight issues discussed by President Carter in the State of the Union address were rank-ordered — on the basis of the number of

[4]Reanalysis from an agenda-setting perspective of earlier gatekeeping studies suggests that the response of the press to its sources is rather immediate. See, for example, M.E. McCombs and D.L. Shaw, "Structuring the 'Unseen Environment'", *Journal of Communication,* 26:18-22 (1976); David Gold and J.L. Simmons, "News Selection Patterns Among Iowa Dailies," *Public Opinion Quarterly,* 29:425-430 (1965). Moreover, a recent study of public response to civil rights coverage in the press over a 23-year period found that the major response by the public occurred within four weeks. See James Winter, "An Agenda-Setting Time Frame for the Civil Rights Issue, 1954-1976." Communication Research Center, Syracuse University, 1979.

stories on each issue — for each of the news media at each of the three time periods. These nine sets of rank-orders were then compared, using Spearman's rho (a rank-order correlation coefficient), to the president's agenda.

FINDINGS

Table 2 shows that, contrary to the hypothesis, the post-speech correlations are weaker for all the news media than the correlations in the period prior to the State of the Union address. Overall, these findings describe a phenomenon of agenda-setting by the press, whereby the issues emphasized by the news media are reflected in the president's priorities, rather than the reverse, presidential influence on the subsequent press agenda.

In addition to this unexpected direction of agenda-setting influence, the data also suggest another pattern, a significant difference between the *local* newspaper, the Washington *Post,* and the *national* news media. Like the New York *Times* and the television networks, the *Post's* post-speech correlation is weaker than the pre-speech correlation. But unlike the other news media, the strongest correlation between the *Post's* coverage and the president's agenda occurs with the synchronous coverage rather than with the pre-speech coverage. Of course, the State of the Union address is, in many ways, a local story for the Washington *Post.* The fact that its synchronous coverage best matches the president's agenda may reflect both this local angle and the *Post's* more numerous connections to the White House as a news source. For the other news media the synchronous correlations are the poorest match between the president and the media.

At first glance, the moderately strong correlations that do exist between the president's agenda and the post-speech emphasis of the New York *Times* and national television networks might suggest some reciprocal agenda-setting influence by the president on the press subsequent to the initial influence of the press on the president. While this interpretation would resurrect, at least partially, the initial research hypothesis, closer scrutiny of the data eliminates any such hope.

Two sets of partial correlations were calculated from the data in Table 1,

TABLE 2
Correlations Between the President's Agenda and the
Media Agendas

	Washington Post	*N.Y. Times*	*TV Networks*
Pre-Speech	.452	.631	.688
Synchronous	.619	.476	.072
Post-Speech	.202	.548	.500

both to test the new hypothesis emerging from the empirical findings (namely, agenda-setting influence by the press on the president's State of the Union address) and to test the possibility of secondary influence by the president on subsequent press coverage.

If the new hypothesis is to be fully sustained and the original research hypothesis completely rejected for both newspapers and the television networks, the empirical relationship between the president's agenda and subsequent press coverage must be demonstrated to be spurious. In other words, the pre-speech coverage (A) influences both the president's address (B) and subsequent press coverage (C); the empirical link between B and C is spurious, existing only because B and C have a common cause. In statistical terms this means that the BC correlations (the last row in Table 2) should be reduced to approximately zero when A is partialled out. Calculation of the partial correlations BC.A for both newspapers and the television networks resulted in the total disappearance of the original positive BC relationship.

To further test the view of no presidential influence on subsequent press coverage – or, antithetically, in an attempt to partially resurrect the original research hypothesis – a second statistical model was posited:

A → B → C.

According to this model early press coverage influences the president's address, which in turn influences subsequent press coverage. The zero order correlations in Table 2 which show positive relationships for both AB and BC are preliminary evidence in support of this model. However, a rigorous test of the model requires calculation of the AC.B partial correlations, particularly for the New York *Times* and the television networks. If this intervening variable model is correct, the AC correlations should be substantially reduced when B is partialled out. However, calculation of the actual partial correlations failed to reduce the original positive relationships between A and C at all. In other words, the model is rejected.

DISCUSSION

Rejection of the intervening variable model leaves the field at this time to the new hypothesis which asserts press influence on the president's address and holds that the empirical relationship between the president's address and subsequent press coverage is spurious. The elegance of the partial correlation analyses just reported as evidence is that opposite results were required – and obtained – to support the new hypothesis of press influence on the president's agenda. Support of the spuriousness model required partial correlations substantially less than the zero-order correlations while rejection of the competing intervening variable model required partial correlations identical to the zero-order correlations. Both were obtained.

This study analyzes only one State of the Union address and the press coverage of those issues. While the information presented here obviously is limited in time and place, its implications are vast.

22 "Keeping the Gates" for Gatekeepers: The Effects of Wire News*

D. Charles Whitney
Lee B. Becker

An enduring concern in the study of journalistic practice is the degree to which news is standardized. A number of commentators have noted that various constraints reduce the variability of news available to audiences. Most of these constraints are tangible, concrete and relatively well documented, such as time, "news hole," or space, money, standardized sources, organizational policy and craft norms.[1] Others are considerably less apparent, and one such "unseen" constraint is the subject of this paper.

Two recent commentaries have reexamined White's classic 1949 "Mr. Gates"

---

*Reprinted from *Journalism Quarterly* (1982, Vol. 59, pp. 60–65) by permission of the editor.

[1]For time, see Robert L. Jones, Verling C. Troldahl and J.K. Hvistendahl, "News Selection Patterns from a State TTs-Wire." JOURNALISM QUARTERLY. 38:303-12 (1961); and Guido H. Stempel III, "How Newspapers Use the Associated Press Afternoon A-Wire." JOURNALISM QUARTERLY. 41:380-384 (1964); for space, see Gaye Tuchman, *Making News: A Study in the Construction of Reality* (New York: Free Press, 1978) and David Manning White, "The Gate-Keeper: A Case Study in the Selection of News," JOURNALISM QUARTERLY, 27:383-390 (1949); for money, see Edward J. Epstein, *News from Nowhere* (New York: Vintage, 1973); for standardized sources, see Warren Breed, "Newspaper 'Opinion Leaders' and Processes of Standardization," JOURNALISM QUARTERLY, 35:277-284, 328 (1955); but for a contrary view, see Guido H. Stempel III, "Uniformity of Wire Content in Six Michigan Dailies," JOURNALISM QUARTERLY, 37:45-48, 129 (1959); for policy, see Breed, "Social Control in the Newsroom; A Functional Analysis," *Social Forces,* 33:326-35 (1955), and John Dimmick, "The Gate-Keeper: An Uncertainty Theory," *Journalism Monographs* No. 37 (November 1974); for craft norms, see Tuchman, "Objectivity as Strategic Ritual," *American Journal of Sociology,* 77:660-679 (1972).

study of the news selection behavior of one Midwestern wire news editor.[2] Both have argued that more remarkable than White's finding that the editor engaged in idiosyncratic, subjective selections and rejections of news items was that the editor apparently unconsciously mirrored selections already made for him by the wire services. Classifying the news available from the wire service into seven content categories (labor, accidents and disasters, crime and vice, human interest, national, political, international), McCombs and Shaw[3] note a Spearman's rho of .64 between ranks of seven news item content categories supplied by the wires and ranks of stories selected by "Mr. Gates," and a Spearman r of .80 for a replication study of the same editor 17 years later.[4]

Gold and Simmons, in a study of 24 Iowa daily newspapers relying solely on one AP wire circuit for state, national and international news found overall coefficient of concordance of .915 between ranks of proportions of content supplied by the wire service and ranks of proportion of content used by the newspapers in 13 categories.[5]

Stempel, in a 1959 content analysis of wire stories used by six small Michigan dailies, found agreement to be relatively low, with only eight of 764 stories used by all papers and with overall agreement at 31% of stories across papers.[6] His 1964 study of 21 metropolitan papers offers findings more directly relevant to the research reported here.[7] Average use of AP A-wire items by all papers was 22% ranging from a low of 11% by a New York paper to 34% by the *Rochester* (N.Y.) *Times-Union*. In the study period, the afternoon AP A-wire transmitted 97 Washington, D.C.-datelined stories (17% of all stories), 298 U.S.-datelined stories (54%) and 159 foreign-datelined stories (29%). While the numbers and proportions of stories bearing these datelines varied substantially, proportions selected by papers within categories did not: 22% of the D.C.-datelined stories, 20% of the U.S.-datelined stories and 24% of the international stories were selected by the papers.

These findings suggest that wire service editors, in broad terms, "set the news agenda" for newspaper news editors, by suggesting the proper "news mix" and proportions within news categories such as accidents and disasters,

---

[2]Paul M. Hirsch, "Occupational, Organizational, and Institutional Models in Mass Media Research; Toward an Integrated Framework," in Hirsch, Peter V. Miller and F. Gerald Kline, eds., *Strategies for Communication Research* (Beverly Hills, CA.: Sage. 1977), pp. 13–42, and Maxwell E. McCombs and Donald L. Shaw, "Structuring the 'Unseen Environment'," *Journal of Communication,* 26:18–22 (Spring 1976).

[3]*Op. cit.,* p. 21.

[4]Paul Snider, "Mr. Gates' Revisited: A 1966 Version of the 1949 Case Study," JOURNALISM QUARTERLY, 44:419–427 (1967).

[5]David Gold and Jerry L. Simmons, "News Selection Patterns Among Iowa Dailies," *Public Opinion Quarterly* 29:425–430 (1965).

[6]*Op. cit.*

[7]*Op. cit.*

crime and vice and human interest news. Two possible explanations present themselves. The first is that the structure of each day's wire file, independent of proportions of content, influences editors' selections. For example, "soft news" such as human interest stories may be transmitted early in a wire cycle, leading to a higher proportionate selection for such early-moving copy, while "hard news" might move closer to deadline.[8] While in an absolute sense editors might value later-moving stories more highly as news, they might not ordinarily alter previously-made news judgments. Whitney, for example, recorded several such non-substitutions in story play in news scripts in a large metropolitan radio newsroom.[9]

A second and perhaps more plausible explanation of the correspondence between wire copy provided editors and their editorial choices is that wire service editors and news editors in media outlets share highly similar news values, and thus a finding that each select news items in similar proportions in news content categories merely reflects similarity of judgment.

If Gold and Simmons and the "Mr. Gates" studies are correct, the wire services "set agendas" for the news play "mix" of these various sorts of stories by transmitting them in varying proportions: if 5% of what is transmitted is labor news, then 5% of what is selected should be as well. Also implied is that the proportions in categories are consistent across time. The proportion of news within the content type becomes an added piece of information for editors to use in making story selections, information that would be absent if equal proportions of news were transmitted in each category.

An adequate test of an hypothesis that wire service editors' assignment of items in varying proportions to news categories influences other editors' selections of a subset of those items in similar proportions, then, would require variations in the wire file proportions assigned to various news categories. Where the file is "stacked," or proportioned much as news is routinely transmitted, editors' selections should mirror proportions transmitted. Where the file is "balanced," several outcomes, amenable to varying interpretations, are possible: a) if selections mirror the "balanced" nature of the "balanced" wire file, the outcome strongly supports the notion that wire editors "set the agenda" for news editors; b) if selections instead follow the proportions of news normally assigned by editors of both wire services and newspaper and television editors, the plausible interpretation is that in normal circumstances, both editors are applying the same news values; c) if, however, selections in a "balanced" condition reflect neither the "usual" proportions nor the "balanced" proportions, this invites an "added information" interpretation—that

---

[8]Cf. Jones, Troldahl and Hvistendahl, *op. cit.*

[9]D. Charles Whitney, " 'Information Overload' in the Newsroom: Two Case Studies," Unpublished Ph.D. dissertation, University of Minnesota, 1978.

where the proportioning approximates "normal" wire service distributions in the categories, it is followed, but when it does not, idiosyncratic selection will apply.

METHODS

Editorial managers of the morning and evening newspapers in Columbus and Dayton, Ohio, and of the three Columbus and two Dayton commercial television stations with regularly-scheduled news broadcasts of 30 minutes per day or more were asked for lists of news employees whose duties included selecting wire service news one or more days per month. Fifty-two such editors were identified, and 46 (88.5%) agreed to participate in the study. Fieldwork dates were May 1–14, 1979, and each editor completed a news selection task and answered a dozen personal interview items. Administration was completed at subjects' offices at the beginning or end of their working days, and about 30 minutes was required of each. Fieldworkers were journalism graduate students.

The selection task was as follows: Two dummy files of what the editors were told were lead paragraphs of wire service news stories were printed on cards. Each file included 98 news items, roughly the number of items that a content analysis of a week of the Ohio AP newspaper wire indicated would be transmitted during a typical day's morning or evening newspaper cycle. About 275 items were selected from current and old newspaper files, from four-year-old wire service items and from fictionalized accounts similar to the newspaper and wire items. Omitted were sports, state and local items, weather and stock market quotations[10] and items of especially important current interest. References to a day of the week were altered to "yesterday" or "today." Stories were coded into the seven categories mentioned in the "Mr. Gates" studies: labor, accidents and disasters, crime and vice, human interest, national, political and international. Stories which could not be reliably coded into a single category by two judges were excluded. When the story files were completed, items were tentatively assigned to two decks. In the first, or "balanced" deck, 14 items were assigned to each of the seven categories; in the second, or "unbalanced" deck, proportions of items were used approximating those reported by Snider for wire items read by "Mr. Gates": labor 5 items

---

[10]Gold and Simmons, *op. cit.,* found such categories to be invariably applied by newspapers, which used a fixed proportion of such copy regardless of what was coming in. Whitney, *op. cit.,* pp. 8–9, has referred to such stories as "policy" stories, since the rules for their selection or rejection are fixed and noncontemporaneous: A weather forecast for a particular region or state has a .0 or a 1.0 chance of being selected for a particular newspaper, regardless of its content on a given day, and the Dow-Jones averages will, or will not, be used by a particular evening newscast, regardless of whether they are up, down or unchanged.

(5.1%); accidents and disasters, 7 items (7.1%); crime and vice, 11 items (11.2%); human interest, 14 items (14.3%); national, 16 items (16.3%); political, 21 items (21.4%); and international, 24 items (24.5%). All items were presented to a panel of five Ohio State University journalism faculty and staff members with news editing experience for ranking on a Likert-type 1–5 "newsworthiness" scale. Their mean item rankings were then used to balance the overall "newsworthiness" within each category across the two decks.

A repeated measures counterbalanced design called for the experimental subjects (the news editors) to select 21 stories, or about the number of wire service items that the largest newspaper in the two cities ran in an average day, from each file. Fieldworkers decided by a coin toss whether the first subject to whom they administered the selection task would select stories from the "unbalanced" or "balanced" deck, or file, first; in subsequent administrations, each fieldworker systematically varied the order of administration. Twenty-four editors selected from the "unbalanced" day first, and 22 from the "balanced."

RESULTS

Of the 46 editors who participated, 38 (82.6%) were male and eight (17.4%) were female; 29 (63%) were newspaper editors with the remaining 17 (37%) working for television stations. The editors spend a mean of 4.04 days per week editing wire news. They had been wire editors for a mean of 7.5 years with the most senior editor having been one for 28 years, and they had been professional journalists for a mean of 13 years.

Editors showed considerable variability in their selections of 21 stories from

TABLE 1
Proportions in Wire File and Proportions Selected by Editors in
"Balanced" and "Unbalanced" Conditions

	Balanced Condition		Unbalanced Condition	
	% in wire file	% selected by editors	% in wire file	% selected by editors
Labor	14.3	11.0	5.1	5.3
Accidents & Disasters	14.3	20.7	7.1	7.3
Crime & Vice	14.3	16.0	11.2	14.5
Human Interest	14.3	11.7	14.3	17.9
National	14.3	22.2	16.3	19.8
Political	14.3	9.7	21.4	21.7
International	14.3	8.7	24.5	13.4
	100.1%	100.0%	99.9%	99.9%

both sets of news leads: in the "balanced" deck, only six stories (6.1%) were selected by no editors, 19 (19.4%) were selected by 25% of the editors, and only seven stories (7.1%) were selected by as many as half the editors. In the "unbalanced" deck, only two stories (2%) were not selected, and 24 (24.5%) were selected by as many as half the editors. The most favored stories in the "balanced" and "unbalanced" set were selected by 38 and 36 editors, respectively. A test for an order-of-administration effect was performed by computing t-tests on the mean number of items selected within each content category by order of administration ("balanced" or "unbalanced" first). In none of the 14 comparisons was the t-value significant at the .05 level (pooled variance estimate). Thus an order of administration effect was considered unlikely.

Proportions of stories in the content categories in the "unbalanced" conditions by and large serve as excellent predictors of editor selections within the categories; only international news varies substantially from the proportion of incoming news, and international news was the *least* favored category in the balanced condition. (Figure 1).

A Pearson correlation coefficient between number of items incoming and number selected in the categories in the "unbalanced" set is $r = .71$ ($p = .037$, $n = 7$); the Spearman rank-order r is .62 ($p = .025$, $n = 7$). For newspaper editors the Pearson r is .71; for broadcast editors, Pearson r is .66. Since there is no variation in the number of stories presented to the editors in the "balanced" set, correlation coefficients between number of incoming and selected items in the "balanced" deck cannot be computed.

The notion that wire editors and news editors share similar conceptions of how many stories should be selected within each of the seven categories can be tested by comparing the number of incoming stories in the unbalanced set with the number of stories selected by editors from the balanced set. As both examination of Figure 1 and reference to correlations suggest, this is not the case; the Pearson r is $- .41$ (n.s.) Spearman r is $- .33$ (n.s.). Examination of the rankings of selected stories in the "balanced" condition reveals no particular pattern of selection, although, as previously noted, it shows that generally editors are least likely to select international news, the category of news that in both White's 1949 and Snider's 1966 "Mr. Gates" studies accounted for the highest proportion of incoming wire news. A final internal check compared editors' selections in the unbalanced condition with selections in the balanced condition; they were virtually unrelated (Pearson $r = - .046$, n.s.; Spearman $r = .07$, n.s.), indicating that selection influence was not closely related to editors' news values.

Further Analysis.   Newspaper editors were more likely in the balanced condition to select accident and disaster, crime, human interest and international stories than were their television counterparts, and the TV editors were more likely to select political, labor and national stories. In the unbalanced

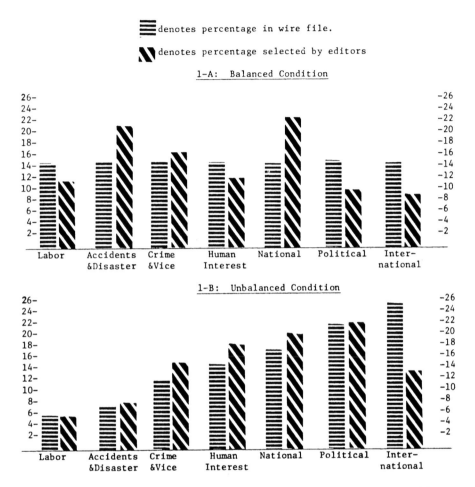

FIGURE 1. Percentages of stories in wire files, and percentages selected by editors, in balanced and unbalanced files in seven content categories.

condition, newspaper editors and television editors are virtually identical in their selection patterns, except that newspaper editors were much more likely to pick human interest stories ($T = 2.34$, 44 $d.f.$, $p = .02$), and TV editors were more likely to select national news items.

Several content variations seem counterintuitive and in some cases contradictory to previous research. Becker has noted that broadcast newsmen are more likely to report they cover controversy and conflict than are print journalists,[11] and Buckalew has noted that for television editors, a visuality

[11]Lee Becker, "Organizational Variables and the Study of Newsroom Behavior." Paper presented to the International Association for Mass Communication Research. Warsaw, Poland, August, 1978, p. 10.

news determinant must be added to the list of traditional news elements judged by print journalists.[12] As such, then, the content variations may represent structural variations not controlled in the experiment.

SUMMARY

Forty-six Columbus and Dayton, Ohio, editors cooperated in a counterbalanced-design field experiment to test whether proportions of news items in seven content categories transmitted by wire services served to cue editors as to proportions which should be selected from these categories. Support for such an hypothesis was found, but little support for an alternative explanation that wire editors and newspaper and television editors share an ongoing set of news values was found. In addition, it was suggested that international news was less valued by the newspaper and television editors than was anticipated.

Gold and Simmons, in a reexamination of content analysis data of small Iowa daily newspapers, finding a similar pattern, noted that "This similarity in patterns of news emphasis may represent similarity of news judgments. An alternative interpretation is that the pattern of emphasis of the wire service, represented by the frequency with which various types of stories are set out, is more or less uncritically accepted by these . . . daily newspapers for their own patterns of emphasis." This study undercuts the notion that the wires and the editors routinely share news values. It supports the idea that news as routinely transmitted in stock categories is indeed "uncritically accepted" in newspaper and television newsrooms.

Sprinkled through the recent research literature on the role of the mass media in setting the political agenda are references to the nagging question of how the media formulate the agenda they present to their audiences.[13] This study suggests quite strongly that the local media, at least, are influenced greatly by the decisions of a relatively few editors operating at the regional, national and international bureaus of the wire services. In other words, the agenda being presented by the media audiences is influenced by the newsgathering procedures of the media and the relationships among the media. The local media are hardly acting alone in shaping the political agenda.

---

[12]James K. Buckalew, "A Q-Analysis of Television News Editors' Decisions," JOURNALISM QUARTERLY, 46:135–137 (1969).

[13]Maxwell E. McCombs and Donald L. Shaw, "The Agenda-Setting Function of Mass Media," *Public Opinion Quarterly*, 37:176–187 (1972); Shaw and McCombs. *The Emergence of American Political Issues* (St. Paul, Minn.: West, 1977).

23 Intermedia Influence and the Drug Issue: Converging on Cocaine*

Stephen D. Reese
Lucig H. Danielian

> *In recent weeks, as the intense attention to drugs has faded, some have asked if the reaction to drugs was appropriate, and how it is that the press and Congress sometimes suddenly discover and then dismiss a major national problem.*
> —*Kerr, 1986, p.1*

Kerr was talking about drug coverage in the media, but the same could be said for many other national issues that rise and fall in prominence with each passing month. Many issues, such as the nuclear threat and the national debt, endure from year to year, but others seem more fleeting.

Big events drive many big stories and draw general attention to the problems they represent. Rock Hudson's death spurred national attention to the AIDS crisis. Spy arrests led to other questions about the quality of national security safeguards, and three major airline crashes in 1985 produced a rash of stories on air safety.

Other stories are less tied to specific events yet become big nevertheless. In the last couple of years such stories have included the famine in Ethiopia, Mideast terrorism, and the farm crisis. The problems behind these stories existed before the media "found" them and continued to exist after attention waned.

Each of these stories was characterized by a rapid convergence of media attention, during which it seemed that all media channels as well as conver-

*Reprinted from *Communication Campaigns About Drugs* (Pamela J. Shoemaker, editor) Lawrence Erlbaum Associates, 1989.

sations on the street are filled with the story. Although this bandwagon tendency among the media is not new in the press, one wonders if it has become more pronounced in recent times. This study is a first attempt to explore what is now a rather impressionistic notion of how the big media converge on a big story, especially those not directly tied to big events. The drug issue, particularly the "cocaine summer" of 1986, is a perfect example of such an issue.

Although the mainstream news media routinely tend to cover the same stories, some stories are tackled with a vengeance. What critics call media "hype" is a visible manifestation of this phenomenon of intermedia convergence. As for the drug issue itself, Edwin Diamond (1987) and his News Study Group at New York University noted that by August 1986, television had begun to reflect on its drug coverage over the summer, questioning whether it had been exaggerated, and media treatment of cocaine became a story itself. Nevertheless, high-profile television coverage continued through early September 1986 with a CBS documentary, "48 Hours on Crack Street," on September 2, and NBC's "Cocaine Country," aired on September 5. Perhaps in response, on September 23, PBS's McNeil/Lehrer Newshour featured a lengthy discussion (22 minutes) on whether the drug problem was hyped by the media.[1]

No one would accuse the media of "hyping" a story if first one paper examined a story, then another, and so on. But when every news organization emphasizes the same story at roughly the same time in a "feeding frenzy," the amount of coverage often seems out of proportion to the problem at hand. ABC reporter John Quinones confirmed that this was the case with the drug issue in 1986, noting that "sometimes we [the media] have a tendency to feed on one another, and the story feeds upon itself" (Diamond, 1987, p. 10).

The drug issue is a good example of a big story that may have been blown out of proportion by the media. For one thing, the story seemed to have a distinct rise and fall of media attention. It fits our notion of media convergence and allows for relatively easy definition and measurement. In addition, any similarities in media coverage of drugs cannot be explained by "pack journalism." The story did not emerge from a special "beat," as do national political stories. The nature of pack journalism on these beats is familiar by now. If several organizations assign reporters to cover the same thing, the resulting coverage tends necessarily to be similar. It deals with similar events and is filtered through the standardizing influence of the pack.

---

[1]Other less mainstream media have also noted the exaggerated coverage given the drug issue. Hatch (1987), for example, characterized the drug "hype" as a carefully orchestrated disinformation campaign promulgated by the Reagan administration to help pursue attacks on domestic freedoms and mask more pressing social problems. Indeed, any number of intrusive drug testing programs have been advocated in the aftermath of the drug summer of 1986.

Although specific events, like the death of Len Bias, did drive some media coverage, the drug issue was not covered by packs nor confined to a specific geographical location. Key editorial decisions were made to give greater treatment to the issue and these decisions were observed by others in the media. Furthermore, the story was not promoted by any one party, candidate, agency, or group. Rather, drugs have been a problem for years, but only recently was a significant convergence of coverage observed.

BACKGROUND

Elite media leadership has not been the subject of much research. No content analysis studies were found that systematically examined the extent of elite media leadership at the national level, and only one study was found below the national level. At the state level, newspapers tended to influence the broadcast agenda for statehouse stories more than the reverse (Atwater, Fico, & Pizante, 1987). Most such research, however, has examined cross-sections of content from different media and found strong similarities (sometimes called "homogeneity," "consonance," or "conformity") in their respective agendas. Newspapers have been compared and found to be similar in the topics covered and in how those topics were treated (e.g., Bigman, 1948; Donohue & Glasser, 1978; Riffe & Shaw, 1982).

Network newscasts have attracted greater attention, and their respective agendas have been found to be very similar (Altheide, 1982; Buckalew, 1969; Capo, 1983; Dominick, 1981; Foote & Steele, 1986; Fowler & Showalter, 1974; Graber, 1971; Hester, 1978; Lemert, 1974; Meeske & Javaheri, 1982; Riffe, Ellis, Rogers, Van Ommeren, & Woodman, 1986; Stempel & Windhauser, 1984; Weaver, Porter, & Evans, 1984). More than any three newspapers, the network newscasts are functionally equivalent, to the extent that Altheide (1982) declared them a national news service.

The original agenda-setting study by McCombs and Shaw (1972) is one of the few studies to compare agendas across media. Comparing agreement on campaign issue coverage by *The New York Times, Time, Newsweek,* NBC, CBS, and four local newspapers showed a high degree of agreement across those media. These similarities have been variously explained as resulting from similar real-world events, standardized organizational structure, and similar journalist socialization experiences. These explanations do not require that news organizations know what the others are doing. They could operate independently of each other and produce similar content. All of these factors no doubt play a part, but another equally important influence on intermedia agreement is the leadership exerted by some news organizations over others. This explanation obviously does require that the newsworkers know what others are doing.

Others have looked at the relationships among the mass media through case studies and participant observation. Media sociologists have documented an intermedia influence phenomenon, making it clear that looking to other media organizations for confirmation of news judgment is an institutionalized practice. Warren Breed (1980), in his classic study of the newsroom, found evidence that suggested this intermedia leadership process. He termed the phenomenon of one newspaper leading others as "dendritic" influence: "The influence goes 'down' from larger papers to smaller ones, as if the editor of the smaller paper is employing, in absentia, the editors of the larger paper to 'make up' his page for him" (p. 195). This pattern of influence, he said, assumed a dendritic or arterial form with the flow of influence from larger papers to smaller ones. Larger papers weren't copied, but their decisions as to the value of certain stories were followed.

This tendency for newsworkers to look to each other for guidance has remained in full force in more recent years. In *Deciding What's News,* Herbert Gans (1979, p. 91) noted that, when entertaining story ideas, editors will have already read the *Times* and *Post,* and will be aware of how those papers' editors have ruled on the idea(s) in question. If another paper has carried the story, it has been judged satisfactory, "eliminating the need for an independent decision" (p. 126). Gans noted that this prior publication is also taken as evidence of audience appeal, a particularly important element in "trend stories" (like cocaine). Gans said that when it comes to "trend" stories, "the prudent story suggester waits for another news medium to take the lead, then sells the idea partly on the basis that it has been reported elsewhere" (p. 170).

Until other media are onto a story it may have difficulty emerging, but once they are, a story can build exponentially. In *Reporters and Officials* Leon Sigal (1973) observed the importance of intermedia processes: "The consensible nature of news may even impede the breaking of stories that lack corroboration from opinion-leading newspapers. Once they do break, however, big stories will tend to remain in the news as first one news organization and then another uncovers additional information or a new interpretation" (p. 40).

After a story has reached a "critical mass" it may continue in this way, floating loose from any moorings to actual newsworthy events. Why is it so important for news organizations to look to each other for confirmation of news judgment? Sigal is among others who have noted that adherence to routine channels provides a way of coping with uncertainty. The similarities of newsworkers' stories reassures them that they know the "real news." Following the lead of another organization serves the same function. Consistency is accuracy.

Certain media are followed on certain types of issues because they are thought to have special expertise and resources. Miller (1978; pp. 16-17), for example, noted that *The New York Times* is regarded as the leader for how to treat international stories, *The Washington Post* is looked to for leadership for national domestic issues, and *Rolling Stone* is regarded as the leader for counterculture antiestablishment stories. In a case study analysis, she noted how the *Stone's* coverage of Americans in Mexican prisons triggered national print and television coverage, as other media picked up the lead and attention mushroomed.

Are the networks looked to by other media for guidance? Although intermedia influence has been assumed to always flow from print to electronic media (e.g., Massing, 1984), recent developments may have altered this equation. When Gannett designed its national newspaper, *USA Today,* it was with television in mind. From the shape of the paper dispensers to the colorful graphics, the publication was pitched to an audience of television viewers. This includes using the television networks to help guide story decisions. Prichard (1987) described how a December 1982 story about a man attempting to blow up the Washington Monument was bumped from page 1A of *USA Today,* having been deemed a local story. It was reinstated after Dan Rather led with it on the "CBS Evening News." Now that the nation knew about the story, it had become page 1 material. The broadcast by a major network had given the story a "verification factor."

In general, however, newspapers look to other newspapers, and television networks monitor each other, with certain "bellwethers" being tracked by all on specialized issues. But is there one general standard looked to by all the news media? Gans noted what is widely felt by many observers—that ultimately *The New York Times* is used as the final arbiter of quality and professionalism, across journalistic formats. Indeed, in the often ambiguous world of journalism, "if the *Times* did not exist, it would probably have to be invented" (Gans, 1979, p. 181).

THE CASE OF COCAINE

This study examines coverage by several national media of the drug issue over a period of time to determine the extent to which they converged on the drug issue and whether one medium can be said to have led the others.

If intermedia agenda setting took place in the drug issue, we would expect to find substantial similarities in when the various media gave the issue most attention. The rise and fall in attention would be expected to occur at about the same times. The intermedia leadership explanation for that similarity would be strengthened if rises in one organization's coverage could be seen to precede a rise in another's. Of particular interest is the relationship between print and television news, often criticized as merely following the lead of the elite media (Massing, 1984). Finally, this study determines which of the elite newspapers played the largest role in covering the drug issue.

RESULTS AND DISCUSSION

Tables 5.1 and 5.2 show how the stories in our sample broke down into the study categories, compared by the 10 news sources. These sources are combined by medium in Table 5.3. The major types of newspaper cocaine stories were crime and "use and abuse," accounting for 62% of the total. Comparing across the five newspapers shows that the proportions of coverage are roughly similar. *The Washington Post* featured cocaine deaths more prominently than the others, due largely to the great amount of coverage given the death of hometown basketball star Len Bias. Table 5.2 shows a similar pattern. Television newscasts and the news magazines give their greatest coverage of cocaine to crime and use and abuse stories. Television gives greater attention, however, to deaths and national policy responses. The three networks show more similarity in their coverage than do the newspapers.

Table 5.3 provides a combined look at the three media. Newspapers, news magazines, and television newscasts show similar amounts of coverage in the study categories. The major difference (enough for a statistically significant chi-square value) was found in the tendency of newsmagazines to focus less on crime and more on the use and abuse of cocaine. The week-to-week nature of the newsmagazines' coverage appears to suit them better to more evaluative trend-type stories than to specific day-to-day crime coverage.

Figures 5.1 through 5.4 take a closer look at media coverage over time by

TABLE 1

Nature of Cocaine Stories in *The New York Times, The Washington Post, The Wall Street Journal, The Los Angeles Times,* and *The Christian Science Monitor*

	Medium				
Story Category	New York Times	Wall St. Journal	Wash. Post	LA Times	Chr. Sci. Monitor
Deaths	7%	0%	24%	1%	0%
Crime	39	39	28	48	35
Antidrug movement	5	0	3	4	0
Use and abuse	26	39	24	17	30
Policy Response					
National	2	4	3	3	4
State/local	5	0	0	1	0
International	6	9	12	11	17
Private sector	2	4	1	0	0
Foreign	5	4	6	14	9
General crisis	2	0	0	0	4
Total	100%	100%	100%	100%	100%
N	(250)	(23)	(98)	(71)	(23)

TABLE 2
Nature of Cocaine Stories Transmitted by the Television
Networks and News Magazines

Story Category	Medium				
	ABC	*CBS*	*NBC*	*Time*	*Newsweek*
Deaths	14%	9%	14%	13%	5%
Crime	37	41	40	26	19
Antidrug movement	3	4	3	4	0
Use and abuse	27	21	24	22	43
Policy Response					
National	17	8	10	13	0
State/local	1	3	1	0	0
International	4	8	5	9	14
Private sector	3	3	6	9	0
Foreign	3	5	5	0	14
General crisis	0	0	0	4	5
Total	100%	100%	100%	100%	100%
N	(70)	(30)	(81)	(23)	(23)

TABLE 3
Overall Nature of Cocaine Stories in Newspapers, News
Magazines, and Television Networks

	Medium		
	Newspapers	*News Magazines*	*Television Networks*
Deaths	9%	9%	12%
Crime	38	23	39
Antidrug movement	4	2	3
Use and abuse	25	32	24
Policy Response			
National	3	7	6
State/local	3	0	2
International	9	11	6
Private sector	1	5	4
Foreign	7	7	4
General crisis	2	5	0
Total	100%	100%	100%
N	(465)	(44)	(231)

Chi square (18) = 29.9, $p < .05$.

newspapers and the television networks (*The Christian Science Monitor* gave cocaine relatively little coverage and was omitted from the newspaper comparison charts). During 1985 it does not appear that there was a distinctive media convergence, but 1986 does show evidence of this phenomenon. *The New York Times* covered the baseball trials, involving cocaine use by some

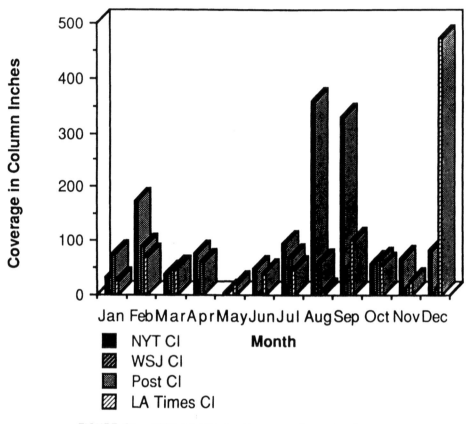

FIGURE 5.1.   1985 newspaper coverage of cocaine issues.

Mets players, heavily in August and September 1985. That was largely a local issue, however, and the other papers did not pay much attention to that story or cocaine generally, until *The Los Angeles Times* printed a major multipart series at year's end. The network newscasts showed a similar pattern in 1985. ABC carried the most coverage early in the year with CBS and NBC picking up the pace later on. Again, the coverage is diffused, and no internetwork agenda similarity is observed. Great similarities are seen in 1986 where both the volume and concentration of coverage increased substantially. The peak of coverage shown graphically in Fig. 5.2 and 5.4 in the summer of 1986 hints at the media convergence phenomenon suggested earlier.

Two different processes are suggested by media coverage in 1985. One process is the leading of one medium by others. For example, television stories show a marked rise in March following a similar increase in the number of

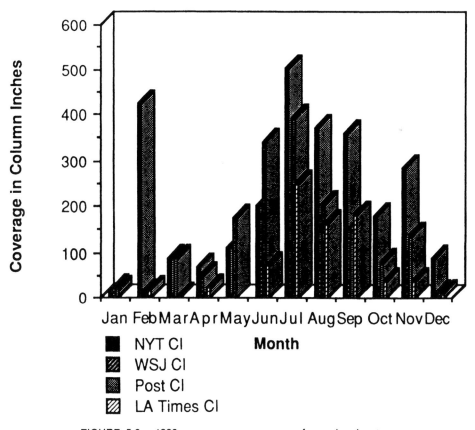

FIGURE 5.2.   1986 newspaper coverage of cocaine issues.

New York Times and news magazine stories the month before. February 1985 saw two cover stories in *Time* and *Newsweek* on cocaine trafficking. The television networks followed this emphasis with stories of their own. Later in the year another process seems to take place. A major event, the baseball drug trials of September, drives the coverage of all three media resulting in a simultaneous peak in coverage.

The evidence suggests a combination of these processes occurring in 1986. The death of athletes Len Bias and Don Rogers in June of that year drew a significant amount of media attention. But that coverage built on previous attention to the cocaine problem. Evidence for media leadership may be found in the fact that three of New York City's major newspapers carried extensive articles on cocaine and crack on May 18. These stories were followed by a rush of coverage in other media in the following months, climaxing in the peak of

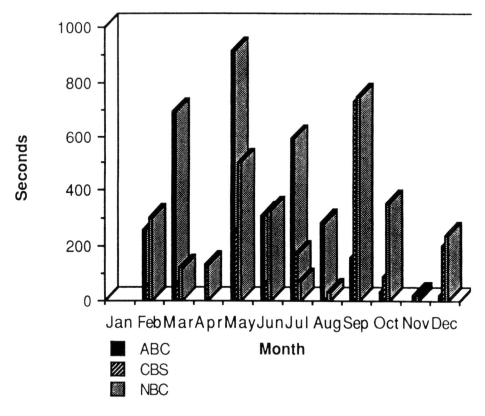

FIGURE 5.3. 1985 network news coverage of cocaine issues.

media attention seen in July. So although the death of the athletes may be considered prominent events driving each medium's agenda, these events probably had the effect of focusing press attention on an issue already set in motion. They provided a hook, or newspeg, on which to hang the cocaine story.

Judging from Fig. 5.2, *The New York Times* took the lead in covering the cocaine issue. The other papers quickly fell in line, though, around mid-year. *The Wall Street Journal* was least likely to follow the others, playing the cocaine story up and down throughout the year, with a slight rise in mid-year. The *Journal* has a specialized audience, however, and tended to run cocaine stories when a major business was involved. After the three New York papers covered the crack/cocaine story in the middle of May, the *Post* ran a long "use and abuse" story of its own a few days later. After the *Times* and the *Post* devoted major attention to the issue in June, *The Los Angeles Times* jumped on and stayed with the issue through September. A loose interpretation of Fig.

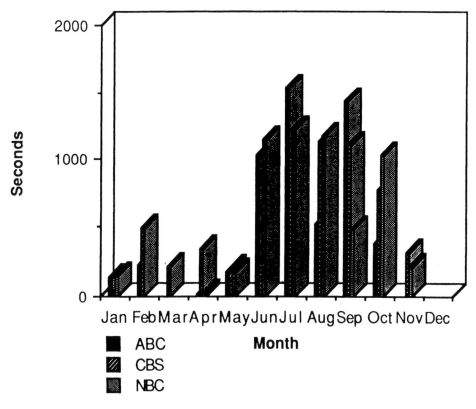

FIGURE 5.4.   1986 network news coverage of cocaine issues.

5.2 suggests that the *Times* laid the groundwork for the story, which gathered strength when the *Post* picked up the story and expanded it with a heavy focus on the Len Bias death. With two elite papers running with the story, *The Los Angeles Times* was obliged to join in.

It appears that the print media, and specifically *The New York Times,* set the agenda for the television networks. Network coverage peaked in September with dual documentaries on CBS and NBC on the cocaine problem, while attention by the print media had already begun to wane. Interestingly, the television networks dropped the issue completely in December while newspapers continued coverage at a lower level. Television news, more than newspapers, appears to follow a smooth attention curve, discovering an issue, playing it strongly, and then moving on to other stories. This tendency may contribute to the notion that the media converge on issues, resulting in a short national attention span.

REFERENCES

Altheide, D.L. (1982). Three-in-one news: Network coverage of Iran. *Journalism Quarterly, 59,* 482–486.

Atwater, T., Fico, F., & Pizante, G. (1987). Reporting on the state legislature: A case of inter-media agenda setting. *Newspaper Research Journal, 8,* 52–61.

Bigman, S.K. (1984). Rivals in conformity: A study of two competing dailies. *Journalism Quarterly, 25,* 127–131.

Breed, W. (1980). Dissertations on sociology: The newspaperman, news and society. New York: Amo Press.

Buckalew, J.K. (1969). News elements and selection by television news editors. *Journal of Broadcasting, 14,* 47–54.

Capo, J.A. (1983). Network Watergate coverage patterns in late 1972 and early 1973. *Journalism Quarterly, 60,* 595–602.

Diamond, E. (1987, February 7). Is TV news hyping America's cocaine problem? *TV Guide,* pp. 4–10.

Dominick, J.R. (1981). Business coverage in network newscasts. *Journalism Quarterly, 58,* 179–185.

Donohue, T. R., & Glasser, T. L. (1978). Homogeneity in coverage of Connecticut newspapers. *Journalism Quarterly, 55,* 592–596.

Foote, J., & Steele, M. E. (1986). Degree of conformity in lead stories in early evening network TV newscasts. *Journalism Quarterly, 63,* 19–23.

Fowler, J. S., & Showalter, S. W. (1974). Evening network news selection. A confirmation of news judgment. *Journalism Quarterly, 54,* 712–715.

Gans, H. (1979). *Deciding what's news.* New York: Random House.

Graber, D. (1971). Press coverage patterns of campaign news: The 1968 presidential race. *Journalism Quarterly, 48,* 502–512.

Hatch, R. (1987). Drugs, politics, and disinformation. *Covert Action Information Bulletin, 28,* 23–27.

Hester, A. (1978). Five years of foreign news in U.S. television evening newscasts. *Gazette, 24,* 88–95.

Kerr, P. (1986, November 17). Anatomy of an issue: Drugs, the evidence, the reaction. *The New York Times,* p. 1.

Lemert, J. B. (1974). Content duplication by the networks in competing evening newscasts. *Journalism Quarterly, 51,* 238–244.

Massing, M. (1984). The network newscasts: Still hot off the presses. *Channels, 47,* 47–52.

McCombs, M., & Shaw, D. (1972). The agenda setting function of the mass media. *Public Opinion Quarterly, 36,* 176–184.

Meeske, M. D., & Javaheri, M. H. (1982). Network television coverage of the Iranian hostage crisis. *Journalism Quarterly, 59,* 641–645.

Miller, S. H. (1978). Reporters and congressmen: Living in symbiosis. *Journalism Monographs, 53,*

Parenti, M. (1986). Inventing reality: The politics of the mass media. New York: St. Martin's Press.

Prichard, P. (1987, October). The McPapering of America: An insider's candid account. *Washington Journalism Review,* pp. 32–37.

Riffe, D., & Shaw, E. F. (1982). Conflict and consonance. Coverage of third world in two U.S. papers. *Journalism Quarterly, 59,* 484–488.

Riffe, D., Ellis, B., Rogers, M.K., Van Ommeren, R.L., & Woodman, K. A. (1986). Gatekeeping and the network news mix. *Journalism Quarterly, 63,* 315–321

Sigal, L. V. (1973). *Reporters and officials: The organization and politics of newsmaking.* Lexington, MA: D.C. Heath. Stempel, G. H., & Windhauser, J. W. (1984). The prestige press revisited: Coverage of the 1980 presidential campaign. *Journalism Quarterly, 61,* 49–55.

Weaver, J. B., Porter, C. J., & Evans, M. E. (1984). Patterns of foreign news coverage on U.S. network TV: A 10-year analysis. *Journalism Quarterly, 61,* 356–363.

Weaver, D., & Wilhoit, G. C. (1986). *The American journalist.* Bloomington, IN: Indiana University Press.

24 The Impact of Campaign Agendas on Perceptions of Issues*

Wenmouth Williams Jr.
Mitchell Shapiro
Craig Cutbirth

McCombs and Shaw's 1972 study of the agenda-setting function of the press has produced much interest in how the mass media influence our priorities of campaign issues.[1] The conclusion from this first study and much of the succeeding research is that the media can set political agendas for their respective audiences. Some researchers are now suggesting that a "theory" of agenda setting may be in order. To this end, McCombs has suggested a variety of methods to build such a theory.[2] One of these methods, the building of matrices comprised of variables impacting the agenda-setting process, was the focus of a study by Williams and Semlak. They concluded that many of the variables originally discussed by McCombs could be organized into two matrices: one for antecedent and the other for intervening variables. Some of the antecedent variables included commitment to a candidate and involvement in a campaign. Dependence on television for campaign information was one intervening variable.[3] Many other studies have replicated these findings and

---

*Reprinted from *Journalism Quarterly* (1983, Vol. 60, pp. 226–232) by permission of the editor.
[1]Maxwell McCombs and Donald Shaw, "The Agenda-Setting Function of the Mass Media," *Public Opinion Quarterly,* 36:176–187 (1972).

[2]Maxwell McCombs, "Agenda-Setting Research: Bibliographic Essay," *Political Communication Review,* 1:1–7 (1976); Maxwell McCombs and Donald Shaw," An Up-to-Date Report on the Agenda-Setting Function," a paper presented to the annual conference of the International Communication Association, Acapulco, Mexico, 1980.

[3]Wenmouth Williams, Jr. and William Semlak, "Campaign '76: Agenda Setting During the New Hampshire Primary," *Journal of Broadcasting.* 22:531–540 (1978).

uncovered additional variables crucial to the understanding of the agenda setting process.[4]

The basic problem with most of these studies is that they concentrate on audience variables such as campaign involvement, almost to the exclusion of many potentially important content or message variables. For example, McCombs in his original bibliographic essay, and other subsequent theory-building articles, focuses on audience variables, with the only significant content variable being whether the voter receives political information from either network television news programs or the daily newspaper. The failure to consider content variables may explain the great variability in results of agenda-setting studies conducted since 1972.[5]

The studies that have considered content or message variables, such as story placement and visual techniques have neglected to study their relative impact on the formation of personal agendas. Two studies, conducted independently by Frank and Hofstetter, involved extensive examinations of how network television covered the 1972 presidential campaign. The basic finding was that the three networks used different methods to communicate about the candidates, but that these differences did not result in any systematic biases favoring either McGovern or Nixon.[6]

One of the few studies to consider the impact of message variables was conducted by Williams and Semlak. By constructing separate agendas for inherent characteristics of television news and for each of the message variables identified by Frank, they found that media impact on audience perceptions of campaign issues depended on which mass medium is used for campaign information and which communication strategies the media use to communicate this information.[7]

A second and much more comprehensive study of content and how it affects the agenda setting process was conducted by Zucker. He found that the perceived importance of issues that can be personally experienced by the audience is not very susceptible to media influence. However, perceptions of issues that cannot be personally experienced, such as foreign relations, can be affected by the media. The general conclusion from this study and the results

[4]David Weaver, "Need for Orientation, Media Uses and Gratifications and Media Effects," paper presented to the annual meeting of the International Communication Association, Chicago, 1978; Lee Becker, "The Impact of Issue Saliencies," in Donald Shaw and Maxwell McCombs, eds., *The Emergence of American Political Issues: The Agenda-Setting Function of the Press* (St. Paul: West Publishing Co., 1977); L. Erwin Atwood, Ardyth Sohn and Harold Sohn "Daily Newspaper Contributions to Community Discussions," *Journalism Quarterly,* 55:570–576 (1978).

[5]Williams and Semlak, *op. cit.;* McCombs and Shaw (1972 and 1980), *op. cit.*

[6]Robert Frank, *Message Dimensions of Television News* (Lexington, Mass.: Lexington Books, 1973); Richard Hofstetter, *Bias in the News: Network Television Coverage of the 1972 Election Campaign* (Columbus: Ohio State University Press, 1976).

[7]Wenmouth Williams, Jr. and William D. Semlak, "Structural Effects of TV Coverage on Political Agendas," *Journal of Communication,* 28:114–119 (1978).

of the Williams and Semlak research is that content variables are important to the study of the agenda-setting process.[8]

One important content variable is how the news media organize their messages. One organizational schema is to order stories based on their relative importance to the audience. For example, the lead event might be an airplane crash. That day's newscast would lead with this item and follow it with interviews of eye witnesses, victims, etc. As many as three or four different stories may be contiguous in the media agenda, all related to the crash. In this hypothetical example, the media have given the audiences a frame of reference,[9] the actual crash, to organize and facilitate understanding of other related issues presented later in the newscast. Other frames might also be used in the same or different newscast. An energy frame may be used to present a story on oil in Saudi Arabia. A similar story might receive a foreign relations frame. A local television news editor might group the first story with others on energy and the second with foreign relations stories at the end of a newscast. Local newspapers might put all international stories on the same page. In simple terms, the media often use frames for events to give them meaning.

Framing is complicated when the media cover political campaigns because they are faced with the problem of competing frames, the "normal" frame as discussed above and the political frame. This second or political frame comprises part of what Lang and Lang call the "second hand reality" of the campaign, or what Swanson labels the "melodramatic scenario."[10] Issues receiving a political frame (i.e., the campaign agenda) are relevant to the campaign and the candidates. Such stories are typically presented as ongoing series.

The reason why framing is potentially important to the understanding of the agenda-setting process is that often the media communicate issues relevant to a campaign, but do not give an implicit campaign frame. The result is that the audience must decide if issues are relevant or irrelevant to the campaign. If the media provide a campaign frame, then the consumer knows the linkage to the candidates or the electoral process. If the media do not provide a campaign frame, then the viewer-reader is left with ambiguities as to the campaign relevance of the story.

Despite these apparent problems of determining campaign relevance for the news editors and consumers, past agenda-setting research has failed to

---

[8]Harold G. Zucker, "The Variable Nature of News Media Influence," In Brent D. Ruben, ed. *Communication Yearbook 2* (New Brunswick: Transaction Books, 1978), pp. 225–240.

[9]Dennis K. Davis and Stanley J. Baran, *Mass Communication and Everyday Life: A Perspective on Theory and Effects* (Belmont: Wadsworth Publishing Co., 1981), pp. 69–70.

[10]Kurt Lang and Gladys Lang, "The Mass Media and Voting," in Eugene Burdick and Arthur Brodbeck, eds. *American Voting Behavior* (New York: Free Press, 1959); David Swanson, "And That's The Way It Was? Television Covers the 1976 Presidential Campaign," *Quarterly Journal of Speech,* 63:239–248 (1977).

consider the impact framing has on perceptions of campaign issue importance. The traditional methodological approach codes all the issues communicated during a portion of the campaign period, regardless of their relevance to the campaign. Respondents are then asked to identify issues most important to the campaign. The assumption is that voters make at least some attempt to process and store this information as it applies to the various candidates.[11] The purpose of the present study was to test this assumption. If the logic of framing pertains to the agenda-setting process, then the media should have the most impact on the perceived importance of campaign issues when they give issues a campaign frame.

METHOD

Two data sets were collected in this study. The first data set consisted of the media agendas presented during the 1980 presidential campaign. The second data set was the audience survey.

Media Agendas.   The time period considered in this study was between Sept. 15 (the beginning of the media campaign) and Oct. 31, 1980.[12] The TV network agenda was determined by initially coding stories into one of 136 content categories. The unit of analysis was the issue and not the story as defined by the networks. For example, if a news item was about the Middle East and devoted a portion of the story to Arab oil prices and a second portion of the same story to foreign relations with Saudi Arabia, the item was coded in the energy category for the first portion and in the foreign policy category for the second portion. The time devoted to each segment or portion was tabulated for each of these two issues and added to the total in their respective categories. The 136 categories were then collapsed into 12. The television agenda was then computed by summing the total number of seconds of each content segment in each category. The categories were then ranked based on the total time. Only weekday, evening newscasts were analyzed.

The newspaper agenda consisted of all stories found on the front and two editorial pages of a central Illinois daily newspaper published from Monday through Friday. Again, the unit of analysis was the content segment and not the story. Column inches, based on a six-column format, were recorded for each segment. Column inches were then summed to determine the rankings of categories.

---

[11]Williams and Semlak, "Campaign '76 *op. cit.;* McCombs and Shaw, "An Up-to-Date," *op. cit.;* Jack McLeod, Lee Becker and James Byrnes, "Another Look at the Agenda Setting Function of the Press," *Communication Research,* 1:131–166 (1974).

[12]ABC for one day and three issues of the daily newspaper were not included.

Campaign agendas were determined by separating each content segment that was directly linked to either Reagan or Carter. John Anderson was not included in this analysis because he received so little media attention. Most stories in the campaign agenda for the television networks were contained in regularly appearing campaign series. However, occasionally direct references were made in other items. Each issue receiving a candidate reference was recorded, as well as the total number of seconds or column inches. Totals for each of the 12 issue categories were then used to determine ranks for the campaign agenda. The non-campaign agenda consisted of all the other stories appearing in the newscasts or newspaper that did not make an implicit link between the issues and the two major candidates.

Audience Agenda.   The audience agenda was determined during telephone interviews administered by trained coders from Oct. 20 to 31, 1980. A list of randomly generated telephone numbers was constructed using the random digit dialing technique. In total 482 residents in central Illinois were initially contacted; 356 were actually interviewed for a completion ratio of 74%. The audience agenda was determined by answers to this question:

When talking to others, what is the most important presidential campaign issue?

This item measures the interpersonal agenda or what issues are discussed by the electorate. Other agendas such as the perceived community agenda (what people perceive is important to their community) or the intrapersonal agenda (what people personally believe is important, but not necessarily discussed) were not included in the questionnaire.[13]

Using responses from the interpersonal agenda question, an audience agenda was constructed by summing the number of respondents naming issues in the twelve categories. The categories were initially developed from the content analysis of the media agendas. The rationale for this procedure, following the logic of the agenda setting process, is that the media present agendas of issues which lead to the formation of the audience agenda. The time order is implicit in the agenda setting research cited earlier. The intercoder reliability was .94.

RESULTS

The 12 issue categories and some examples were:

1. Integrity in government-ABSCAM, Billy Carter, Richard Nixon.
2. Nuclear energy-power plants, energy shortages.

---

[13]Williams and Semlak, "Campaign '76," found the interpersonal and intrapersonal agendas to be highly correlated.

TABLE 1
Intermedia Correlations for Campaign and Non-Campaign
Agendas

	CBS		NBC		Newspaper	
	Non-Campaign	Campaign	Non-Campaign	Campaign	Non-Campaign	Campaign
ABC						
Non-Campaign	.72*	−.07	−.60*	−.04	.44	−.33
Campaign	.35	.71*	.04	.64*	.14	.49
CBS						
Non-Campaign			.79*	.07	.78*	−.22
Campaign			−.13	.87*	.31	.66*
NBC						
Non-Campaign					.52	−.13
Campaign					.19	.75*

*Significant $p < .05$.

3. Social problems-abortion, birth control, crime, aid to cities.
4. Foreign policy-Afghanistan, detente, El Salvador.
5. Campaign-non-issue information.
6. Debates-televised candidate debates.
7. Social rights-bussing, capital punishment, civil rights.
8. Defense-arms limitations, military strength, the draft.
9. Inflation-gold prices, government spending, stock market prices.
10. Jobs-industry issues, unemployment.
11. Iran hostages-stories about them and their release.
12. Iran war-with Iraq.

Ten of the 12 categories were used in assessing the agenda-setting effect. The two categories dealing with the campaign (non-issues) and the debates were not included in the following analysis because they were not considered campaign issues. Further, most previous research has not considered time/space devoted to campaign non-issues relevant to the agenda-setting process.[14]

Intermedia Correlations. Spearman Rho rank order correlations were computed to determine the inter-relationships between the four news sources considered in this study. The 24 correlations computed to determine these relationships appear in Table 1. All of the campaign/campaign and non-campaign/non-campaign comparisons for the three television networks were statistically significant ($p < .05$). Only three of the six relationships (campaign/

---

[14]Leonard Tipton, Roger Haney and John Baseheart, "Media Agenda-Setting in City and State Election Campaigns," *Journalism Quarterly,* 52:15–22 (1975).

campaign and non-campaign/non-campaign) between the network and the newspaper agendas were significant. No significant correlations were found for any of the 12 non-campaign/campaign agenda comparisons. Within the media, the non-campaign/campaign correlations were: ABC (.22), CBS (.18), NBC (– .13) and the newspaper (– .04).

Media and Audience Correlations. Two sets of correlations were computed to determine the agenda setting impact of the four news sources: one set for the non-campaign agendas and the second set for the campaign agendas.[15] The results for the non-campaign agendas were: ABC (.37), CBS (.04), NBC (– .12) and the newspaper (– .10). Correlations for the campaign agendas were: ABC (.60), CBS (.64), NBC (.78) and the newspaper (.22). All three TV correlations were statistically significant. All four media campaign/audience correlations were substantially greater than their corresponding figures for the non-campaign agendas.

A clearer understanding of how the campaign agendas affected the respondents in this study resulted when only Carter and Reagan supporters were considered in the audience agendas.[16] The campaign agendas for the television networks and the newspaper were divided into two segments, one including only the stories directly linked to Carter and a second comprised of items only linked to Reagan. These two agendas were labelled the candidate agendas. The three network agendas were combined to form a television agenda for each candidate because of the statistical similarities of the campaign and candidate agendas (all were significantly correlated).

Four correlations were then computed between the Reagan and Carter media agendas and their respective supporters. The resulting correlations for Carter supporters were television, .80, and newspaper, .42. Correlations obtained for Reagan supporters were: Television, .68, and newspapers, .38. The correlations between the television/candidate and supporter agendas were statistically significant.

DISCUSSION

The general conclusion from this study is that framing is a crucial content variable in the agenda-setting process. The substantially larger correlations

---

[15]Audiences were defined as respondents able to name a favorite anchorman. Correlations reported here use only the audience of the three networks and respondents reading the newspaper at least once a week. Other correlations computed, controlling for the amount of newspaper reading, showed little impact of media use on the agenda setting process in this study. Also, a majority (69%) of the respondents reported reading the newspaper at least five times a week.

[16]Candidate supporters were defined by response to this question: Who is your favorite candidate in the upcoming presidential race?

obtained between the audience and campaign agendas, as compared to the relationship between the non-campaign and audience agendas, suggest that voters require obvious links between candidates and issues to determine the political relevance of these issues to a campaign. The assumptions of past agenda-setting research that respondents can either consciously or subconsciously make these links is clearly not valid, and may explain some of the inconsistencies in previous studies. The media must perform what Wright labels the correlation function, or clarify how issues interrelate and are applicable to daily lives.[17]

The importance of framing as a message variable is also evident when the candidate agendas are considered. Direct links to either Reagan or Carter had a substantial agenda setting impact on what their respective supporters perceived as important to the campaign. This finding suggests some support for selective retention, or at least selective perceptions. Clearly, the issues presented by the candidates that also received media coverage were judged important by committed respondents in this study.

The other results of this study support much past agenda-setting research. Network television presented a fairly homogenous view of the campaign and non-campaign issues. The very high correlations suggest almost identical agendas for the three networks. Similar results were not evident for the newspaper, also supporting some previous studies. This finding may be explained by the tendency of many local newspapers to be fairly partisan in elections, as compared to the nonpartisan nature of network television news. The newspaper in this study was published in a highly Republican area and typically endorses Republican candidates. This partisanship was not evident in the total amount of coverage (column inches) devoted to Reagan as compared to Carter. However, partisanship no doubt was very important in the editorial endorsements and other items published on the editorial pages included as part of the newspaper agenda in this study.

The agenda-setting impact of television, relative to the daily newspaper, also supports many earlier studies. For example, McCombs found newspapers to be most influential early in the campaign process. However, television "catches up" as election day approaches.[18] This study demonstrates the impact television news can have on political agendas late in a campaign, especially when framing is included as a message variable.

The results of this study indicate that voters need a frame or a point of reference for determining the campaign relevance of issues. This finding has many implications for journalists and future agenda setting research. For journalists, if the intent of a news story is to show how issues relate to campaigns, merely publishing them in election periods is not sufficient. Direct

---

[17]Charles Wright, *Mass Communication* (New York: Random House, 1959).

[18]Donald Shaw and Maxwell McCombs, eds., *The Emergence of American Political Issues: The Agenda-Setting Function of the Press* (St. Paul: West Publishing, 1977).

links must be made between issues and candidates for audiences to perceive their campaign relevance. Further, the results of this study point to the potential significance of special campaign series in newspapers and on television. However, these series must stress issue positions of the candidates and how specific campaign appearances relate to these positions, not just the candidate's activities.

For agenda setting research, these findings underscore the importance of message variables. More attention should be devoted to other content variables such as source attribution and the placement of campaign series. Future research studies should also consider the theoretical implications of including a third matrix of agenda-setting variables devoted entirely to message characteristics.

VI NEW APPROACHES TO AGENDA-SETTING

This final section assesses the contributions and limitations of agenda-setting studies. It also provides guidance for future research. "The agenda-setting hypothesis . . . attributes to the media at one and the same time too little and too much influence," Kurt and Gladys Lang assert. The Langs and other authors in this section address this criticism by discussing fresh ways of thinking about the agenda-setting formulation.

Oscar Gandy, Jr. contends that agenda-setting research has suffered from overemphasizing the media's impact on the public's agenda. He challenges researchers to go "beyond agenda-setting" by examining how media content is itself shaped by powerful societal forces. Gandy focuses on the use of "information subsidies" by interest groups and bureaucracies to influence journalistic priorities and work routines.

The reading by Kurt and Gladys Lang offers a new approach to agenda-setting that arises from their analysis of the Watergate scandal. The Langs call Watergate a "high threshold" issue, one that is removed from people's direct experiences. They state that such issues require widespread and sustained media attention to rise on the public's agenda of concerns. Only when Watergate received this attention, in large measure because of actions taken in political and governmental arenas, did the scandal become salient enough to topple the Nixon presidency. To the Langs, "agenda-building" — the process by which media and other societal institutions interact over time to focus attention on an issue — is a more apt phrase for capturing the way agendas are set than the conventional "agenda-setting" notion.

Gene Burd's essay provides a normative assessment of the evolution of agenda-setting research. He finds many desirable trends, including the growth of multidisciplinary studies and the increased willingness to use agenda-setting as a handle for understanding larger questions about media and society. On the other hand, he criticizes some of the underlying assumptions and approaches of agenda-setting researchers. He calls for a broader reliance on qualitative research methods, and a less static view of the general public.

The readings in this section present various challenges to the conventional definitions and approaches of agenda-setting researchers. These challenges are worth summarizing here. First, the agenda-setting formulation is said to suffer occasionally from conceptual ambiguity. For example, does "agenda-setting" refer to changes in people's priorities but not their opinions, as though the two are always separate? Does "issue salience" include changes in *personal* priorities as well as *societal* or *policy* priorities?

Then there are questions about the unit of analysis that is being studied. By agenda-setting, do we mean media effects on individuals, groups or larger societal units? Can the term *agenda* be used in the same way for describing media, public, and policy priorities? And do public agendas matter in the making of media and policy agendas?

Other questions are raised about the directionality of agenda-setting effects. Do media affect public and policymaker priorities, or do they themselves reflect the concerns of their audiences? To what extent do interpersonal relations outside of mass communication (e.g., between journalists and policymakers or interest groups) influence media content and citizen priorities? Finally, is it meaningful to suggest that media "effects" can occur in a linear direction in a society that is complex and rapidly changing?

Clearly, these questions suggest that more research is needed before the agenda-setting quest is completed. While much has been accomplished since the early formulations of Lippmann, Cohen, and McCombs and Shaw, fresh endeavors using innovative methods will further advance our understanding of the agenda-setting role of mass media. Hopefully, this need will not escape the priorities of future scholars.

25 Beyond Agenda-Setting*

Oscar Gandy

BEYOND AGENDA SETTING

Some 10 years before its explicit formulation by McCombs and Shaw, Kurt and Gladys Lang had begun to specify an agenda-setting function for the mass media. They argued that the mass media structured a reality which was so pervasive and so obtrusive that it was difficult, if not impossible, to escape its influence. On the basis of their analysis of the presidential campaigns of 1948 and 1952, they concluded that there was an important role for the media in defining the limits of political debate, and specifying the issues upon which voters would decide how to vote.[1]

Although based in part on the earlier work of Berelson, Lazarsfeld, and McPhee,[2] the work of the Langs offered some important insights that either had eluded researchers or had presented them with insurmountable methodological problems. They rejected Joseph Klapper's "limited effects"[3] view of media power, describing such findings as artifacts of the dominant research paradigm. Research then, as now, focused primarily on the period of the electoral campaign. And, as they suggest,

> the very emphasis on change *within* the span of a campaign makes it almost inevitable that whatever realignments occur are limited by the more permanent identifications and loyalties existing at the time the study is started. . . . All these

*Reprinted with permission of Ablex from *Beyond Agenda Setting: Information Subsidies and Public Policy* by Oscar H. Gandy, Jr. Copyright © 1982 by Ablex.

habits and orientations have their roots outside the campaign . . . examination of change within this short span fails altogether to account for the cumulative impact of media exposure.[4]

In their view, *all* news is relevant to the vote, not merely the speeches made during the campaign. Media coverage of important events, the state of the economy, and relations with foreign governments all contribute to the public's impression of the kind of leadership they will accept at that particular moment in history.

In arguing for the extension of the boundaries of research on mass media, public opinion, and political behavior, they provided the theoretical basis upon which contemporary agenda-setting research is built.

Building on the work of the Langs, and incorporating similar theoretical departures in the area of political socialization (cognitive development and attitude formation), McCombs and Shaw provided the first empirical verification of what they called the agenda-setting function of the mass media.[5] By selecting a sample of undecided voters, they hoped to avoid the tendency toward selective exposure attributed to political partisans. Subjects were asked to identify the key issues in the campaign as they saw them, without regard to the positions on those issues taken by candidates. A content analysis of selected media provided a list of 15 categories of issues of major and minor importance to the press, as reflected in the number of appearances of those issues. The high correlation between what the media treated as important, and what the undecided voters considered to be important, was taken as evidence of the media's power to influence the salience of issues, thereby setting the public agenda.

This publication stimulated a great number of attempts to replicate the main effect, to see if it varied across media and across classes of issues.[6] As with other studies of mass media effects,[7] agenda-setting research efforts revealed the complexity of the phenomenon as different variables were used as the basis for comparisons. There were differences in the strength of the relationship between content and public agendas as researchers examined different contingent conditions. Media users were seen to differ in the extent to which they were interested in public affairs, were knowledgeable of issues and candidates' positions on them, engaged in discussion of political issues with family and friends, or expressed a "need for orientation" within a swirl of media content. These differences were reflected in varying degrees of agreement between media and personal agendas.

Methodological concerns about the measurement of media and public agendas have also been expressed.[8] It matters greatly how one asks respondents about the nature of their priorities. Black people, who have tended to set themselves apart from and in opposition to the policies and concerns of the Reagan administration, would give one response to the question: "What are the most important problems facing the government today?," and quite another to the question: "What are the most important problems facing black people today?"

It matters greatly whether one limits the assessment of the media agenda to the news items covered by the networks, or includes the agenda of problems faced by the principal characters in prime-time fiction. The strength of the correlations between public and media agendas varies with the number of categories or items arranged in any list of priorities—the longer the list, the lower the correlation.

There are even problems associated with determining just what the temporal relationship ought to be between media attention to an issue and its elevation to a place of importance in the public agenda.[9] Some kinds of issues or events move easily to the public agenda, others take more time, and the theoretical base of agenda-setting research is incapable of predicting just what that optimal lag should be. This problem of time is addressed by the Langs in their examination of Watergate as an issue that moved quite late onto the public agenda, despite its early coverage in the media.[10]

They describe certain issues as being "low threshold" issues, and because of the link between these issues and an individual's personal well-being, items covered in the press are of immediate importance. Those issues that do not touch the lives of most members of the audience are seen to have a high threshold, and require considerable media attention to achieve the same level of salience in the public consciousness. This notion may be seen to be somewhat akin to Gerbner et al.'s notion of *resonance,* where objective conditions and experiences serve to heighten the impact of media portrayals of violence or other social realities.[11] In the specific case of Watergate, the Langs also suggest that in addition to the fact that the break-in did not impinge on anyone's lives, the story "appeared outlandish to most people," and the "phenomenon of incredulity" served to keep the scandal off the public agenda for a long period of time.[12]

The list of conditions and cautions associated with gathering scholarly evidence in support of the existence of an agenda-setting effect is lengthy, and bound to grow longer. Researchers, anxious to earn additional publications through the presentation of significant differences, or strong, positive correlations, will continue to offer their own idiosyncratically defined formulations of the basic relationship between media and public consciousness. In the end, the conclusions will be the same as those always offered by the armies of equivocation: some media coverage will affect the agendas of some people, regarding some issues, some of the time.

By pursuing the infinite regress of individual differences, there is no question that research will find variations in the impact of media agendas. But does that really matter? Is it a difference that makes a difference in the final analysis of power?

As the Langs suggest,[13] the agenda-setting formulation is both too little and too much at the same time. All consciousness is not based on exposure to media. Although the amount is smaller all the time, *some* awareness is based on direct experience with our environment. At the same time, public issues and political action are not determined solely by the knowledge and perceived importance of issues and events. However, because McCombs and his colleagues[14] want to limit the agenda-setting construct to matters of issue salience, I suggest that we have to go beyond agenda-setting to determine who sets the media agenda, how and for what purposes it is set, and with what impact on the distribution of power and values in society.

In developing answers to these questions, I have turned toward political economy, and away from the traditional social-psychological base upon which much of the empirical work in mass communications is built. Knowledge and information are seen to have economic and political value through their relation to power, or to control over the actions of others. In capitalist societies in general, and in the United States in particular, the power of knowledge and information has been amplified by the tendency of such societies to transform essentially public goods into private property.

In addition, as with other commodities that are produced for sale in capitalist markets, the market for information is characterized by both shortage and surplus. Some information, like advertising and other promotional messages, is over-produced, and is provided free to its consumers. Indeed, in many cases, people are paid indirectly to consume advertising messages when the sources of the information sponsor entertainment or news in the mass media. Other information, such as that necessary to evaluate the risks associated with genetic research and development, is not available to the general population at any price.

Because information is at the heart of individual and collective decision making, control of information implies control over decision making. And, since the exchange of information is determined largely on an economic basis, maldistribution in economic resources will be reflected in maldistribution of information. Such an economic perspective makes it possible to see control over the decisions and actions of others as flowing from the power to control their access to information.

Within a capitalist society, manipulation of prices is one way to control the consumption of information. With information, as with most commodities, when the price is lowered, the amount consumed increases; when the price is raised, the amount consumed generally decreases. Those with the power to control the price of information not only control its consumption, they also influence the decisions that are based on that information. Thus, if information opposed to the development of nuclear energy were made available at a lower price than that set for information in support of its use, more of the critical information would be consumed, and by extension, decision makers would be inclined to restrict its development. Persons who favor the development of nuclear energy would, therefore, have an incentive to lower the price of favorable information.

Indeed, all who have an interest in such decisions have an incentive to influence the prices faced by others for information related to those decisions. Efforts to reduce the prices faced by others for certain information, in order to increase its consumption, are described as *information subsidies*.[15] It is through the provision of information subsidies to and through the mass media that those with economic power are able to maintain their control over a capitalist society.

In turning away from social psychology in order to understand the role of information and media in the maintenance of the status quo, I have also turned away from the traditional focus on the audience or consumer as the target of mass communications. While the impact of information subsidies on individual and collective decision making is important to our understanding of power, much is already known. What we do not know, and what this book seeks to explore, are the relatively unknown dimensions of source behavior and the structural conditions that facilitate the use of information as an instrument of social control.

FOCUS ON THE SOURCE

There are a great many ways in which one can begin to characterize the sources of mass media content. The media may be viewed collectively, as is often the case in those agenda-setting studies that seek to demonstrate how "the media" set the public agenda with regard to the most important issues of the day. Other studies may divide the media into subgroups, print and electronic, in an effort to determine which wings of the monolith are more important and influential in setting the agenda of audience groups. In either approach, the media content is taken as given, and only peripheral interest is shown in determining how the agenda is set from day to day, from edition to edition.

A much smaller group of researchers begins with media content, but attempts to draw inferences about the nature of media organization on the basis of consistencies or patterns of attention and emphasis that characterize some sources and not others. Just as psychiatrists are able to draw inferences about the psychological "states" of their patients, content analysts draw inferences about the "managerial assumptions" that determine the content of mass media.[16]

A more direct approach, characterized by Gerbner as institutional process analysis,[17] uses the techniques of participant and nonparticipant observation to describe the procedures, pressures, and constraints that result in the production of a characteristic symbolic structure. This regularity in content is seen to be the result of the interplay of various institutional pressures imposed on the media by various sources of power, including

> the authorities who issue licenses and administer the laws; the patrons who invest in or subsidize the operation; organizations, institutions and loose aggregations of publics that require attention and cultivation; (and) the managements that set policies and supervise operation.[18]

Although Gerbner identified nine major sources of power or influence over message production, the bulk of mainstream research has been focused on the group he calls the Experts—the creative talent, technicians, or professionals who create, organize, and transmit media content. Within this group, the focus is even narrower, where researchers have tended to concentrate on the work of journalists, reporters, and editors as they operate the gates of the capitalist press. These "gatekeeper" studies traditionally view news content as the result of individual action, and seek to understand that action by understanding the background and personality of journalists.

The first, and perhaps the most important, of these studies was David Manning White's 1950 study of news selection by the opinionated "Mr. Gates."[19] White sought to discover the reasons behind the wire editor's selection of only 10% of the stories available to him during a given week. He classified the reasons given most frequently by the editor, and noted with particular interest the ideological character of many of the editor's comments. Stories were rejected because they were "propaganda" or "too red," and occasionally, because they were probably false, as indicated by the "B.S." label applied by Mr. Gates. Most important of all, however, was the limitation of space. Stories that made their way past other more personal filters were rejected because there was not enough space for their publication. In spite of this, White concluded that the editor had considerable independent power over media content and that "the community shall hear as a fact only those events which the newsman, as the representative of his culture, believes to be true."[20]

Walter Gieber, writing in 1963, had a somewhat more realistic view of the constraints or limits on the power of individual journalists or editors:

> the fate of the local news story is not determined by the needs of the audience or even by the values of the symbols it contains. The news story is controlled by the frame of reference created by the bureaucratic structure of which the communicator is a member.[21]

Paul Hirsch, in pursuing this structuralist view somewhat further, suggests that the requirements of the organization far outweigh any individual preferences that may guide any single gatekeeper.[22] His reanalysis of White's original study calls our attention to the surprising degree of consistency in the percentage of stories of a given type supplied by the wire services, and the percentages finally selected by the editor. While Mr. Gates may have had any number of *reasons* or personal justifications for the selections he made, he was "exercising discretion only within the latitude permitted for selecting particular stories to fit standard, widely agreed-upon categories, in the usual (expected) proportions that characterize a medium-sized, midwestern daily with a predominately conservative readership."[23]

GATEKEEPERS AND THEIR SOURCES

Within the context of organizational or structural requirements, recent studies of the nature of newswork have taken notice of the relationship between journalists and their sources. For some, this relationship is seen as social; for others, it is essentially economic. Herbert Gans, for example, uses a primarily social metaphor:

> The relationship between sources and journalists resembles a dance, for sources seek access to journalists, and journalists seek access to sources. Although it takes two to tango, either sources or journalists can lead, but more often than not, sources do the leading.[24]

Stephen Hess suggests that a kind of personal affinity brings journalists and their sources into contact. "Some news sources are automatic—people who must be approached because of the positions they hold. But otherwise, reporters seek news sources they prefer to be with . . . they like each other— and hate each other—because they are so much alike."[25] Hess suggests that certain sources, because of their styles, their use of bureaucratic language, and their reliance on documents and "boring statistics," are almost repellent to journalists.

Others suggest that regular contact between journalists and their sources may lead to some degree of personal identification, which may result in a hesitancy on the part of those journalists to reveal information that might harm or otherwise erect a barrier between them and their friends. This is seen to be particularly true for science writers, who because they are highly trained in their specialization, and are frequently in contact with scientists on a collegial basis, are "less likely to report science in a way that deviates from the norms of the scientific community, particularly in areas of controversy involving scientists."[26] Edie Goldenberg suggests that this interaction between journalists and their sources will, over time, tend to separate the reporters from their readership as the primary targets of their writing. Rather than writing for the mass audience, journalists who are in regular contact with government officials, and other reporters on the city hall beat, come to write instead for the friends they see each day.[27]

As important as these social explanations may seem to be, it is possible to reduce them to their basic economic considerations. Even social interaction can be seen in terms of costs and benefits, investments and rewards. Journalists have to meet deadlines, editors have to fill space, producers must fill the time between the commercials. In order to reduce their uncertainty about meeting these fairly standard organizational requirements, journalists enter into relationships of exchange with their sources that have many of the qualities of traditional economic markets. Although there is no exchange of cash, except in those few cases of "checkbook journalism," where reporters pay their sources for information, there is still an exchange of value. Journalists decide whether to invest time in the pursuit of one source rather than another, based on their estimation of the probable returns such an investment will produce. Those sources who have proved their value in the past are selected over those who are either unknown or have reduced their value by providing false information, or information in a form that was not easily converted into a publishable story.

Certain classes of sources have been identified as being more reliable than others. Official bureaucracies, or bureaucratically organized institutions, tend to be the most reliable, and as a result, bureaucratically supplied information comes to dominate mass media channels. Mark Fishman sees bureaucratic sources as doing much of the work of journalists.[28] Even when a journalist is aware that there is substantial self-interest involved in a particular controversy, and with a little effort the reporter could construct a balanced examination of the issues, Fishman suggests that the rule of least effort usually guides journalistic behavior:

> If reporters see that an agency in the beat territory has already claimed a controversy . . . then reporters will not take it upon themselves to assemble a constellation of interests around the event or establish a common framework with which accounts are brought into correspondence. This work is already done for them by officials.[29]

Investigative reporting, or enterprise news, is time-consuming, and journalists have only so much time to invest in the production of a story. Where the average journalist may generate one "think piece" a week, the use of bureaucratic sources facilitates the production of two or more routine stories each day. In Goldenberg's terms, "reporters had to have great energy and dedication to ferreting out stories to emerge from the overwhelming number of stories handed to them and do investigative journalism."[30]

Reliance on bureaucratic sources is facilitated by the tendency of journalists to accept information from these routine sources as factual. When the factual nature of information is not questioned, journalists need not invest valuable time in an effort to obtain verification. While journalists resist the implication that they are the victims of bureaucratic propaganda efforts, and vehemently deny the possibility that they hold any sources as being above suspicion, Dan Nimmo would respond that the proof is in the pages.[31] Far too many news releases are successful in achieving publication for each to have been subjected to more than a cursory review.

Leon Sigal's analysis[32] of the stories appearing on page one of *The New York Times* and *The Washington Post* supports Nimmo's conclusion. Of nearly 1,200 stories, 58.2% were identified as coming through routine bureaucratic channels — official proceedings, press releases and conferences, and nonspontaneous or planned events. Only 25.8% of the most important stories in these elite newspapers could be identified as the product of investigative or enterprise journalism. And, to the extent that interviews, the largest category of enterprise channels, could also be seen as the result of routine access to bureaucratic spokespersons, very little of the news has its origin in an investigatory mode.

Even when journalists are sure that the information bears checking, there are other economic considerations that lead them to go with the flow, to follow the pack. In Fishman's discussion of the case of a police department-created "crime wave,"[33] a newly created police unit sought publicity by leaking stories about an increase in attacks by black and Hispanic youths against poor elderly whites. Despite the fact that police statistics had shown an actual decrease in such crimes, journalists were unable to resist the pressure to follow this "non-story." Because other journalists and other media channels were covering the story, and publishing each new report as it was issued by the police unit, it was less costly to go along with the trend than to risk criticism or to invest in producing a more attractive alternative.

It is clear that journalists and other gatekeepers benefit from the relationships they establish with sources best able to meet their needs. It is also easy to see how they come to favor those bureaucratic sources who can provide a regular, credible, and ultimately usable flow of information, insight, and imagery with which to construct the news. But what value does the source receive in return?

The value of controlled access to target audiences through mass media channels is found ultimately in its contribution to source control over decisions made by the targets. Information is an important input in the production of influence, and the news media are primary means for the delivery of information. Because of the credibility normally associated with news, in comparison with that associated with commercial speech, sources would prefer to have their message delivered in a 30-second news item, than in a 60-second commercial.

In choosing between reporters and techniques for attracting the reporter's attention, sources are concerned with questions of cost-effectiveness. Press releases, briefings, and press conferences are seen to be economically efficient because they provide sources with access to several reporters at the same time, saving the time that would be spent in individual interviews. Some of the newer forms of what Dom Bonafede refers to as "socialized journalism" are even more efficient.[34] Special breakfasts and luncheon meetings where key officials and politicians are invited to speak before a select group of reporters have become popular with sources as well as reporters. These events not only "offer the guests an opportunity to get 15 or so interviews out of the way at once," but do it in a more highly controlled atmosphere where the "invitations-only" nature of the event serves to screen out the "kooks," who tend to ask embarassing questions or fail to follow the rules of the game regarding the use of background or off-the-record information.

Because the targets of these information subsidies vary from source to source, they will differ in their use of techniques to meet a journalist's needs. Altheide and Johnson suggest that bureaucrats generally aim their information subsidies at specialized rather than mass audiences.[35] Thus, they will select those channels which are used more regularly by high-level government officials and policy makers. Although it might take less effort to gain access to the editorial pages of several small-town newspapers, the expected value from such exposure is almost nonexistent when compared to that derived from positive editorial treatment in *The Washington Post*.

It is the goal of all sources to influence decisions by changing the stock of information upon which those decisions are based. Since the public is generally only marginally involved in the determination of public policy, and because the costs of molding public opinion are often quite high, sources have greater incentives to use the press to *define* public opinion than to influence it directly. Still, there are times when an effort to mobilize grass-roots support is economically justified. Then sources select those techniques that ensure the widest coverage for the least effort. Very often this means concentrating on the wire services and papers like *The New York Times*. A press release that is successful in gaining access to the Associated Press (AP) or United Press International (UPI) wires is more efficient than individual releases sent to each newspaper in the nation. And just as the wire services set the front page agendas of the nation's urban papers, the elite papers like the *Times* set the agenda for the networks. Assignment editors spend their mornings reading the *Post* and the *Times*. Adams and Albin suggest that "there are many topics that get newspaper coverage while being scarcely covered by television. There are virtually no topics that receive television news attention that are non-issues in elite newspapers."[36] In Gitlin's words, "the *Times* is, in fact, one of the main channels through which network newsworkers form pictures of the world, what is happening there, and what, within that world, deserves coverage."[37]

Often the value of an information subsidy for any source is increased to the extent that the source can disguise the promotional, partisan, self-interested quality of the information. This is often accomplished when news stories convey the desired information without identifying its source. Information that would be accepted only with caution if its source were identified as a partisan in a debate is much more powerful if it is received as objective fact, reported by an uninterested journalist.

On occasion, government policy deliberations involve struggles within the administration, or between administration and bureaucracy. Sources that want to influence the debate without risking the wrath of superiors seek journalists who will allow them to "leak" the information into the news media. Leaks are also important as techniques for launching "trial balloons." A policy maker who wishes to test public sentiment, or the receptiveness of others in the policy arena, without associating herself with a losing policy option, can avoid that risk by leaking the information first and taking responsibility for it later, if the response to the idea is favorable.

Whereas the journalist selects from an array of sources and events on the basis of perceived utility in producing news that will meet organizational requirements, sources select from an even larger array of techniques on the basis of their relative efficiency in the production of influence over the knowledge, attitudes, and behavior of others.

NOTES

1. Lang, Kurt, and Lang, Gladys. (1971). The mass media and voting. *In* W. Schramm, and D. Roberts (Eds.), "The Process and Effects of Mass Communication," revised ed., pp. 678–700. Urbana, Illinois: University of Illinois Press.

2. Berelson, Bernard, Lazarsfeld, Paul F., and McPhee, William M. (1971). Political power: the role of the mass media. *In* W. Schramm, and D. Roberts (Eds.), "The Process and Effects of Mass Communication," revised ed., pp. 655–667. Urbana, Illinois: University of Illinois Press.

3. Klapper, Joseph. (1960). "The Effects of Mass Communication." New York: The Free Press.

4. Lang, Kurt, and Lang, Gladys. Page 683 in footnote 13, 1971.

5. McCombs, Max, and Shaw, Donald. (1972). The agenda-setting function of mass media. *Public Opinion Quarterly 36* (Summer), 176–187.

6. A comprehensive review of agenda setting and related studies is published *in* D. Shaw, and M. McCombs (Eds.). (1977). "The Emergence of American Political Issues: The Agenda-Setting Function of the Press." St. Paul, Minnesota: West Publishing.

7. McLeod, Jack, and Reeves, Byron. (1980). On the nature of mass media effects. *In* Stephen B. Whithey, and Ronald P. Abeles (Eds.), "Television and Social Behavior: Beyond Violence and Children." Hillsdale, New Jersey: Lawrence Erlbaum Associates.

8. De George, William F. (1981). Conceptualization and measurement of audience agenda. *In* G. Wilhoit, and H. de Bock (Eds.), "Mass Communication Review Yearbook," Vol. 2, pp. 219–224. Beverly Hills, California: Sage Publications.

9. Eyal, Chaim, Winter, James P., and De George, William F. (1981). The concept of time frame in agenda setting. *In* G. Wilhoit, and H. de Bock (Eds.), "Mass Communication Review Yearbook" Vol. 2, pp. 212-218. Beverly Hills, California: Sage Publications.

10. Lang, Gladys, and Lang, Kurt. (1981). Watergate: an exploration of the agenda-building process. *In* G. Wilhoit, and H. de Bock (Eds.), "Mass Communication Review Yearbook," Vol. 2, pp. 447-468. Beverly Hills, California: Sage Publications.

11. Gerbner, George, Gross, Larry, Morgan, Michael, and Signorielli, Nancy. (1980). The main-streaming of America: violence profile no. 11. *Journal of Communication 30* (No. 3) (Summer), 10-25.

12. Lang, Gladys, and Lang, Kurt. Pages 458-459 in footnote 22, 1981.

13. *Ibid.,* pp. 465-466.

14. McCombs, Maxwell. (1981). Setting the agenda for agenda-setting research; an assessment of the priority idea and problems. *In* G. Wilhoit, and H. de Bock (Eds.), "Mass Communication Review Yearbook," Vol. 2, pp. 209-211. Beverly Hills, California: Sage Publications.

15. Bartlett, Randall. (1973). "Economic Foundations of Political Power." New York: The Free Press.

16. Gerbner, George. (1964). On content analysis and critical research in mass communications. *In* L. Dexter, and D. White (Eds.), "People, Society, and Mass Communications," pp. 476-500. New York: The Free Press.

17. Gerbner, George. (1972). Communication and social environment. *Scientific American 227* (No. 3), 153-160.

18. *Ibid.,* pp. 156-157.

19. White, David M. (1964). The gatekeeper: a case study in the selection of news. *In* L. Dexter, and D. White (Eds.), "People, Society, and Mass Communications," pp. 160-172. New York: The Free Press.

20. *Ibid.,* p. 171.

21. Gieber, Walter. (1964). News is what newspapermen make it. *In* L. Dexter, and D. White (Eds.), "People, Society, and Mass Communications," p. 178. New York: The Free Press.

22. Hirsch, Paul. (1977). Occupational, organizational, and institutional models in mass media research: toward an integrated framework. *In* P. Hirsch, P. Miller, and F. Kline (Eds.), "Strategies for Communication Research," pp. 13-42. Beverly Hills, California: Sage Publications.

23. *Ibid.,* p. 23.

24. Gans, Herbert J. (1979). "Deciding What's News: A Study of CBS Evening News, NBC Nightly News, Newsweek and Time," p. 116. New York: Pantheon Books.

25. Hess, Stephen. (1981). "The Washington Reporters," p. 126. Washington, D.C.: The Brookings Institution.

26. Donohue, George A., Tichenor, Phillip J., and Olien, Clarice N. (1973). Mass media functions, knowledge, and social control. *Journalism Quarterly 50* (No. 4) (Winter), 656.

27. Goldenberg, Edie N. (1975). "Making the Papers," p. 79. Lexington, Massachusetts: D.C. Heath.

28. Fishman, Mark. (1980). "Manufacturing the News," pp. 45-46. Austin, Texas: University of Texas Press.

29. *Ibid.,* p. 132.

30. Goldenberg, Edie N. Page 80 in footnote 39, 1975.

31. Nimmo, Dan. (1978). "Political Communication and Public Opinion in America," p. 207. Santa Monica, California: Goodyear Publishing.

32. Sigal, Leon V. (1973). "Reporters and Officials," pp. 119-130. Lexington, Massachusetts: D.C. Heath.

33. Fishman, Mark. Pages 5-10 in footnote 40, 1980.

34. Bonafede, Dom. (1981). Reporters' breakfast and lunch groups — good reporting or "socialized journalism?" *National Journal* (March 21), 487–491.

35. Altheide, David, and Johnson, John. (1980). "Bureaucratic Propaganda," pp. 18–21. Boston, Massachusetts: Allyn and Bacon.

36. Adams, William, and Albin, Suzanne. (1980). Public information on social change: TV coverage of women in the work force. *Policy Studies Journal 8* (No. 5) (Spring), 729.

37. Gitlin, Todd. (1980). "The Whole World is Watching," p. 299. Berkeley, California: University of California Press.

26 Watergate: An Exploration of the Agenda-Building Process*

Gladys Engel Lang
Kurt Lang

The conviction that mass communications are a powerful political force has survived the frustration of researchers trying to tease out direct effects from the fabric of surrounding social influences. During the past decade the conviction has gained new strength from studies documenting the correspondence between the amount of media attention a problem receives and the amount of public concern, findings that have been cast into the language of "agenda setting." The theorem that the mass media set the public agenda boils down to the proposition that, during a political campaign and on other occasions, "people learn from the media what the important issues are." As a result, the search for political effects has changed direction. The focus of inquiry has turned away from persuasion and toward changes in the salience of certain objects on the political landscape; away from the content of public opinion (what people think) and toward the things about which the public has opinions (what people think about).

The apparent simplicity of this reformulation helps explain much of its attractiveness. Almost any observed correlation between aggregate measure of content on one hand and the cognitions of the audience on the other is consistent with the agenda-setting hypothesis. This is certainly how McCombs and Shaw,[1] in introducing the neologism into communication research, interpreted the match they found between what voters said were key issues in

*Gladys Engel Lang and Kurt Lang, *Mass Communication Review Yearbook,* (Vol. 2, pp 447–453, 455–456, 459, 464–468) copyright 1981 by Sage Publications Inc. Reprinted by permission of Sage Publications Inc.

the 1968 election and the emphasis given these issues in the media coverage of the campaign.

The hypothesis also rests firmly on a simple and highly plausible premise: The perceptions people have of the larger universe, of the things they cannot see for themselves, which includes most of the political environment, are rarely the result of direct observation and experience. They are, as Lippmann[2] was among the first to point out, known only secondhand, derived mostly from mass media reports. In the political realm, other organized and interpersonal channels, important and effective as they may be, play only a supplementary role, operating within a larger symbolic context provided by media messages. Public recognition by media can also add a new dimension to people's experience, even where the objects or events in the news are familiar or already directly known to them.[3]

Since the publication of McCombs and Shaw's trend-setting article, there has been a host of "quick, almost casual, empirical forays" into agenda-setting.[4] The value of many of these studies, which we have no intention of reviewing here, is diminished both by certain methodological inadequacies and the lack of a clear theoretical framework. There is no question that such a framework is needed, and it is toward this objective that the present paper, drawing on material about Watergate, makes a modest step. We start from the observation that the agenda-setting hypothesis—the bland and unqualified statement that the mass media set the agenda for political campaigns—attributes to the media at one and the same time too little and too much influence. The whole question of how issues originate is sidestepped, nor is there any recognition of the process through which agendas are built or through which an object that has caught public attention, by being big news, gives rise to a political issue. In other words, while agenda-setting research, like most research, suffers from methodological shortcomings, the more basic problems are conceptual.

SOME CONCEPTUAL PROBLEMS

What follows is a brief annotated catalogue of some of these problems. First, there is the distinction between content and salience. What people think may not be as easily separable from what they think about, as the various formulations of agenda-setting have implied.[5] On the contrary, many differences of opinion originate from the different weights people attach to elements in a complex situation.[6] Therefore, the clever campaigner will seek to persuade by focusing on those issues that work in his or her favor while deliberately playing down those that might work for the opponent. Salience is related to content insofar as a problem with only minimal recognition by the media may be perceived as welcome news and judged important because it is the preferred talking point of one's candidate or party. Watergate—to cite the issue that serves as a vehicle for illuminating agenda-setting—was perceived as a McGovern issue throughout the 1972 campaign and therefore considered important by many of his more dedicated supporters.[7] What they thought about the break-in and its implications made them think it important. Most people did not think about it because they did not think it a serious matter.

Second, some of the observed correlations between salience and media content may be nothing more than an artifact of the subject categories under which specific news items are classified. In other words, that they may be produced by the research method and not by the media can best be illustrated by a comparison of the original study by McCombs and Shaw and another by Robert Frank,[8] who used questions from the Gallup Poll to see if news emphasis matched public concerns. The first of these studies found an impressive correlation of +.979, concluding that the composite of the media coverage was reflected in the judgment of voters on five major issue categories: foreign policy, law and order, fiscal policy, public welfare, and civil rights. Foreign policy ranked far above the other four both in media coverage and as the object of voter concern in 1968. Frank's 1972 data showed "international problems" to be the most overrepresented network news category, in the sense that the public "could not care less" about this part of the news; contrariwise, the Vietnam war was of "even greater interest to the American people than the relatively large amount of airtime devoted to the subject."[9] These discrepancies showed up only because Frank had put all Vietnam items into a separate category instead of subsuming them under foreign policy, as had McCombs and Shaw. Granted, the two studies were conducted four years apart, but would the 1968 study have found as great a correlation had Vietnam been introduced as a sixth category distinct from other international problems faced by the United States?

The third question relates to the matter of causal influence. Instantaneous effects are improbable except under conditions of crisis, where the reported event signals a danger threatening most everyone, so that a media buildup is generally expected to precede any rise in public concern. According to one study, the strongest relationship between media emphasis and issue salience was obtained when correlations were lagged by four months.[10] However, the time element may vary, and the number of other factors that operate during the buildup period with potentially reinforcing effects on the issue's salience should make us cautious about the direction of any media effect. Salience can dictate media coverage. Some events, moreover, operate as sleepers; concern rises as media attention diminishes. For example, a school strike usually receives maximum coverage during its early days but becomes a cause of increasing concern, even with sporadic news treatment, as children who miss their classes fall further and further behind in their school work. Coverage usually picks up again, briefly, until a settlement reduces parental concern.

A fourth question turns on the unit of analysis: Is it the individual who is made aware of a problem and comes to recognize its importance after having learned of it from the mass media, or is agenda-setting a process through which an issue develops? Although we clearly opt for the latter alternative, it remains indisputable that individuals have different thresholds of sensitivity and that not everyone is apt to respond to the same coverage in the same way. How much an individual's awareness and perceptions of salience are affected by the amount of coverage depends on certain dispositional factors. In particular, it is the potential utility of news items — that is, the belief that they depict developments with some bearing on their own situation — that makes some people pay attention. Others with no perceived stake in the outcome of events may follow the same developments, mainly to satisfy a more diffuse interest in political news of all kinds. Different dispositions can make a problem reported by the press salient for both groups, even where the coverage is less than phenomenal. To the extent that this happens, stepping up the amount of news cannot do much to raise the salience the problem has for this group — a ceiling has already been approached. This ceiling effect may, at a stage in the development of the issue, yield empirical observations that at first glance seem to refute the agenda-setting function of the mass media. After an issue has made headlines for some time, the largest increases in salience are recorded not among the most interested but among the least interested and therefore the least exposed to the mass media. It does not follow from this finding that media exposure has a negative effect. Such findings only demonstrate, first, how much it can take for an issue to break through to public consciousness and, second, that patterns of individual responses need always to be analyzed within the framework of a larger collective process — in the case of Watergate, the framework of the transformation of the problem from campaign infighting readily dismissed to a matter of national importance.

This raises the fifth and probably most basic question: What is an issue? Without a clear definition, the concept of agenda-setting becomes so all-embracing as to be rendered practically meaningless. Thus, when Becker et al., in their review article,[11] have it cover *any* causal relationship "between the media coverage and the salience of topics in the minds of individuals in the audience," they obliterate any distinction between the personal and the political, between the many things that may enter discussion among intimates and the systemic agenda that stands for the range of the controversies that fall within the legitimate concern of the polity.[12] In fact, issues have been variously conceptualized as (1) *concerns,* the things about which people are personally worried; (2) *perceptions of key problems* facing the country, about which the government should do something; (3) the existence of *policy alternatives* between which people must choose (whether or not to support SALT II, an antiabortion amendment, and so on); (4) a *public controversy,* such as the one over Watergate; and (5) the "reasons" or underlying *determinants of political cleavage* (the "issue" most closely related to an electoral outcome or certain objective interests, such as class/occupation or race, even though these symbols may not enter the debate).

There is naturally some overlap in what would be included within each of the five definitions. A personal concern can also be identified as one of the most important problems facing the country, as an object of considerable public controversy or as the basis for an electoral decision. When there is much anxiety about its passage, even a policy alternative can become a matter of grave personal concern. To illustrate the point by a concrete example: McCombs and Shaw[13] asked respondents to name the "key" issues in the campaign — namely, the things the "government should concentrate on doing something about." The wording allows for a good deal of leeway but basically invites respondents to state their uppermost concerns (such as rising prices or crime in the streets), their perceptions of the most important "problem" (the economy or energy shortages), and the main "controversies" connected with a campaign (peace in Vietnam). The examples, though hypothetical, should make clear that the "issues" elicited as responses are not necessarily those critics have in mind when they blame the press for not paying more attention to the policy differences between the candidates. Nor are the "issues" apt to be named those on which electoral decisions are normally based.[14]

Most voters, whatever their specific concerns, still vote for the man or the party they believe has their own best interest at heart or simply for the one they believe would do the "better job."[15] This holds even for members of single-issue constituencies, who are guided by endorsements rather than by what the candidates say or avoid saying. Yet most people, when asked what they see as the "issues," are not at all hesitant to name one or the other, and the ones most often mentioned are those the candidates have stressed and the media have singled out for attention. They name issues even when they do not perceive differences in the candidates' positions on the issues named or even incorrectly associate their own policy preference with the candidate of their choice. Thus, in 1972, McGovern failed to hold enough of the natural "dovish" constituency that he needed to win, mainly because they had come to doubt his ability to make good, even on peace in Vietnam. While for them peace was the big issue facing the country, it was not at issue in their vote.

What is an issue? In the last analysis, it is whatever is in contention among a relevant public. The objects of potential controversy are diverse. A policy, a party and its platform or past performance, a personality, a particular act, or even a theory about such things as the state of the economy or the causes of a disease can stir public debate. Of course, many controversies — even political ones — remain invisible. Discussion may be confined to the political bodies legally charged with responsibility for making decisions. They may seek expert advice or be responsive to special interests. But it is not with politics on the more esoteric level that agenda-setting research is concerned. The public agenda, as opposed to the various institutional agendas, consists of only those issues on which "the people" form opinions and are inclined to take sides. This degree of participation can develop only through some medium of communication that links the polity and the public at large. In assessing the role of the media, one is compelled to take account of the different thresholds of attention, not only among individuals but also among issues.

ISSUE THRESHOLDS

Some issues arise out of conditions that *directly affect nearly everybody* in the same way, such as inflation, high taxes, and gasoline shortages, and therefore exhibit a strong propensity to show up as personal concerns. A different type is related to a situation whose effects are *selectively experienced,* such as urban congestion or draft calls. Last, there are conditions and developments whose effects are *generally remote* from just about everyone, such as the plight of refugees from Vietnam or wrongdoing high up in the government. The three categories, we argue, have vastly different thresholds of sensitivity, and the nature of the influence exerted by the media varies accordingly.

Economic conditions that affect nearly everyone tend to have low thresholds. The problem would be of general concern even without attention from the news media. However, concern is apt to be boosted in two ways: through media recognition that puts the problem into the public domain and through statements by political figures trying to mobilize certain constituencies with promises, by fixing blame, or courting support for some kind of political action. The "economic" issue moves onto the political agenda quite naturally. As it does, the political relevance of the voters' own economic position compared with that of the previous year recedes while the relevance of their perception of the state of economic affairs increases.[16] These perceptions are basically media generated, though as the number feeling personally worse off continues to increase, it becomes more difficult to believe prosperity is just around the corner, whatever is reported.

On other matters that are more selectively experienced, such as urban crime, the problem itself is made more visible and concern increased by media recognition. Reports of a crime wave can make even those not personally victimized cautious about walking the streets, even when there is little potential danger. Sensational media coverage can exaggerate the dimensions of a problem; it can also create a problem where none exists. For instance, speculations about an impending oil shortage helped spawn a run on existing supplies that led to a real shortage.[17] While continuing attention by the media helps keep a problem alive, lagging media recognition can slow the rise of concern, particularly when those most directly affected are few and/or powerless. The majority either remains unaware of the problem or downgrades its importance, as in the case of ghetto conditions that suddenly erupt into riots.[18]

The potential influence of the media is greatest when the public has no direct contact with the problem. Whether or not a major event, like the launching of the first Soviet sputnik or an American moon landing, becomes an issue depends on whether it is reported in a context of crisis and partisanship or as a unifying achievement. The style of coverage reflects, in turn, the existing political situation and the ability of political figures to seize on the event as an issue.

Problems compete for attention.[19] Therefore, the salience an issue has for elites or for the mass public is not just an absolute but to some extent a relative matter. A potentially explosive issue surfacing at the wrong time, when other controversies are dominating the polity and the news media, is apt to be ignored until the time is ripe for it. Here, too, thresholds are relevant. High-threshold issues encounter greater difficulties in gaining the attention of the news media, and even when they do (as through some sensational expose or foreign policy crisis) much depends on the ability of an administration, party, or candidate to identify with the cause or to steer clear of the negative implications. The controversy may affect political support without entering the list of most important problems. By contrast, low-threshold issues, because of their link to personal concerns, almost compel attention from political elites as well as the news media. This increases the likelihood that they will either displace or become assimilated into issues already on public agendas.

In analyzing the role of the mass media in structuring the issues of a campaign or the controversies of an era, one must go beyond a search for simple correspondences between the treatment of certain topics in the press and the extent to which the mass public is aware, informed, and concerned about these matters.

Watergate provides a prima facie case through which to consider the role of the mass media in agenda-setting. It allows us to examine, first, the failure of Watergate to become a significant factor in the outcome of the 1972 election and, second, the way Watergate erupted into a major controversy just five months later. As to the election, the press has been criticized for not giving sufficient coverage to Watergate and thereby burying the issue. On the other hand, the media have been lavishly praised for their key role in mobilizing the public; without their dogged pursuit of the facts, the scandal would have expired and the Nixon administration would not have been held accountable. Neither version quite accords with the evidence. . . .

Watergate obviously belongs in the category of high threshold "issues." The problem it signified was outside the range of most people's immediate concerns. The details of the incident seemed outlandish and their import difficult to fathom. Surfacing during a campaign, the whole story could more easily be dismissed, since denunciations of the opposition for unfair election-eering methods and low-level campaign tactics are endemic to American politics. Still, it is not unheard of for such charges as those leveled by McGovern to stick and for "corruption" and "dirty politics" to become a concern and provoke controversy in the heat of a campaign. Whether this happens is more contingent on recognition of the problem by the media than in the case of problems that directly impinge on everyone. For the "high threshold" issue mere recognition is not enough. It requires a buildup, which is a function of more than the amount of space and/or time the media devote to the story. The latter may push it past the threshold of inattention, but one must also look at the kind of coverage to explain how a remote incident like Watergate becomes an issue.

The apparent lack of impact of the Watergate news coverage can only be understood if one takes account of the political context: the fact that the story broke during an electoral contest and that it had to compete for attention against other political controversies. . . .

A half-year after Nixon's landslide victory, Watergate had become the center of a full-blown political controversy. Not only was nearly everybody aware of it,[42] but far more people than during the election expressed concern. Even before the televised hearings of the Senate Watergate Committee were to begin in May, Watergate had made its way, for the first time, onto the Gallup list of "most important problems facing the country today." Though clearly still lagging behind such low-threshold issues as "the high cost of living," mentioned by three out of five people, "Watergate and/or corruption in government" with 16 percent was in close competition with "crime and lawlessness" (17 percent) and "drugs" (16 percent) for second place.[43]

Meanwhile, the number of people willing to play ostrich and simply write the whole matter off as "just more politics," though still a plurality, had been steadily dwindling, and the number for whom the "bugging attempt" was "really something serious" had been going up correspondingly. ORC found that just three percent of their respondents believed in February that Nixon had ordered the break-in. Gallup and Harris, which did not resume polling on Watergate until April, registered similar increases in seriousness.

What first breathed new life into a story that had almost expired was the start of the trial of the Watergate defendants. It was scheduled and held in Washington with its unique concentration of news staffs. For much of January, the trial provided a continuous flow of news for the networks. But the real breakthrough did not come until much later. On March 23, the day his sentence was to be set, McCord's letter was read in open court. A bombshell, it spoke of "political pressure" on all the defendants to remain silent, of perjury during the trial, of higher-ups (not named) who were implicated in the Watergate operation. From this point on the disclosures began to fit together.

They had too much plausibility not to call for answers. The possibility of a scandal could no longer be ignored, even by the regional press still favorable to Nixon. After a brief break in Watergate headlines in early April, every one of five papers examined gave Watergate continuous and prominent coverage through the entire month before the Senate hearings. During this same month, 56 percent of the evening newscasts over the 23 weekdays led off with a Watergate story. No longer was it the "bugging incident." Enough evidence was out to persuade even the more hesitant editors that a major scandal was shaping up.

To create a Watergate issue, the media had to do more than just give the problem publicity. They had to stir up enough controversy to make it politically relevant, not only on the elite level but also to give the bystander public a reason for taking sides. By spring 1973, the public, for the most part, was still not outraged, but it was making its presence felt. The intense press coverage made it evident to political actors that, as more and more people were taking Watergate seriously, they would probably react negatively to anything that gave the appearance of a continuing attempt at coverup. Those in Congress insistent on a full investigation were able to exploit the widespread feeling that the whole truth about Watergate had not yet come out and maneuver the opposition into a corner. The many things from the closed hearings that found their way into the press stirred up enough controversy for the Watergate issue to mushroom into a full-blown scandal. As yet it did not appear as a personal threat, personally touching people's lives, as it would later, when the extent to which the administration had engaged in illegal electronic eavesdropping and other retribution against political enemies became public knowledge. But the public could not be called "apathetic," as it had been as late as March.[59]

AGENDA-BUILDING

To say that they set the agenda is to claim both too much and too little for the media of mass communication. There are, after all, concerns that do not originate from the media, in that they fall within most people's direct experience. Media recognition helps put these concerns into the public domain. What was a widespread concern is thereby "politicized." With regard to high-threshold issues, the media assume a still more important role. Except for the news reports about Watergate, most people would not have even known there was a problem. Media attention was a necessary condition for the emergence of the Watergate issue. Without it there would not have been the same amount of controversy. But the media do not operate in total autonomy from the political system, and their gradual saturation with Watergate news must be viewed in relation to political developments in which the press itself was one of the movers. Agenda-building is a collective process with some degree of reciprocity.

The Watergate issue had broken into public consciousness only after the media, by covering developments and by the way it covered them, had created a sense of real crisis. It was not something they had created out of whole cloth. The coverage, which stirred interest, was dictated by events, but the media were themselves part of the field of action. Political figures made use of whatever publicity they could attract to advance their own goals and interests, increasing the number of Watergate events there to be covered until the coverage escalated to reach saturation level, with Watergate on the front page and on the evening news day after day. The headlines alone would not have been enough to transform a problem so removed from most people's daily concerns into an issue, but there was enough continuity to rivet attention to the developing story. The process was circular with media exposure, political interest, and events on the elite level feeding one another.

Let us summarize the part played by the news media. First, the news media highlight some events, activities, groups, personalities, and so forth to make them stand out. Different kinds of issues require different amounts and kinds of coverage to gain attention. This common focus affects what people will think or talk about.

Second, the object that is the focus of attention still needs to be framed. It must come to stand for something — some problem or concern. The media can play up or down the more serious aspects of a situation.

The third step in the buildup links the object or event to secondary symbols, so that it becomes a part of the recognized political landscape. Something like interest aggregation is involved, since the line of division on the particular issue does not always coincide with the cleavage between the organized political parties or between other sharply defined groups. The media tend to weave discrete events into a continuing story, often a political one.

Finally, spokesmen who can articulate demands must make their appearance. Their effectiveness stems in good part from their ability to command media attention.

The process is a continuous one, involving a number of feedback loops, most important among which are the way political figures see their own image mirrored in the media, the pooling of information within the press corps, and the various indicators of the public response. We argue that a topic, problem, or key concern to which political leaders are or should be paying attention is not yet an *issue*. Important as the media may be in focusing attention, neither awareness nor perceived importance makes an issue. However, once the above-mentioned links are established, a topic may continue to be an issue even if other topics receive greater emphasis from the media.

NOTES

1. M.E. McCombs and D.L. Shaw (1972) "The Agenda-Setting Function of Mass Media." *Public Opinion Quarterly,* 36, pp. 176–187.

2. Walter Lippmann (1922) *Public Opinion.* New York. Lippmann developed his ideas during service with the Inter-Allied Propaganda Commission, and his bitterness at the "peace" settlement to World War II makes for fascinating reading in Ronald Steel, *Walter Lippmann and the American Century.* Boston, 1980.

3. See W.P. Davison (1960) "Political Significance of Recognition via Mass Media—an Illustration from the Berlin Blockade. *Public Opinion Quarterly,* 20, pp. 327–333.

4. M.E. McCombs (1979) *Setting the Agenda for Agenda-Setting Research.* Communication Research Center, Newhouse School of Public Communication, Syracuse University, June 1979 (mimeo), p. 3 states that fifty papers were produced in six years.

5. This formulation comes from Bernard Cohen, *The Press and Foreign Policy.* Princeton, N.J.: Princeton University Press, 1963, p. 120. Our own words, likewise cited by McCombs and Shaw in the above article, were "the mass media force attention to certain issues by suggesting what individuals in the mass should think about, know about, have feelings about." See also Kurt Lang & Gladys E. Lang, "The Mass Media and Voting," in E. Burdick and A.J. Brodbeck (eds.) *American Voting Behavior.* New York: Free Press, 1959, p. 232.

6. A. Lawrence Lowell (1913) *Public Opinion and Popular Government.* New York: Longman's, Green.

7. T.E. Patterson and R.D. McClure (1976) *The Unseeing Eye; the Myth of Television Power in National Politics.* New York: Putnam, p. 27.

8. R.S. Frank, *Message Dimensions of Television News.* Lexington, Mass.: Lexington Books, 1973.

9. Ibid, p. 61.

10. J.P. Winter, "An Agenda-Setting Time Frame for the Civil Rights Issue 1954–1976." Presented at the annual meeting of the American Association for Public Opinion Research, May 1979.

11. L.B. Becker, M.E. McCombs and J.M. McLeod (1975) "The Development of Political Cognitions," in S.H. Chaffee (ed.) *Political Communication.* Beverly Hills, Cal.: Sage, p. 38.

12. R.W. Cobb and C.D. Elder (1971) "The Politics of Agenda-Building: An Alternative Perspective for Modern Democratic Theory." *Journal of Politics,* 33, pp. 892–915.

13. McCombs and Shaw, op. cit.

14. A. Campbell et al. (1960) *The American Voter.* New York: John Wiley.

15. S. L. Popkin et al. (1976) "Toward an Investment Theory of Voting." *American Political Science Review,* 70, pp. 779–805.

16. D.R. Kinder and D.R. Kiewiet (1979) "Economic Discontent and Political Behavior: The Role of Personal Grievances and Collective Economic Judgments in Congressional Voting." *American Journal of Political Science,* 23, pp. 495–523.

17. H.M. Kepplinger and H. Roth (1979) "Creating a Crisis: German Mass Media and the Oil Supply in 1973–1974." *Public Opinion Quarterly,* 43, pp. 285–296.

18. National Advisory Commission on Civil Disorder (1968) *Report.* Washington: GPO.

19. T.W. Smith (1980) "America's Most Important Problem—A Trend Analysis." *Public Opinion Quarterly,* 44, pp. 164–180.

20. J. Perry (1973) *Us and Them; How the Press Covered the 1972 Election.* New York: Clarkson N. Potter.

21. B. Bagdikian (1973) "The Fruits of 'Agnewism.' " *Columbia Journalism Review,* Jan./Feb., p. 12.

22. The most complete study of the television coverage of the 1972 by Hofstetter does not have a category for Watergate but subsumes this subject under either "Republican party affairs" or

"government functioning." C. Richard Hofstetter (1976) *Bias in the News.* Columbus: Ohio State University Press. Our conclusion is based on (1) an unpublished paper by Lawrence W. Lichty, "Network News Reporting of Watergate During the 1972 Election," Madison, Wisconsin, 1974; (2) Diamond, op. cit.; and (3) Patterson and McClure, op. cit. for television; and on J. R. Holz (1976) "Watergate and Mass Communication: A Case Study in Public Agenda-Setting." Unpublished Master's thesis, University of Pennsylvania for the New York *Times* coverage. This has been supplemented by an analysis of the four papers indexed in the Bell & Howell Newspaper Index. For a comparison between television and newspapers, see D. A. Graber (1976) "The Press and TV as Opinion Resources in Presidential Campaigns." *Public Opinion Quarterly,* 40, pp. 285-303.

23. Gallup Opinion Index, 1935-1937.

24. ORC data were made available through the courtesy of Harry O'Neill and is gratefully acknowledged.

25. H. Mendelsohn and G. J. O'Keefe (1976) *The People Chose a President.* New York: Praeger, p. 200.

26. According to a Harris poll in mid-September 1972, 84 percent considered the attempt to wiretap another party's headquarters "a basic violation of individual freedom."

27. The same Harris poll showed 57 percent believing it a commonplace occurrence with another 15 percent uncertain.

28. ORC, August 28-30, 1973.

29. Ibid.

30. Both the Harris and the Time/Yankelovich polls give evidence of slippage.

31. The Harris Survey.

32. A.H. Miller and W.E. Miller (1975) "Issues, Candidates and Partisan Divisions in the 1972 American Presidential Election." *Journal of Political Science,* 5, pp. 393-434.

33. D.H. Weaver et al. (1975) "Watergate and the Media: A Case Study of Agenda-Setting." *American Politics Quarterly,* 3, pp. 452-472.

34. A byline story by Ronald Kessler.

35. We have omitted here any discussion of the controversy over the delay and the alleged reduction in the length of the second part of this enterprise.

36. Bagdikian, op. cit.

37. E.R. May and J. Fraser, eds. (1973) *Campaign '72: The Managers Speak.* Cambridge: Harvard, p. 207.

38. Popkin et al., op. cit.

39. *The Harris Yearbook 1972,* p. 70, 72. In October, a majority believed that McGovern would get peace on the wrong terms and nearly as many thought his election would slow down the return of American prisoners as thought would speed it up.

40. Miller and Miller, op. cit.

41. A.S. Edelstein and D. P. Tefft (1976) "Media Credibility and Respondent Credulity with Respect to Watergate." *Communication Research,* 4, pp. 426-439.

42. Gallup showed public awareness of "Watergate" at 52 percent in September 1972, at 83 percent in early April, 91 percent in mid-May. ORC showed it at near-saturation (85 percent) as early as mid-February.

43. *Gallup Opinion Index* ;ns 100, October 1973, p. 11.

44. *The Harris Yearbook 1973.*

45. Ibid.

46. The exact Gallup question was "Do you approve or disapprove of the way Nixon is handling his job as President?"

47. The exact Harris questions were "How would you rate the job President Nixon is doing as President? . . . on inspiring confidence in the White House personally? . . . on handling corruption in the government?"

48. The net rating (i.e., the percentage of positive minus the percentage of negative responses) in the Harris poll was +35 in May − down from +48 in February.

49. New York *Times,* April 20, 1973.

50. New York *Times,* April 26, 1973.

51. From transcript of telephone conversation, April 25, 1973, as published in the New York *Times,* November 22, 1974, p. 20.

52. Holz, op. cit.

53. Based on an examination of the Bell & Howell Index for four newspapers—the Chicago *Tribune,* the Los Angeles *Times,* the New Orleans *Times-Picayune,* and the Washington *Post.*

54. Based on the *Television News Index and Abstracts,* Vanderbilt University. This index is not suited for a full content analysis but enables us to trace increases in time devoted to Watergate.

55. The criterion for saturation is four successive days, five out of seven, six out of nine and no break for longer than three days. This was done largely to allow for Sunday and Monday doldrums in the coverage. For television, the criterion was four out of five successive weekdays.

56. Weaver et al., op. cit.

57. Edelstein and Tefft, op. cit.

58. The Harris Survey, May 8, 1973—Special Bonus Column.

59. On March 25, 1973, the New York *Times* editorially despaired of the "monumental apathy" of Americans in the face of this serious trend in corruption.

27 A Critique of Two Decades of Agenda-Setting Research

Gene Burd

Agenda-setting research is at its best when it is empirical and cautious, but also eclectic and congenial to multiple methods and different disciplines. At its worst, agenda-setting scholarship is mass media-centric, excessively enamored with the exaggerated power and effects of media technologies, and tied naively to a largely rational notion of human nature and the myth of an objective "public interest."

Unfortunately, too many agenda-setting researchers rely on a linear, one-dimensional, assembly-line model for the production and manufacture of public opinion and policy. Seemingly implicit in this technological pipeline is the use of the mass media as giant educational machines to socialize the public to accept policies that are manufactured by professional journalists and policy elites. One gets an image of a public that is made up of atomized individuals waiting "out there" in an amorphous mass society to be acted upon as they are being fed a presumably accurate account of the real world (which, in fact, is a world dominated by the progressive middle-class values of American journalism).

Despite its more recent conciliatory spirit, agenda-setting research retains a rather strong positivist position about the experience, observation, and reporting of reality. Communication is often seen as the transmission of manifest objective content from sources to receivers. As with journalists, more is often seen as better and more effective, until the communication act is successful.

This approach may neglect human communication that is nonrational, ritualistic, and symbolic. Such communication is a shared social construction that creates a picture of reality that is beyond mass media; that exists instead in the minds of individuals. Happily, agenda-setting research has become more receptive to the social construction of agendas by adjusting neat, clean hypotheses about mass media mechanics of communication to the dynamic, changing nature of audiences.

Another hallmark of agenda-setting research is a rather unchallenged assumption that the general public has a general public interest or agenda that can or should be implemented by rational policymakers. Such policymakers are seen as capable of planning the future of local communities or the nation. This ideal was popular in the 1960s. Today, a more realistic approach is to view the polity as a symbiotic ecology of games that contains competing and overlapping agendas, with newspapers and other media being just another "game in town" with their own routines and rituals. No one game controls the total community scene, although the press is a kind of "fourth branch of government," with the newspaper "the prime mover in setting the territorial agenda," as political scientist Norton Long espoused the agenda-setting hypothesis in 1958. Although he conceded "perhaps the existence of some kind of general public," Long suggested that "The common interest, if such there be, is to be realized through its institutional interactions rather than through the self-conscious rationality of a determinate group charged with its formulation and attainment" (Long, 1958 p. 255).

Thirty years later, Hilgartner and Bosk (1988) proposed an empirically testable public arenas model for the rise and fall of social problems wherein media merely compete with other symbiotic ecologies (i.e., organizations, institutions, groups) for the scarce resource of public attention. They suggest that agenda-setting for social problems may be the result of collective assessments that do not necessarily describe objective conditions.

Noting also recently that media and other agenda-setting influences take an objectivist approach, sociologist Douglas Maynard (1988) contended that language and interaction, "the stuff and substance of social life" and "an organized domain in its own right," offer a different starting point for social problem agendas. Instead of studying issues that elites consider to be important, they instead focus on problems that ordinary citizens consider salient in routine discourse.

In fact, agenda-setting research is finding increasingly that informal, interpersonal communication outside of mass media may shape the agendas of journalists and policymakers as well as citizens. Recent studies have shown that reporters and officials sometimes collaborate to achieve mutually beneficial agenda-setting changes (Cook et al.). This overlap of the legitimate government and the "other shadow government" of the press (Rivers, chapter 16, this volume) may be a reminder that a multidimensional ecology exists with perhaps several different agendas. Similar dimensions have been found in the interpersonal awareness levels (Benton & Frazier, chapter 6, this volume) and selective priming of audiences over time (Lang & Lang, chapter 26, this volume).

However, perhaps the major contribution of agenda-setting research remains its empirical testing of the old common sensical question, "Does news matter?" In doing this, it has utilized multiple research methods through the marriage of content analysis and survey research, the use of macro-case histories (and polls) over long periods of time (Funkhouser, chapter 4, Smith, chapter 8), and more recent receptivity to experiments (Iyengar, Peters, & Kinder, chapter 9).

Research in journalism and mass communication has become more interdisciplinary through studying agenda-setting, although it has not adequately embraced the sociological notion that newsgathering routines may affect profoundly the ideology of media content (Tuchman, Fishman, Gitlin, Gans). But there have been moves in this direction (Gandy, chapter 25, Lang & Lang, chapter 26). Certainly, agenda-setting research has come a long way from the primitive readership surveys toward examining the link between media content and audiences. Lippmann (chapter 1), Long (1958), Cohen and others have been somewhat vindicated. Studies have joined minds and methods, communities and communication, and embraced both print and electronic media coverage of a wide range of substantive political and social issues from the economy and ecology to crime and civil rights.

The inclusive and comprehensive climate of agenda-setting has accommodated personal and group experience and perceptions on issues arising in the real world of the audience (Erbring et al.), as well as awareness, attributes, curiosity, and interpersonal communication among audiences seeking information (Hill, chapter 15, Weaver, chapter 14). It has matched social indicators with news coverage (MacKuen), and warmed up to still another approach – the meaning and method of history – by relating the national agenda to the stream of selectively recorded events in the real world over time (Funkhouser, chapter 4).

In a somewhat related manner, agenda-setting research has exhumed rich possibilities for extended debate about some questions. Is print better than television as an agenda-setter? How does community experience (direct and indirect) and information type (obtrusive and inobtrusive) relate to dependence on media (Palmgreen & Clarke, chapter 11; Atwood, Sohn, & Sohn, chapter 12; Zucker)? Is television creating a national community agenda with excessive emphasis and preoccupation with the presidency (Iyengar, Peters, & Kinder)? Such questions address basic concerns about American governance.

These normative issues raised by agenda-setting research are highly relevant to the practice of journalism. If the agenda-setting hypothesis is proved conclusively, then journalists may finally abandon the newsroom mythology that news is objective while editorials are reserved for media's influential role.

Will any pretense at fairness and objectivity disappear if news alone has power? Will less glamourous media (like local newspapers and their agenda-setting potential) be neglected for national television?

Unlocking the "atomic secrets" of communication science may help set new research and professional agendas. Who sets the agenda (Gandy, chapter 25) may take on even more importance. How pseudo events shape news and missing and hidden agendas may get renewed attention, as well as new looks at content analysis (Turk, chapter 20) and gatekeeping (Reese & Danielian, chapter 23). If professional journalists are convinced that news does matter, they may be more receptive to revealing news-gathering norms rather than hiding behind the myth that news is "whatever happens."

As to the future, agenda-setting might embrace rather than be bashful about using methodologies which will enrich the study of communication from the viewpoint of the actor who is observed. Oral histories and participant-observation, for examples, belong in the methodological repertoire of agenda-setting researchers. The rituals and routines, the legends and lore, the personal documents and life experiences are part of the living history—and thus the agendas—of mass media audiences. Such qualitative data might be taken more seriously by agenda-setting scholars who lament the lack of an obtainable, objective record. Nonetheless, agenda-setting scholars have increasingly managed to blunt some of the sharp edges of the quantitative-qualitative swords in journalism education and research circles. Receptivity to additional research approaches and inclusive rather than exclusive models have both opened up communication within and outside the discipline. This open and eclectic atmosphere is a refreshing change from some of the closed and exclusive positions of some previous and contemporary scholars, and has been one of the most valuable contributions in the quest to test the agenda-setting hypothesis.

REFERENCES

Hilgartner, S., & Bosk, C.L. (1988). The rise and fall of social problems: A public arenas model. *American Journal of Sociology, 94* (1), 53–78.

Long, N. (1958). The local community as an ecology of games. *American Journal of Sociology, 64* (3), 251–261.

Maynard, D. W. (1988). Language, interaction, and social problems. *Social Problems, 35* (4), 311–334.

Bibliography

PUBLISHED REFERENCES

Anokwa, K., & Salwen, M.B. (1988). Newspaper agenda-setting among elites and non-elites in Ghana. *Gazette, 41,* 201–214.

Asp, K. (1983). The struggle for the agenda: Party agenda, media agenda, and voter agenda in the 1979 Swedish election campaign. *Communication Research, 10*(3), 333–355.

Atwater, T., Fico, F., & Pizante, G. (1987). Reporting on the state legislature: A case study of inter-media agenda-setting. *Newspaper Research Journal, 8*(2), 53–62.

Atwater, T., Salwen, M.B., & Anderson, R.B. (1985). Media agenda-setting with environmental issues. *Journalism Quarterly, 62,* 393–397.

Atwater, T., Salwen, M.B., & Anderson, R.B. (1985). Interpersonal discussion as a potential barrier to agenda-setting. *Newspaper Research Journal, 6*(4), 37–43.

Atwood, E., Sohn, A., & Sohn, H. (1978). Daily newspaper contributions to community discussion. *Journalism Quarterly, 55,* 570–576.

Atwood, L.E. (1981). From press release to voting reasons: Tracing the agenda in a congressional campaign. In D. Nimmo (Ed.), *Communication yearbook 4* (pp. 467–482). New Brunswick, NJ: Transaction.

Becker, L.B. (1977). The impact of issue saliences. In D.L. Shaw & M.E. McCombs (Eds.), *The emergence of American political issues: The agenda-setting function of the press* (pp. 121–131). St. Paul, MN: West.

Becker, L.B. (1982). The mass media and citizen assessment of issue importance: A reflection on agenda-setting research. In D.C. Whitney & E. Wartella (Ed.), *Mass communication review yearbook 3* (pp. 521–536). Newbury Park, CA: Sage.

Becker, L.B., & McCombs, M.E. (1978). The role of the press in determining voter reactions to presidential primaries. *Human Communication Research, 4,* 301–307.

Becker, L.B., McCombs, M.E., & McLeod, J.M. (1975). The development of political cognitions. In S.H. Chaffee (Ed.), *Political communication: Issues and strategies for research* (pp. 21–63). Newbury Park, CA: Sage.

Becker, L.B., & McLeod, J.M. (1976). Political consequences of agenda-setting. *Communication Research, 3,* 8–15.

Becker, L.B., Weaver, D.J., Graber, D.A., & McCombs, M.E. (1979). Influence on public agendas. In S. Kraus (Ed.), *The great debates: Carter vs. Ford, 1976* (pp. 418–428). Bloomington, IN: Indiana University Press.

Behr, R., & Iyengar, S. (1985). Television news, real-world cues, and changes in the public agenda. *Public Opinion Quarterly, 49,* 38–57.

Beniger, J.R. (1978). Media content as social indicators: The Greenfield index of agenda-setting. *Communication Research, 5,* 437–453.

Benton, M., & Frazier, P.J. (1976). The agenda-setting function of mass media at three levels of information holding. *Communication Research, 3,* 261–274.

Black, E.R., & Snow, P. (1982). The political agendas of three newspapers and city governments. *Canadian Journal of Communication, 8,* 11–25.

Blood, W. (1982). Agenda setting: A review of the theory. *Media Information Australia, 26,* 3–12.

Bowers, T.A. (1973). Newspaper political advertising and the agenda-setting function. *Journalism Quarterly, 50,* 552–556.

Bowers, T.A. (1977). Candidate advertising: The agenda is the message. In D.L. Shaw & M.E. McCombs (Eds.), *The emergence of American political issues: The agenda-setting function of the press* (pp. 53–67). St. Paul, MN: West.

Boyer, P.J. (1989). Famine in Ethiopia: The TV accident that exploded: In M. Emery & T.C. Smythe (Ed.), *Readings in mass communication: Concepts and issues in the mass media* 7 (pp. 293–298). Dubuque, IA: Brown.

Brosius, H.B., & Kepplinger, H.M. (1990). The agenda-setting function of television news: Static and dynamic views. *Communication Research, 17,* 183–211.

Caspi, D. (1962). The agenda-setting function of the Israeli press. *Knowledge: Creation, diffusion, utilization, 3*(3), 401–414.

Chaffee, S.H., & Izcaray, F. (1975). Mass communication functions in a media-rich developing society. In S.H. Chaffee (Ed.), *Political communication: Issues and strategies for research* (pp. 367–395). Newbury Park, CA: Sage.

Chaffee, S.H., & Wilson, D.G. (1977). Media rich, media poor: Two studies of diversity in agenda-holding. *Journalism Quarterly, 54,* 466–476.

Cobb, R.W., & Elder, C.D. (1971). The politics of agenda-building: An alternative perspective for modern democratic theory. *Journal of Politics, 33,* 892–915.

Cobb, R.W., & Elder, C.D. (1972). *Participation in American politics: The dynamics of agenda-building.* Baltimore: Johns Hopkins University Press.

Cobb, R.W., Ross, J.K., & Ross, M.H. (1976). Agenda building as a comparative political process. *American Political Science Review, 70,* 126–137.

Cohen, B.C. (1963). *The press and foreign policy.* Princeton, NJ: Princeton University Press.

Cook, F.L. (1981). Crime and the elderly: The emergence of a policy issue. In D.A. Lewis (Ed.), *Reactions to crime* (pp. 123–147). Newbury Park, CA: Sage.

Cook, F.L., & Skogan, W.G. (1990). Agenda setting and the rise and fall of policy issues. *Government and Politics* 4 (November 1990).

Cook, F.L., Tyler, T.R., Goetz, E.G., Gordon, M.T., Protess, D., Leff, D.R., & Molotch, H.L. (1983). Media and agenda setting: Effects on the public, interest group leaders, policy makers, and policy. *Public Opinion Quarterly, 47,* 16–35.

Crouse, T. (1973). *The boys on the bus.* New York: Ballantine Books.

Danielian, L., & Reese, S. (1989). A closer look at intermedia influences on agenda setting: The cocaine issue of 1986. In P. Shoemaker (Ed.), *Communication campaigns about drugs* (pp. 47–66). Hillsdale, NJ: Lawrence Erlbaum Associates.

Dearing, J.W. (1989). Setting the polling agenda for the issue of aids. *Public Opinion Quarterly, 53,* 309–329.

DeGeorge, W.F. (1981). Conceptualization and measurement of audience agenda. In G.C.

Wilhoit & H. de Bock (Ed.), *Mass communication review yearbook 2* (pp. 219-224). Newbury Park, CA: Sage.

Demers, D.P., Craff, D., Yang-Ho, C., & Pessin, B.M. (1989). Issue obtrusiveness and the agenda-setting effects of national network news. *Communication Research 16*, 793-812.

Downs, A. (1972). Up and down with ecology: The issue-attention cycle. *The Public Interest, 28*, 38-50.

Eaton, Howard, Jr. (1989). Agenda-setting with bi-weekly data on content of three national media. *Journalism Quarterly, 66*, 942-948, 959.

Edelstein, A.S. (1988). Communication perspectives in public opinion: Traditions and innovations. In J. Anderson (Ed.), *Communication yearbook 11* (pp. 502-533). Newbury Park, CA: Sage.

Einsiedel, E.F., Salomone, K.L., & Schneider, F.P. (1984). Crime: Effects of media exposure and personal experience on issue salience. *Journalism Quarterly, 61*, 131-136.

Entman, R.M. (1989). *Democracy without citizens: Media and the decay of American politics.* New York: Oxford University Press.

Erbring, L., Goldenberg, E., & Miller, A. (1980). Front-page news and real-world cues: A new look at agenda-setting by the media. *American Journal of Political Science, 24*, 16-49.

Eyal, C.H. (1981). The roles of newspapers and television in agenda-setting. In G.C. Wilhoit & H. de Bock (Eds.), *Mass communication review yearbook 2* (pp. 225-234). Newbury Park, CA: Sage.

Eyal, C.H., Winter, J.P., & DeGeorge W.F. (1981). The concept of time frame in agenda-setting. In G.C. Wilhoit & H. de Bock (Eds.), *Mass communication review yearbook 2* (pp. 212-218). Newbury Park, CA: Sage.

Eyal, C.H., Winter, J.P., & McCombs, M.E. (1980). The agenda-setting role of mass communication. In M. Emery & T. Smythe (Eds.), *Readings in mass communication: Concepts and issues in the mass media* (pp. 15-20). Dubuque, IA: William C. Brown.

Eyestone, T. (1978). *From social issues to public policy.* New York: Wiley.

Fan, D. (1988). *Predictions of public opinion from the mass media.* Westport, CT: The Greenwood Press.

Fan, D.P., & Tims, A.R. (1989). The impact of the news media on public opinion: American presidential election 1987-1988. *International Journal of Public Opinion Research, 1*(2), 151-163.

Fishman, M. (1980). *Manufacturing the news.* Austin: University of Texas.

Funkhouser, G.R. (1973). The issues of the sixties: An exploratory study in the dynamics of public opinion. *Public Opinion Quarterly, 37*, 62-75.

Funkhouser, G.R. (1973). Trends in the media coverage of the issues of the 60's. *Journalism Quarterly, 50*, 533-538.

Gadir, S. (1982). Media agenda-setting in Australia: The rise and fall of public issues. *Media Information Australia, 26*, 13-23.

Gandy, O. (1982). *Beyond agenda-setting.* Norwood, NJ: Ablex.

Gans, H.J. (1979). *Deciding what's news: A study of CBS Evening News, NBC Nightly News, Newsweek and Time.* New York: Pantheon Books.

Gilbert, S., Eyal, C.H., McCombs, M.E., & Nicholas, D. (1980). The state of the union address and the press agenda. *Journalism Quarterly, 57*, 584-588.

Gold, D., & Simmons, J.L. (1965). News selection patterns among Iowa dailies. *Public Opinion Quarterly, 29*, 425-430.

Gordon, M.T., & Heath, L. (1981). The news business, crime, and fear. In D.A. Lewis (Ed.), *Reactions to crime* (pp. 227-251). Beverly Hills, CA: Sage.

Gormley, W.T., Jr. (1975). Newspaper agendas and political elites. *Journalism Quarterly, 52*, 30-38.

Hauser, J.R. (1986). Agendas and consumer choice. *Journal of Marketing Research, 23*, 199-212.

Heeter, C., Brown, N., Soffin, S., Stanley, C., & Salwen, M. (1989). Agenda-setting by electronic text news. *Journalism Quarterly, 66,* 101–106.

Hill, D.B. (1985). Viewer characteristics and agenda-setting by television news. *Public Opinion Quarterly, 49,* 340–350.

Hubbard, J., DeFleur, M., & DeFleur, L. (1975). Mass media influences on public conceptions of social problems. *Social Problems, 23,* 22–34.

Iyengar, S. (1979). Television news and issue salience: A reexamination of the agenda-setting hypothesis. *American Politics Quarterly, 7,* 395–416.

Iyengar, S. (1988). Commentary on Rogers and Dearing: New directions of agenda-setting research. In J. Anderson (Ed.), *Communication yearbook 11* (pp. 595–602). Newbury Park, CA: Sage.

Iyengar, S., & Kinder, D.R. (1985). Psychological accounts of media agenda setting. In S. Kraus & R. Perloff (Eds.), *Mass media and political thought* (pp. 117–140). Newbury Park, CA: Sage.

Iyengar, S., & Kinder D.R. (1986). More than meets the eye: TV news, priming, and public evaluations of the president. In G. Comstock (Ed.), *Public communication and behavior* (Vol. 1, pp. 135–171). New York: Academic Press.

Iyengar, S., & Kinder, D.R. (1987). *News that matters: Agenda-setting and priming in a television age.* Chicago: University of Chicago Press.

Iyengar, S., Peters, M.P., & Kinder, D.R. (1982). Experimental demonstrations of the "not so-minimal" consequences of television news programs. *American Political Science Review, 76,* 848–858.

Iyengar, S., Peters, M.P., Kinder, D.R., & Krosnick, J.A. (1984). The evening news and presidential evaluations. *Journal of Personality and Social Psychology, 46,* 778–787.

Kaid, L.L., Hale, K., & Williams, J.A. (1977). Media agenda-setting of a specific political event. *Journalism Quarterly, 54,* 584–587.

Kepplinger, H.M., Donsbach, W., Brosius, H-B., & Staab, J.F. (1986). Media tenor and public opinion-a longitudinal study of media coverage and public opinion on Chancellor Kohl. *Kolner Qeitschrift fur Soziologie und Sozialpsychologie, 38,* 247–279.

Kingdon, J.W. (1984). *Agendas, alternatives and public policies.* Boston: Little, Brown.

Kraus, S., & Davis, D. (1976). *The effects of mass communication on political behavior.* University Park: Pennsylvania State University Press.

Lambeth, E.B. (1978). Perceived influence of the press on energy policy making. *Journalism Quarterly, 55,* 11–18, 72.

Lang, G.E., & Lang, K. (1981). Watergate: An exploration of the agenda-building process. In G.C. Wilhoit & H. de Bock (Eds.), *Mass communication review yearbook 2* (pp. 447–468). Newbury Park, CA: Sage.

Lang, G.E., & Lang, K. (1983). *The battle for public opinion: The president, the press, and the polls during Watergate.* New York: Columbia University Press.

Leff, D., Protess, D., & Brooks, S. (1986). Changing public attitudes and policymaking agendas. *Public Opinion Quarterly, 50,* 300–314.

Light, P.C. (1982). *The president's agenda.* Baltimore: John Hopkins University Press.

Linsky, M. (1986). *Impact: How the press affects federal policy-making.* New York: W.W. Norton.

Linsky, M., Moore, J., O'Donnell, W., & Whitman, D. (1986). *How the press affects federal policy making: Six case studies.* New York: W.W. Norton.

Lippmann, W. (1922). *Public opinion.* New York: Macmillan.

MacKuen, M.B., & Coombs, S.L. (1981). *More than news.* Beverly Hills, CA: Sage.

Manheim, J.B. (1986). A model of agenda dynamics: In M.L. McLaughlin (Ed.), *Communication yearbook 10* (pp. 499–516). Newbury Park, CA: Sage.

Manheim, J.B., & Albritton, R.B. (1984). Changing national images: International public relations and media agenda setting. *American Political Science Review, 73,* 641–647.

Mazur, A. (1981). Media coverage and public opinion on scientific controversies. *Journal of Communication, 31,* 106–115.

McClure, R.D., & Patterson, T.E. (1976). Setting the political agenda: Print vs. network news. *Journal of Communication, 26,* 23–28.

McCombs, M.E. (1976). Agenda-setting research: A bibliographic essay. *Political Communication Review, 1,* 1–7.

McCombs, M.E. (1977). Newspaper versus television: Mass communication effects across time. In D.L. Shaw & M.E. McCombs (Eds.), *The emergence of American political issues: The agenda-setting function of the press.* St. Paul, MN: West.

McCombs, M.E. (1978). Public response to the daily news. In L.K. Epstein (Ed.), *Women and the news* (pp. 1–14). New York: Hastings House.

McCombs, M.E. (1981). The agenda-setting approach. In D.D. Nimmo & K.R. Sanders (Eds.), *Handbook of political communication* (pp. 121–140). Beverly Hills, CA: Sage.

McCombs, M.E. (1981). Setting the agenda for agenda-setting research: An assessment of the priority ideas and problems. In G.C. Wilhoit & H. de Bock (Eds.), *Mass communication review yearbook 2* (pp. 219–224). Newbury Park, CA: Sage.

McCombs, M.E., & Gilbert, S. (1986). News influences on our pictures of the world. In J. Bryant & D. Zillmann (Eds.), *Perspectives on media effects* (pp. 1–15). Hillsdale, NJ: Lawrence Erlbaum Associates.

McCombs, M.E., & Masel-Waters, L. (1976). Agenda-setting: A perspective on mass communication. *Mass Communication Review, 3,* 3–7.

McCombs, M.E., & Shaw, D.L. (1972). The agenda-setting function of mass media. *Public Opinion Quarterly, 36,* 176–187.

McCombs, M.E., & Shaw, D.L. (1976). Structuring the 'unseen environment.' *Journal of Communication, 26*(2), 18–22.

McCombs, M.E., & Weaver, D.H. (1985). Toward a merger of gratifications and agenda-setting research. In K.E. Rosengren, L.A. Wenner, & P. Palmgreen (Eds.), *Media gratifications research: current perspectives* (pp. 95–108). Newbury Park, CA: Sage.

McLeod, J.M., Becker, L.B., & Byrnes, J.E. (1974). Another look at the agenda-setting function of the press. *Communication Research, 1,* 131–166.

Megwa, E.R., & Brenner, D.J. (1988). Toward a paradigm of media agenda-setting effect: Agenda-setting as a process. *Howard Journal of Communications, 1*(1), 39–56.

Mendelsohn, H. (1989). Socio-psychological construction and the mass communication effects dialectic. *Communication Research, 16,* 813–823.

Miller, A., & MacKuen, M. (1979). Learning about the candidates: The 1976 presidential debates. *Public Opinion Quarterly, 43,* 326–346.

Miller, W.E., & Stokes, D.E. (1963). The politics of agenda-building: An alternative perspective for modern democratic theory. *Journal of Politics, 33,* 892–915.

Molotch, H., Protess, D., & Gordon, M. (1987). The media-policy connection: Ecologies of news. In D. Paletz (Ed.), *Political communication research* (pp. 26–48). Norwood, NJ: Ablex.

Mullins, L.E. (1977). Agenda-setting and the young voter. In D.L. Shaw & M.E. McCombs (Eds.), *The emergence of American political issues: The agenda-setting function of the press* (pp. 133–148). St. Paul, MN: West.

Nelson, B.J. (1978). Setting the policy agenda: The case of child abuse. In J.V. May & A.B. Wildavsky (Eds.), *The policy cycle* (pp. 17–41). Beverly Hills, CA: Sage.

Nelson, B.J. (1984). *Making an issue of child abuse.* Chicago: University of Chicago Press.

Neuman, W.R., & Fryling, A.C. (1985). Patterns of political cognition: An exploration of the public mind. In S. Kraus & R.M. Perloff (Eds.), *Mass media and political thought* (pp. 223–240). Newbury Park, CA: Sage.

Paletz, D.L., & Boiney, J. (1988). Commentary on Edelstein: Interest groups and public opinion. In J. Anderson (Ed.), *Communication yearbook 11* (pp. 534–546). Newbury Park, CA: Sage.

Paletz, D.L., & Ertman, R.M. (1981). *Media power politics.* New York: The Free Press.

Palmgreen, P., & Clarke, P. (1977). Agenda-setting with local and national issues. *Communication Research, 4,* 435–452.

Patterson, T.E. (1980). The *mass media election: How Americans choose their president.* New York: Praeger.

Patterson, T.E., & McClure, R.D. (1976). *The unseeing eye: The myth of television power in national politics.* New York: Putnam.

Phillips, D. (1979). Suicide, motor vehicle fatalities, and the mass media: Evidence toward a theory of suggestion. *American Journal of Sociology, 84,* 1150-1174.

Phillips, D. (1980). Airplane accidents, murder, and the mass media: Towards a theory of initiation and suggestion. *Social Forces, 58,* 1001-1024.

Phillips, D. (1983). The impact of mass media violence on U.S. homicides. *American Sociological Review, 48,* 560-568.

Pritchard D. (1986). Homocide and bargained justice: The agenda-setting effect of crime news on prosecutors. *Public Opinion Quarterly, 50,* 143-159.

Protess, D., Cook, F.L., Curtin, T.R., Gordon, M.T., Leff, D.R., McCombs, M.E., & Miller, P. (1987). The impact of investigative reporting on public opinion and policymaking. *Public Opinion Quarterly, 51,* 166-185.

Protess, D., Leff, D.R., Brooks, S.C., & Gordon, M.T. (1985). Uncovering rape: The watchdog press and the limits of agenda-setting. *Public Opinion Quarterly, 49,* 19-37.

Rabinowitz, G., Prothro, J.W., & Jacoby, W. (1982). Salience as a factor in the impact of issues on candidate evaluation. *Journal of Politics, 44,* 41-63.

Ramaprasad, J. (1983). Agenda-setting: Is not a 1984 or is a 1984 view. *Gazette, 32,* 119-135.

Reese, S., & Danielian, L. (1989). Intermedia influence and the drug issue: Converging on cocaine. In P. Shoemaker (Ed.), *Communication campaigns about drugs* (pp. 29-46). Hillsdale, NJ: Lawrence Erlbaum Associates.

Rivers, W.L. (1982, March). The media as shadow government. *Quill,* pp. 11-15.

Roberts, D.F., & Bachen, C.M. (1981). Mass communication effects. *Annual Review of Psychology, 32,* 307-356.

Roberts, D.F., & Maccoby, N. (1985). Effects of mass communication. In G. Lindzey & E. Aronson (Eds.), *The handbook of social psychology* (3rd ed., pp. 539-598). New York: Random House.

Rogers, E.M., & Dearing, J.W. (1988). Agenda-setting research: Where has it been, where is it going? In J. Anderson (Ed.), *Communication yearbook 11* (pp. 555-594). Newbury Park, CA: Sage.

Salwen, M.B. (1988). Effect of accumulation on issue salience in agenda setting. *Journalism Quarterly, 65,* 100-106, 130.

Schoenfeld, A.C., Meier, R.F., & Griffin, R.J. (1979). Constructing a social problem: The press and the environment. *Social Problems, 27,* 38-61.

Schoenbach, K., & Weaver, D.H. (1985). Finding the unexpected: Cognitive bonding in a political campaign. In S. Kraus & R.M. Perloff (Eds.), *Mass media and political thought* (pp. 157-176). Newbury Park, CA: Sage.

Schmeling, D., & Wotring, C. (1976). Agenda-setting effects of drug abuse public service ads. *Journalism Quarterly, 53,* 743-746.

Shaw, D.L. (1977). The press agenda in a community setting. In D.L. Shaw & M.E. McCombs (Eds.), *The emergence of American political issues: The agenda-setting function of the press* (pp. 19-31). St. Paul, MN: West.

Shaw, D.L., & Clemmer, C.L. (1977). News and the public response. In D.L. Shaw & M.E. McCombs (Eds.), *The emergence of American political issues: The agenda-setting function of the press* (pp. 33-51). St. Paul, MN: West.

Shaw, D.L., & McCombs, M.E. (Eds.). (1977). *The emergence of American political issues: The agenda-setting function of the press.* St. Paul, MN: West.

Shaw, D.L., & McCombs, M.E. (1989). Dealing with illicit drugs: The power—and limits—of mass media agenda setting: In P. Shoemaker (Ed.) *Communication campaigns about drugs* (pp. 113-120). Hillsdale, NJ: Lawrence Erlbaum Associates.

Shaw, E.F. (1977). The agenda-setting hypothesis reconsidered: Interpersonal factors. *Gazette, 23,* 230–240.

Shaw, E.F. (1977). The interpersonal agenda: In D.L. Shaw & M.E. McCombs (Eds.), *The emergence of American political issues: The agenda-setting function of the press* (pp. 69–87). St. Paul, MN: West.

Shaw, E.F. (1979). Agenda-setting and mass communication theory. *Gazette, 25,* 96–105.

Siune, K., & Borre, O. (1975). Setting the agenda for a Danish election. *Journal of Communication, 25,* 65–73.

Smith, K. (1987). Newspaper coverage and public concern about community issues. *Journalism Monographs,* No. 101.

Smith, K.A. (1988). Effects of coverage on neighborhood and community concerns. *Newspaper Research Journal, 9,* 35–47.

Smith, T. (1980). America's most important problem: A trend analysis, 1946–1976. *Public Opinion Quarterly, 44,* 164–180.

Soderland, W.C., Wagenberg, R.H., Briggs, E.D., & Nelson, R.C. (1980). Regional and linguistic agenda-setting in Canada: A study of newspaper coverage of issues affecting political integration in 1976. *Canadian Journal of Political Science, 13,* 348–356.

Sohn, A.B. (1978). A longitudinal analysis of local non-political agenda-setting effects. *Journalism Quarterly, 55,* 325–333.

Spector, M., & Kitsuse, J.I. (1977). *Constructing social problems.* Menlo Park, CA: Cummings.

Stone, G.C., & McCombs, M.E. (1981). Tracing the time lag in agenda-setting. *Journalism Quarterly, 58,* 51–55.

Sutherland, H., & Galloway, J. (1981). Role of advertising: Persuasion or agenda setting. *Journalism Quarterly, 58,* 51–55.

Swanson, D.L. (1988). Feeling the elephant: Some observations on agenda-setting research. In J. Anderson (Ed.), *Communication yearbook 11* (pp. 603–619). Newbury Park, CA: Sage.

Swanson, L.L., & Swanson, D.L. (1978). The agenda-setting function of the first Ford-Carter debate. *Communication Monographs, 45,* 330–353.

Tardy, C.H., Gaughan, B.J., Hemphill, M.R. & Crockett, N. (1981). Media agendas and political participation. *Journalism Quarterly, 58,* 624–627.

Tichenor, P.J. (1988). Commentary on Edelstein: Public opinion and the construction of social reality. In J. Anderson (Ed.), *Communication yearbook 11* (pp. 547–554). Newbury Park, CA: Sage.

Tipton, L.P., Haney, R.D., & Baseheart, J.B. (1975). Media agenda-setting in city and state election campaigns. *Journalism Quarterly, 52,* 15–22.

Turk, J.V. (1986). Public relations' influence on the news. *Newspaper Research Journal, 7,* 15–27.

Walker, J.L. (1977). Setting the agenda in the U.S. senate: A theory of problem selection. *British Journal of Political Science, 1,* 432–445.

Watt, J.H., Jr., & van den Berg, S. (1981). How time dependency influences media effects in a community controversy. *Journalism Quarterly, 58,* 43–50.

Weaver, D. (1977). Political issues and voters need for orientation. In D.L. Shaw & M.E. McCombs (Eds.), *The emergence of American political issues: The agenda-setting function of the press* (pp. 107–120). St. Paul, MN: West.

Weaver, D. (1980). Audience need for orientation and media effects. *Communication Research, 7,* 361–376.

Weaver, D. (1984). Media agenda-setting and public opinion: Is there a link? In R.N. Bostrom (Ed.), *Communication yearbook 8* (pp. 680–691). Newbury Park, CA: Sage.

Weaver, D. (1987). Media agenda-setting and elections: Assumptions and implications. In D. Paletz (Ed.), *Political communication research* (pp. 176–193). Norwood, NJ: Ablex.

Weaver, D., & Elliott, S.N. (1985). Who sets the agenda for the media? A study of local agenda-building. *Journalism Quarterly, 62,* 87–94.

Weaver, D., Graber, D.A., McCombs, M.E., & Eyal, C.H. (1981). *Media agenda-setting in a presidential election: Issues, images, and interests.* New York: Praeger.

Weaver, D., McCombs, M.E., & Spellman, C. (1975). Watergate and the media: A case study of agenda-setting. *American Politics Quarterly, 3,* 458–472.

Westley, B.H. (1976). Setting the political agenda. What makes it change? *Journal of Communication, 26,* 43–47.

Whitney, D.C., & Becker, L.B. (1982). "Keeping the gates" for the gatekeepers: The effects of wire news. *Journalism Quarterly, 59,* 60–65.

Williams, W., Jr., & Larsen, D.C. (1977). Agenda-setting in an off-election year. *Journalism Quarterly, 54,* 744–749.

Williams, W., Jr., & Semlak, W.D. (1978). Structural effects of TV coverage on political agendas. *Journal of Communication, 28,* 114–119.

Williams, W., Jr., & Semlak, W.D. (1978). Campaign '76: Agenda-setting during the New Hampshire primary. *Journal of Broadcasting, 22,* 531–540.

Williams, W., Jr., Shapiro, M., & Cutbirth, C. (1983). The impact of campaign agendas on perceptions of issues in 1980 campaign. *Journalism Quarterly, 60,* 226–231.

Winter, J.P. (1981). Contingent conditions in the agenda-setting process. In G.C. Wilhoit & H. de Bock (Eds.), *Mass communication review yearbook 2.* (pp. 235–244). Beverly Hills, CA: Sage.

Winter, J.P., & Eyal, C.H. (1981). Agenda-setting for the civil rights issue. *Public Opinion Quarterly, 45,* 376–383.

Winter, J.P., Eyal, C.H., & Rogers, A.H. (1982). Issue-specific agenda-setting: The whole as less than the sum of the parts. *Canadian Journal of Communication, 8,* 8–10.

Zucker, H.G. (1978). The variable nature of news media influence: In B.D. Ruben (Ed.), *Communication yearbook 2* (pp. 225–240). New Brunswick, NJ: Transaction Books.

UNPUBLISHED REFERENCES

Allen, R.L., Tan, C.Z., & Reagan, J. (1984). *Mass media and agenda diversity.* Paper presented at the International Communication Association.

Anokwa, K., & Salwen, M.B. (1986). *Newspaper agenda-setting among elites and non-elites in Ghana.* International Division of the Association for Education in Journalism and Mass Communication.

Atwood, L.E., Sohn, A., & Sohn, H. (1976). *Community discussion and newspaper content.* Association for Education in Journalism.

Auh, T.S. (1977). *Issue conflict and mass media agenda-setting during Bayh-Lugar senatorial campaign of 1974.* Theory and Methodology Division, Association for Education in Journalism.

Auh, T.S. (1977). *Issue conflict and mass media agenda-setting.* Unpublished doctoral dissertation, Indiana University, Bloomington.

Becker, L., & McCombs, M.E. (1977). *U.S. primary politics and public opinion: The role of the press in determining voter reactions.* International Communication Association.

Bloj, A.G. (1975). Into the wild blue yonder: Behavioral implications of agenda setting for air travel. In M.E. McCombs & G. Stone (Eds.), *Studies in agenda setting.* Syracuse, NY: Syracuse University, Newhouse Communications Research Center.

Blood, R.W. (1981). *Unobtrusive issues in the agenda-setting role of the press.* Unpublished doctoral dissertation, Syracuse University, Syracuse, NY.

Chaffee, S.H. (1979). *Mass media vs. interpersonal channels: The synthetic competition.* Speech Communication Association.

Cohen, D. (1975). *A report on a non-election agenda-setting study.* Association for Education in Journalism.

Eyal, C.H. (1979). *Time-frame in agenda-setting research: A study of the conceptual and methodological factors affecting the time frame context of the agenda-setting process.* Unpublished doctoral dissertation, Syracuse University, Syracuse, NY.

Ferguson, M.A. (1984). *Issue diversity and media: Nominal, attributive and field diversity as correlates of media exposure and diversity.* International Communication Association.

Fryling, A. (1985). *Setting the congressional agenda: Public opinion in a media age.* Unpublished doctoral dissertation, Massachuesetts Institute of Technology.

Hezel, R.T., Andregg, C., & Lange-Chapman, D. (1986). *The agenda-setting function of TV movies: Newspaper coverage of TV movie social issues.* Association for Education in Journalism and Mass Communication.

McCombs, M.E., Gilbert, S., & Eyal, C.H. (1982). *The state of the union address and the press agenda: A replication.* International Communication Association.

McCombs, M.E., & Weaver, D.H. (1973). *Voters' need for orientation and use of mass communication.* International Communication Association.

McCombs, M.E., & Weaver, D.H. (1977). *Voters and the mass media: Information seeking, political interest, and issue agendas.* American Association for Public Opinion Research.

Megwa, E.R., & Brenner, D.J. (1986). *Toward a paradigm of media agenda-setting effects: Agenda-setting as process.* Political Communications Division, International Communication Association.

Moreno, L.M., Ramirez, I.A., Schael, D.C., & Vernon, C.R. (1977). *Importancia tematica en prensa y publicode la cuidad de Mexico,* (Thesis). Universidad Iberoamericana, Departamento De Communicacion, Mexico.

Mullins, L.E. (1973). *Agenda-setting on the campus: The mass media and learning of issue importance in the '72 election.* Association for Education in Journalism.

Neuman, W.R. (1985). *The threshold of public attention.* American Political Science Association.

Protess, D. (1987). *Muckraking matters: The societal impact of investigative reporting.* Evanston, IL: Institute for Modern Communications Monograph Series.

Salwen, M.B. (1985). *Agenda setting with environmental Issues: A study of time process, media dependency, audience salience, and newspaper reading.* Ph.D. Dissertation, Michigan State University.

Salwen, M.B. (1985). *An agenda for agenda-setting research: Problems in the paradigm.* Speech Communication Association.

Salwen, M.B. (1986). *Time in agenda-setting: The accumulation of media coverage on audience issue salience.* International Communication Association.

Schoenbach, K. (1982). *Agenda-setting effects of print and television in West Germany.* International Communication Association.

Schoenbach, K., & Weaver, D.H. (1983). *Cognitive bonding and need for orientation during political campaigns.* International Communication Association.

Shaw, E.F. (1984). *Some interpersonal dimensions of the media's agenda-setting function.* Paper presented at the conference on the Agenda-Setting Function of the Press, Syracuse University.

Shoemaker, P.J., Wanta, W., & Leggett, D. (1987). *Drug coverage and public opinion, 1972-1986.* American Association for Public Opinion Research.

Stevenson, R., & Ahern, T. (1979). *Individual effects of agenda-setting.* Association for Education in Journalism.

Wanta, W. (1986). *The agenda-setting effects of dominant photographs.* Association for Education in Journalism and Mass Communication.

Weaver, D. (1978). *Need for orientation, media uses and gratifications, and media effects.* International Communication Association.

Weaver, D. (1983). *Media agenda-setting and public opinion.* Public Opinion and Communication Seminar.

Weaver, D. (1984). *Media agenda-setting and public-opinion: Is there a link?* International Communication Association convention.

Weaver, D., Auh, T.S., Stehla, T., & Wilhoit, T. (1975). *A path analysis of individual agenda-setting during the 1974 Indiana senatorial campaign.* Association for Education in Journalism.

Weaver, D., Becker, L.B., & McCombs, M.E. (1976). *Influence of the mass media on issues, images, and political interest: The agenda-setting function of mass communication during the 1976 campaign.* Midwest Association for Public Opinion Research.

Winter, J.P. (1980). *Differential media-public agenda-setting effects for selected issues, 1948-1976.* Unpublished doctoral dissertation. Syracuse University, 1980.

Winter, J.P., Eyal, C., & Rogers, A. (1980). *Issue specific agenda-setting: Inflation, unemployment, and national unity in Canada, 1977-1978.* International Communication Association.

Index